Cybersecurity for Executives
In the Age of Cloud

Teri Radichel

Copyright © 2020 Teri Radichel
All rights reserved.
ISBN: 9781652474814

DEDICATION

To everyone trying to protect what they value most, and all the people in the world who are trying to do the right thing.

CONTENTS

	Acknowledgments	i
1	Why executives should care more about cybersecurity	1
2	How network traffic got me into cybersecurity	13
3	Cybersecurity strategy - Ask the right questions	25
4	CVEs: Security bugs that bite	34
5	Exponential increases in cyber risk due to Internet exposure	45
6	High-risk ports: The chink in your network armor	59
7	Data access: Protect your gold	71
8	Trust is overrated	79
9	The aftermath of stolen and abused credentials	96
10	The password problem	115
11	Encryption at rest	132
12	Encryption on wired and wireless networks	150
13	The right cybersecurity training	171
14	Testing your cybersecurity	185
15	Preparing for cybersecurity disasters	204
16	Security policies that reduce risk	213
17	Security exceptions are the norm	226
18	Deployment systems – danger or defense	239
19	How well do you know your vendors	256
20	Efficacy of security products and services	274
21	The attackers are in your network – now what?	283
22	Security automation: Do more with less	297
23	Is the likelihood of a data breach going up or down?	311
24	Change is constant	322

ACKNOWLEDGEMENTS

Thanks to Bill Knaffl (security review), Stephen A. Clark (executive review), and Gregory Shanahan (editor). Thanks also to Julie Smith, Kaitlyn Rodmyre, and Lucas Rodmyre (proofreaders). Thanks also to Sam Rodmyre, who was simultaneously testing my security class labs.

Thanks to my dad for getting me interested in computers before they were a household item, and my mom for dropping a TI-BASIC programming book on the table next to me in sixth grade.

Thanks to my boss at my first corporate job, Joe Beer, who allowed me to attend many different types of technical training despite my lack of experience and even though I was a woman. Thanks also to Carol Cabe for inspiring me to get a master's in software engineering. Thanks to the customers of my previous company, Radical Software, Inc., where I learned and researched many things in this book.

Thanks to Dave Stevens, who let me take a cloud architecture class at a time when we were not allowed to use cloud technology at Capital One, and Terren Peterson for inviting me to work on the Capital One cloud team. Thanks to Wayson Vannatta for giving me the opportunity to work as a cloud architect and director moving a security product to the cloud and your on-going support. Thanks to Paul Henry for taking the time to talk to me when I was wondering if I should drop out of the SANS Master's Degree in Information Security Engineering program. I finished and now have a GSE.

Thank you to everyone who gave me any other form of assistance or support over the years to keep moving forward in my life and career. I could list a lot more people here. This book would not have been possible without all of you.

1
WHY EXECUTIVES SHOULD CARE MORE ABOUT CYBERSECURITY

Most executives say they care about cybersecurity. If that is true, why do we still have so many security breaches? While I was writing this book, Risk Based Security published a report that stated breaches are up 33% over the previous year (Risk Based Security, 2019), and 2019 was on track to be the worst year on record. Organizations need to take a closer look at their approach to cybersecurity.

What is causing this rise in data breaches, even though we have worked on this problem for so long? We have high-level technical answers in some cases based on news articles and reports like the ones I will share with you in this book. The root cause will be mostly speculative at this point because we don't have all the details behind every data breach. However, I have been working both in security and software for over 25 years. I will share my experiences in this book showing how cybersecurity problems creep into technology projects and infiltrate companies that are trying to do the right thing.

Data breaches are like shoplifting and fraud; they are an on-going problem that will never go away. However, I believe we can do better. We are in an exciting time where software and security are converging in new ways that can help us solve security problems. The cloud, in part, is driving this intersection of disciplines and technologies. New ways of working have emerged that break through past barriers that created bottlenecks and roadblocks that slowed things down in the past. At times, organizations need to balance speed and ambition with a thoughtful understanding of the risk of each decision. How can a decision maker understand the risk if they don't understand the variables involved in the equation?

Although I have written articles and white papers about how the cloud can make some organizations more secure, this is not the case if organizations cast tried and true security principles aside as they move to the cloud. Moving to the cloud exacerbated security problems for some organizations. In most cases, though, it wasn't the fault of the major cloud providers — it was the way the organizations moved to the cloud. Some cloud platforms offer capabilities that can help companies protect data better than they do internally, but not without proper architectures and security controls. If organizations don't leverage the security benefits of cloud platforms and implement cybersecurity fundamentals, cloud platforms may increase risk. Merely turning on cloud security services is not enough.

Cybersecurity is not simple. It is an esoteric field, with many nuances, where a single mistake amongst a million things done right can cause a breach. However, at the broadest level, cybersecurity is about statistics, sound judgment calls, and managing risk. It will be difficult for executives to make the right decision if they do not understand the basics of cybersecurity and how breaches occur. This book aims to provide that knowledge in a manner that executives can understand. Armed with this knowledge, they can take actionable steps to improve cybersecurity within their organizations and reduce the number and impact of security breaches.

I've worked on e-commerce and banking systems for the better part of my career. I see many parallels between security and finance. Organizations invest millions of dollars into technology and processes to make sure their money is going to the right place and that their financial data is accurate. Account reconciliation occurs daily. I've helped implement reports to find misapplied and failed transactions for things like e-commerce purchases, investment fund transfers, dividends, and cost basis.

I believe this same level of scrutiny and reconciliation principles can be applied to cybersecurity to help reduce the number of breaches and make organizations more secure. Just as companies measure how much money they have in the bank, they can track where their data exists within their organization and how it flows from one location to another. Companies can implement segregation of duties in systems that manage data the same way they implement segregation of duties for financial processes. Companies can measure gaps in cybersecurity controls the same way they measure fraud, discrepancies, and reconciliation errors.

Cost-Benefit Analysis

Most executives probably understand that data breaches cost organizations money in terms of fines, fees, and legal battles, but let's break this down in a bit more detail. At one point, I heard a security professional suggest not to use the cost of a breach as a basis for more investment because the losses associated with a breach do not offset the upside of skipping security. I disagree with this argument as I believe people prematurely underestimated the full cost of security incidents. Security incidents incur long-term losses that organizations need to consider, which involves more than the fines and fees associated with the number of records affected or the rise and fall of a stock price.

Additionally, when looking at breach statistics, the cost-benefit analysis will be relative to the organization and the size of the security incident. Looking at average numbers can cause logic flaws, as explained in Fooled by Randomness by Nassim Nicholas Taleb (Taleb, 2005). If a catastrophic event occurs that costs your company hundreds of millions of dollars, the average in single-digit millions becomes meaningless. Smaller companies store less data and, as a result, experience less significant breaches, which factors into that average. Organizations should consider worst-case scenarios if the value of their information is high, and plan accordingly.

This equation is also changing now that fees, fines, and lawsuit settlements are rising. GDPR (General Data Protection Regulation) can cost an organization 4% of its worldwide annual revenue for non-compliance (European Union, 2016). Many other countries and states are considering, or have already passed, privacy and data breach laws that may incur fines on top of that, even if you don't serve European customers. The state of California passed the California Consumer Privacy Act (CCPA) in 2018 that allows consumers to seek damages for data breaches and imposes fines on companies of up to $7,500 for each violation (California State Legislature, 2018). Fast Company wrote an article explaining that the law could result in a $375 million fine for a breach of 50,000 customer records (Captain, 2020).

Organizations should also consider that more legislation will come if companies do not take responsibility for information security in more effective ways. New privacy legislation is delaying business initiatives and costing many companies money, as explained by the CISO of Sumo Logic, George Gerchow, in a security podcast I was on with him (Gerchow, George, Radichel, & Hansen, 2019). Legislation such as Sarbanes-Oxley exists as a result of a financial crisis. The government stepped in to ensure companies took appropriate actions to limit financial risk. New laws could arise to address cybersecurity risk as well if companies do not take action on their own.

What is the cost of a data breach?

The average cost of a database breach per the Ponemon Institute in 2018 was $3.86 million (Ponemon Institute, IBM, 2018). For some companies, this may not be a large number. That dollar figure is going to hurt smaller companies more than larger companies. But remember, this is also an average. There are different sizes of data breaches, and a large company with more money or data may be a bigger target. Ponemon estimates the cost of a breach of 1 million or more records is $40 million, and the cost of a mega-breach to be $350 million (Ponemon Institute, IBM, 2018).

After IBM and Ponemon released this study, a proposed settlement for the Equifax breach with the U.S. Federal Trade Commission, the Consumer Financial Protection Bureau, 48 states, the District of Columbia, and Puerto Rico initially came in at $700 million. As it turns out, if Equifax made the proposed payment of $125 to each person affected, that settlement would not have covered all the costs. Later, a judge reduced the amount to $425 million, which is still higher than the average. Likely many people affected will not receive $125. However, $425 million is still a significant amount of money. The lowered payment was, of course, dependent on that particular judge's decision in that specific courtroom. Organizations should consider the risk of a different judge making a different decision, the cost of appeals, and the risk of ultimately higher fines in an alternate final decision.

The harm to the brand of an organization after a data breach may be hard to quantify but consider this: the cost of the breach includes lost revenue if customers choose not to use your product, invest in your company, or buy from your store or website after a breach. Although some companies bounce back after a breach, who can say that they would not have had even greater success without the breach? How far ahead did their competitors advance while they were dealing with the incident? A 2016 report shows that financial institutions risk losing 12–28% of their customers after a data breach (Identity Theft Resource Center, 2016).

Lost time is also a factor in a data breach. Do you want to spend your time talking to lawyers and the news media, and having your support staff explain to customers what happened and whether they are affected? I have seen entire support teams tied up dealing with an incident. Other staff members had to set aside important work and get on phones to cover emergencies the existing support staff could not handle alone. I've also seen teams pulled off big projects to triage security issues when sufficient resources were not deployed in advance to understand and prevent the problem. What positive things could your business do if they did not have to deal with a data breach?

Consider the people who will leave the company after a security incident, no longer wanting to be associated with the organization. Hiring new employees may also be affected as people do not want to be part of a failed security program. This exodus could make it even harder for a company to recover from a breach. I've read personal accounts on LinkedIn from staff members about poor morale after a breach, which will impact performance. The distraction reduces overall productivity within the organization, ultimately affecting your products, your customers, and your brand.

Executives and board members may be personally affected

In the past, cybersecurity and privacy issues may have hurt the company itself in some way. Perhaps the company lost some revenue, the breach tarnished their brand, or their stock temporarily dropped. Cybersecurity breaches, laws, and regulations are now affecting executives and board members. Here are a few examples:

- Recent large-scale data breaches have resulted in CEOs testifying in front of Congress, including the Equifax and Marriott breach (Fazzini, 2019).

- Facebook's CEO, Mark Zuckerberg, met with the Irish Parliament to discuss social media regulations (Irish Central Staff, 2019).

- After some data breaches, including those at Target (BBC News, 2014) and Equifax (Arnold, 2017), CEOs, CIOs, CISOs, and others lost their jobs.

- Hiding an incident did not go well for the subsequently fired CISO of Uber (Riley, 2017).

- U.S. lawmakers have proposed legislation that could result in jail time for executives (Holmes, 2019).

- The Parliament of Australia passed a law that includes imprisonment of up to three years for company executives that allow users to publish violent content on their platforms (Brown, 2019).

The article "Breaches in the boardroom: What directors and officers can do to reduce the risk of personal liability for data security breaches by Goodwin Proctor" (Sharton & Stegmaier, 2018) sums up a landmark case and provides some recommendations for moving security from the server to the boardroom:

> In its 1996 Caremark decision, the Delaware Chancery Court declared that, in such actions, directors could be held personally liable for failing to "appropriately monitor and supervise the enterprise." The court emphasized that a company's board of directors must make a good-faith effort to implement an adequate corporate information and reporting system. Failing to do so can constitute an "unconsidered failure of the board to act in circumstances

in which due attention would, arguably, have prevented the loss."

Executives and board members should factor in personal liability and their own employment when making cybersecurity decisions. When deciding to take a seat on a board, an executive may want to ask the company about cybersecurity practices. Before taking on a role at a company, ensure that the company is willing to invest appropriately in security. When making security decisions, consider the personal impact of a data breach.

We are in a cyberwar

This statement is not political; and it is a global concern. It applies to any organization in any country where people care about the well-being of their families and fellow citizens. It is not an attempt to spread FUD (fear, uncertainty, and doubt). It is just a fact. I have been researching cybersecurity for years — since my first data breach and through my time working on the security research team for a security vendor. I am a member of InfraGard[1], a partnership between the FBI (Federal Bureau of Investigation) and members of the private sector, and other organizations that provide information about cyberattacks and breaches. I spent over five years getting a master's degree in information security engineering from the top cybersecurity professionals in the country who have worked for elite security firms and government organizations. I have also taught classes to government organizations and individuals involved in national security. I hold a SANS GIAC Security Expert (GSE) certification. I continue to research cybersecurity almost daily.

A cyberwar is going on between organized crime and organizations, and between countries. This statement may sound like scare tactics to some people, but nations have employed hackers to carry out cyberattacks for years. I will cite several

---

[1] Infragard https://www.fbi.gov/about/partnerships/infragard

examples throughout this book. The United States is in the midst of a conflict with Iran at the time of this writing. Organizations may think this doesn't concern them. However, top cybersecurity experts such as Christopher C. Krebs, the director of the Cybersecurity and Infrastructure Security Agency at the Department of Homeland Security (DHS), are warning about potential cyberattacks from Iran in retaliation (Kanno-Youngs & Perlroth, 2020). Iran has already demonstrated the ability to carry out such attacks.

David Kennedy, CEO of TrustedSec and a fellow IANS Research faculty member, spoke with CNBC about Iran's tactics and the fact that many organizations are ill-prepared for nation-state attacks (Kennedy, Iran's key cybersecurity threat is ransomware: Former NSA hacker, 2020). Note that CNBC reported the most significant threat is ransomware, but that's not what Kennedy said. He warned about attacks on critical infrastructure such as banking and power plants, among other things. The CEO of FireEye warned about malware from Iran designed to completely wipe out data with no option to pay a ransom to get it back (Hulquist, 2020). After the conflict transpired, the amount of network traffic looking for system vulnerability increased 1800%, according to Andrew Morris, Founder of GreyNoise Intelligence in a post on Twitter (Morris, 2020). You will learn about different nation-state attacks throughout this book.

Reports indicate that countries are working together with those involved in organized crime (Galeotti, 2017). Foreign governments and criminals have leveraged propaganda to sway opinions (Radichel, 2017). Many computer systems and IoT devices are being controlled by C2 (command and control) servers to do their bidding (Fruhlinger, 2018). Organizations are losing proprietary information in data breaches that cause loss of business and competitive advantage. The government cannot protect you against all these attacks because the government doesn't control the configuration of your computer systems and networks. The government may also be unable to do anything about attackers in a foreign country, even if they know who they are, due to lack of jurisdiction. You will learn the primary ways attackers compromise systems in this book. By taking action to minimize the potential for attacks, you can reduce your cyber risk and defend yourself from these threats.

What you need to know is that your systems are under attack. In some cases, even though the attack may not harm your business or your network (you may not even notice it), attackers may use the compromised systems to hurt other people and systems. No matter what country you live in, you may have a vested interest in protecting systems against cyberattacks that could ultimately harm hospitals, industrial control systems, communications systems, election systems, financial organizations, and more. The ultimate damage could be worse than a data breach contained within your organization.

Each organization needs to work to keep their systems secure to help prevent data breaches not only in their environments but globally. Each infected system, and every service provider that allows attackers to reside on their network, is aiding and abetting cybercriminals. Once you understand how these criminals operate, you can do something about it. Build up or employ a cyber army for your organization and create defenses to protect intellectual property, data, employees, and customers. By taking the steps outlined in this book, you will be on a path to understanding where your cyber risk lies and how to reduce it.

Hacking words

A lot of long-time security and technical professionals may be slightly perturbed with my use of the word "hacker" in this book. That's because its original meaning did not have a negative connotation or refer to criminal activity. It meant something along the lines of solving problems in interesting ways, though definitions vary (Raymond, 2001). You may find online and at conferences that some security professionals get annoyed and complain about the use of the word hacker in connection with crimes.

I highly respect those who have this deep history and knowledge of the past and origins of the current state of cybersecurity. However, I imagine the people I am writing this book for, who are executives and people who did not grow up in the original hacker culture, associate the word with criminal or nefarious activity thanks to the news media, movies, books, and other sources. The definition of the word "hacker" in the dictionary has changed to include what most people probably believe the word means: "A person who illegally gains access to and sometimes tampers with information in a computer system (Merriam-webster, 2020)." That is why I chose to use the term in a way that is unfavorable to some cybersecurity individuals.

I find that many times people debate the meaning of words — especially in technology and cybersecurity! Although I attempt to be precise and cite many references, I am not a fan of etymological debates. To me, it is more important that we understand each other and solve the problems at hand, and that's what I attempt to do in this book. I tend to go with dictionary definitions, but in one case where spelling was in question, I took two unscientific polls of my followers on Twitter: Pentester or Pen Tester? The results were almost a tie, but I went with the word most security professionals preferred based on the comments and the variation that won in both cases: "Pentester." I find both commonly used in online resources.

Additionally, some researchers scoff at the use of Wikipedia as a reference. Wikipedia[2] can change and may be edited by people over time. It is not the best primary source of information. However, often, it has countless resources and citations. While writing the book, I sometimes found it to have the most precise

---

[2] Wikipedia https://www.wikipedia.org/

description with more information than other sources. I urge readers to explore the sources on any Wikipedia page I reference to validate further the claims made on those pages. Additionally, help out Wikipedia with a donation if you can to help ensure it can continue as a crowd-sourced information site with editors who attempt to validate the content and citations.

Please keep all this in mind if you are a cybersecurity professional and read something mainstream or described at a high level lacking every technical detail. I am attempting to explain some complex and somewhat esoteric concepts in a way people who don't do this for a living can hopefully understand. The goal here is to reduce data breaches. Sometimes detailed, precise, and historical definitions don't make a difference when trying to achieve that objective. In fact, they may distract from the actual problems I'm trying to help people solve. If you are looking for a basic understanding of cybersecurity, this book is for you. If you want to dive deeper, I include countless references, footnotes, and recommendations for further reading.

2
HOW NETWORK TRAFFIC GOT ME INTO CYBERSECURITY

I ran a software engineering business for over ten years before my current business: creating web applications and e-commerce sites for companies, among other things. For a while, I co-located my servers at companies that provided network connectivity and server racks. I would bring in the servers, configure them with various parts purchased from a variety of vendors, stack them, and maintain everything end to end. It wasn't my favorite thing. I am much happier running applications in cloud environments now so I can focus more on my code and less on the underlying hardware and networking.

To be honest, the first place I hosted web servers was in the basement of a guy who had a T1 line[3], and the mail server was in my condominium. I ended up hosting an e-commerce website in that basement for a business that later became a multi-million-dollar company. That was around 1999, and yes, people used to run small businesses that way back in the day. I wasn't the only

---

[3] Large companies used A T1 line at that time to connect to the Internet. https://en.wikipedia.org/wiki/T-carrier

one. Large companies, on the other hand, would host their servers in their corporate offices and buildings and connect everything with private leased lines. I know this because I helped manage telecommunications bills for a large oil company just after college. Many felt the Internet was not secure enough to use for highly sensitive business transactions and data. A lot of small companies were setting up servers and websites any way they could to get things running.

Technically, my first security incident involved an FTP[4] folder that a friend of mine who worked in IT set up for me on one of the servers in that basement. The IT people in those days were responsible for setting up all the technical infrastructure in companies, as is mostly still the case with on-premises networks and data centers. An FTP folder is a place where files can be stored on a remote server. My IT friend configured the folder to allow both upload and download to the remote file server. No one would find it, right?

The guys with the T1 line called me up one day to ask why I was using up all their bandwidth — almost the entire capacity of their Internet connection. I said I wasn't. We looked into it and figured out someone had "borrowed" that FTP folder to serve up a Warez[5] site (illegal, unlicensed software downloads). I learned the importance of never allowing both upload and download on an FTP folder. This incident was the early precursor to the S3 bucket problems people currently experience on AWS[6]. Without getting into the technical differences, an S3 bucket is the modern version of an FTP folder where you can store files in the Amazon cloud. I also learned that day that if you leave something open on the Internet, people will find it even if you don't tell them it's there.

---

[4] FTP (File Transfer Protocol) https://en.wikipedia.org/wiki/File_Transfer_Protocol

[5] Warez https://en.wikipedia.org/wiki/Warez

[6] Amazon Web Services (AWS). https://aws.amazon.com/

I later hosted systems at a colocation[7] facility provided by Internap in Seattle for a while. I had no problems with Internap. At first, I thought it was cool to scan my hand in the biometric[8] reader like they do in the movies where people get into high-security buildings. But at some point, after dropping my palm on the reader to reboot systems in the middle of the night one too many times and trying to remotely configure a load balancer[9] over the phone with a Cisco-certified engineer, I decided to move to a managed hosting provider[10]. For me, dealing with the physical servers wasn't as fun as writing software. It was a royal pain. Everything would go wrong at the worst possible time, like when I was on a plane or that part of the highway on the coast of California where you get no cell reception.

The managed hosting provider would set up the servers and operating systems, networking equipment, firewalls, and load balancers. I just installed my software on top of that. One reason I decided to make this change was that I thought they would know more about security than me. That was an incorrect assumption. Please note that I moved my servers to this large hosting company that some of you out there reading this are still likely using. But they are not the only one out there that had similar issues — so don't assume my story applies only to that organization.

Although I had a Master of Software Engineering at the time of this incident, no one ever taught me security. I didn't even know anyone who worked in security. I did my best to try to follow the published best practices (which were few and far between at the time). I installed SSL certificates and reduced my liability by never storing credit cards, which was all handled by the processor. I thought no one would bother with me since there was nothing to steal. Many small businesses believe attackers won't bother with

---

[7] Colocation https://www.inap.com/colocation/
[8] Biometrics https://www.dhs.gov/biometrics
[9] Load Balancing. https://en.wikipedia.org/wiki/Load_balancing_(computing)
[10] Managed hosting. https://www.rackspace.com/en-us/managed-hosting

them because they are small. The first-hand experience I had in the early 2000s and the security research I continue to do proves this is not true.

By inspecting network traffic, I ultimately discovered and proved my first data breach was happening. I presented the information to my hosting provider, whom I expected to help me. They didn't. They told me they scanned my system with a virus checker, and it didn't find anything, so everything was fine. I knew it wasn't. I saw strange network traffic every time I restarted my little customized open-source Jetty[11] web server. It would receive five random web requests from computers around the world, and then the traffic would stop. I wasn't getting as many orders suddenly, and I knew something was wrong. When I told this story to the hosting provider, they told me not to worry about it. But the thing is, I was losing money, and I knew it. I didn't like that so much. So no, I wasn't about to "not worry about it."

I wasn't sure what to do, but I knew it had something to do with that network traffic. Those web requests were just odd. I did not believe there were five customers out there just waiting for my little website to come back online who all happened to go to the web page every time I restarted my web server. I went back to support and asked to turn on all the firewall logs. They were only showing me denied traffic. I thought maybe something in the allowed traffic would give me a clue. I wanted to see active connections to my computer. It was just a guess, and I had no idea what I was doing at the time. I didn't even know how to use a packet sniffer[12] to inspect traffic or what to look for in the logs.

The first support person I asked could tell I was clueless. He refused to turn on the logs and told me it would be too much traffic. I wondered how my little web server that got a few orders a week could generate "too much traffic." His words did not deter

---

[11] Jetty web server https://www.eclipse.org/jetty/
[12] Packet sniffer or analyzer. https://en.wikipedia.org/wiki/Packet_analyzer

me. I hung up and waited for the night shift. Now I knew what was possible and what to ask. I also was aware that the night shift is typically a little more lenient, shall we say. I called up and confidently asked the support person to turn on all my firewall logs. He did it happily and without any questions.

At this point, I discovered something even more intriguing. There was a large amount of traffic going out of my server that was indicative of email messages. I didn't know how to look at network packets to see what was in them as I do now, but I knew that email traffic ran on a specific port. I'll explain ports in chapter 5, but it was traffic on port 25 for those who know something about SMTP[13] and email. I knew it was too much email traffic for what I was running on that server. I sent about eight email messages per day.

As a side note, I was sending minimal email from this server because I had outsourced all my email hosting to a provider that could stop spam and fix email problems. I was frustrated because I was getting 900 spam messages per day. I started investigating all the email traffic a few months before this incident. I had discovered that the same spam would arrive five times, and the originating computer address showed the messages came from big companies like Microsoft, HP, and other small businesses. It seemed like, somehow, attackers had compromised these companies, and they didn't know it!

I tried to contact the companies sending the spam, but all the means of contacting them had no effect. I don't know if they were inundated and not reading the emails, or the spammers had infected those mailboxes as well, so no one ever got the messages. All the spam-fighting services out there couldn't make a significant impact until Postini came along (since purchased by Google and now part of Gmail). That was the first product I found

---

[13] SMTP (Simple Mail Transfer Protocol)
https://en.wikipedia.org/wiki/Simple_Mail_Transfer_Protocol

that could make a dent in the spam problem. If you want to know the whole incredible story about spam back then — how organized crime rings in Russia sent it, and criminals threatened business owners and their families who tried to stop the spammers — I recommend you read a book by Brian Krebs called *Spam Nation* (Krebs, 2015).

When I saw the mysterious email traffic in the firewall logs, I turned off the email application on my server. Doing so should have stopped it from sending any emails, but when I checked, the rogue traffic was still there! I wasn't running anything on my server that would have created that type of network traffic. I thought my hosting company would surely believe me now. I took the logs back to them and explained what I'd done to uncover it. Once again, they said it was no problem. "Don't worry about it." *Really*?

But it gets even weirder. I have often wondered if there was an insider at this company working with foreign spammers, and they just thought I wouldn't figure it out. Or maybe they just thought I was a dumb girl, and what I said didn't matter; maybe they had no clue what was going on. I can make up all sorts of outlandish theories and a good movie plot to go along with it, but the fact is I was trying to run my business and get by. I wasn't concerned with any of that at the time. I just wanted to get orders on my e-commerce website and pay my bills. I don't know for sure what the story was internally, but here's what happened next.

I had to figure out through trial and error how to get the malware off my system. I gave up on talking to my hosting company's support team because that was, clearly, useless for this particular matter. I had no idea what to do about malware, but I figured something had to be running on my system to create this traffic. I looked at every application running on my server for anything that wasn't supposed to be there. Eventually, I started turning services[14] off, one by one. I proceeded to crash the system a few times and had to call support to reboot it, but other than that, I was on my own. I wouldn't even have known who to call to help me with the problem at that time. Eventually, I turned off one of the services, and the traffic stopped! I felt triumphant.

I didn't know how to find the malware or figure out how it got on the machine, but this — and 900 spam messages per day — are the reasons I'm writing this book today, speaking at conferences, and providing cloud security training and consulting services to companies. I have since learned how to use sniffers, handle security incidents, and reverse engineer malware, among other things, on my educational journey. I now hold the GSE[15] certification, which some claim is one of the hardest to achieve in the industry.

But as you can see from my story, even if you don't have people on staff who know how to do all that, or who hold cybersecurity certifications, you hopefully have someone on your team who can look at network traffic logs. These logs can tell you a lot. They can probably tell you if you have a security breach right now. This is one of the reasons I emphasize the importance of network security in this book. Even if an attacker compromises a computer system to the point that all the operating system software is providing false information, the attacker cannot hide their traffic entirely on the network. They also generally cannot make their activities in the memory invisible on the computer system, but sometimes the network traffic is easier to investigate.

My story does not end there. After I figured out how to turn off the malware, I went back to my hosting company. I didn't bother to tell them what I'd discovered because, at this point, it seemed futile. I just asked them to deny outbound network access I didn't need. My computer didn't initiate outbound connections to

---

[14] Operating system services https://www.w3schools.in/operating-system-tutorial/services/
[15] The SANS GSE https://medium.com/cloud-security/the-sans-gse-1b4741a819fe

anything. It only replied to requests it received. I only wanted to allow the most minimal traffic required for my applications to run correctly. They argued with me! They said no one bothers with outbound traffic. I said I didn't care what everyone else does. I wanted to block it. In the end, like everything else in this story, I figured out how to do it myself. I had very restrictive network rules in my firewall settings that only allowed what the applications on my server required.

And magically, after doing all that and stopping the malware, the orders on my website jumped back up. The malware did not come back. What I didn't know then was that I had made it nearly impossible for C2 (command and control) traffic to function on my server. That's another topic I will explain further in chapter 5. I was happily getting some nice side money from my hostel booking venture for about a month, and then even stranger things happened.

Before finishing the rest of this story, I need to explain how I ended up creating this e-commerce website in the first place. At some point in the mid 2000's I went to live in Manly Beach near Sydney, Australia, for three months because I needed an escape. The business I helped grow to a multi-million-dollar company had shafted me. The owner sold the company and all the technology that my company (and mostly I) had built. She made promises about future work and then left me hanging with several contracts, which I couldn't afford to pay when the new owners took over. I trusted her so I didn't get these promises in the form of a legal document. I had just lost my lawyer, who wasn't answering my emails because I was his smallest client and didn't want to fight them anyway. At this point, I just wanted to get away to see the other side of the world and start over. I figured I'd have to get a "real job" after this setback. I even considered moving to Australia permanently, but that didn't happen.

While I was there, I started talking to this hostel owner. He was complaining about the cost of hostel booking websites he was using to advertise. When I got back to the U.S., I created a booking website for him and just took a cut of the bookings instead of charging him for it. I was pretty good at SEO[16] (getting web pages high up in Google and other search engine rankings), and my idea was that I was going to create an online hostel booking website and make a zillion dollars so it would be worth it.

At some point prior to the security incident, the owner of the hostel in Australia contacted me and said there was a new owner. I was okay with that as long as I was still getting paid. I didn't know what was going on at Manly Beach in Australia. Also, intriguing was that after I found and stopped the malware on my server, this new owner, assuming that's who he was, contacted me. He complained that he was getting too much business. Who complains about making too much money? He also complained that the prices of the hostel bookings were too high. I didn't set those prices — he had control over that. And people were paying them! None of this made sense.

I had shut down one function of the site I suspected to be involved in the attack, and he complained about that as well. I restored the functionality as he requested, but as mentioned had made changes to better protect the system, such as closing unnecessary network ports. I had also created my very own web application firewall (WAF)[17] — a term that did not exist at the time. I was inspecting every single web request and rejecting any that looked like possible attacks. I researched website security vulnerabilities like the OWASP Top 10[18]. I tried to subvert anything that looked suspicious, even if I wasn't positive it was an attack. I made a few mistakes and learned a lot in the process. The malware did not

---

[16] SEO (search engine optimization)
https://en.wikipedia.org/wiki/Search_engine_optimization
[17] A web application firewall (WAF)
https://en.wikipedia.org/wiki/Web_application_firewall
[18] Open Web Application Security Project (OWASP) Top 10 List
https://www.owasp.org/index.php/Category:OWASP_Top_Ten_Project

come back even after restoring the suspect functionality. If you are not familiar with the things I just mentioned, I'll explain them later in this book.

Oddly enough, a few months after fixing the security problem on the hostel site and ensuring it did not come back, the hostel owner contacted me to cancel his service and move it elsewhere. At this point, the website was generating a lot more business for him than before (as far as I know). The breach never affected him financially, only me. When my web server was compromised, I wouldn't get my fee. People would still show up at the hostel, and he'd get his portion of the payment for the booking. But I wasn't getting my cut. I find the whole thing a bit strange because he was happy the site was not producing many reservations. Once the website was generating much more business and was also giving me my cut, he moved the site. I presume someone was diverting the leads from my site somewhere else. Perhaps it was a coincidence. I wasn't one to argue with customers to try to get them to stay, so I helped him migrate the domain name and never heard from him again.

We are still not quite at the end of the story. Another strange thing happened. A short time after I got the malware off my server, my hosting company contacted me and offered to pay me two months of hosting fees to go away. I thought this was odd. However, I had not been asking them for any help at this point, and I didn't tell them, but I was not impressed with their service (*understatement!*) and was planning to leave anyway. I took the money and moved to another hosting provider.

A few weeks after I moved my servers, a story appeared in one of the many cybersecurity or IT-related news sources I was following at the time. The headline was something like, "Most servers ever were hacked" in data centers and were spewing out stock spam. The malware had an embedded Kaspersky virus checker. I was able to find a reference to this malware on the SecureWorks site in 2006 (Stewart, 2006): "The SpamThru bot has the capability to scan the system for other malware using a pirated copy of Kaspersky Anti-Virus."

The malware wanted to make sure no other sloppy malware co-existed that might cause someone to discover their spam-generating software. *Genius.* The hosting company scans the system. No viruses. All is well. I wonder what virus checker that big hosting company was using at the time. Kaspersky, perhaps? I was pretty sure this was the same malware on my system, but I wasn't using the same hosting company anymore, nor was I on that compromised server, so I could not verify anything. At that time, I also didn't have the skills I have now to investigate systems and networks after breaches to determine what happened.

After experiencing this data breach and building software to protect my websites better, I tried to pitch my WAF to investors and sell it to other customers. Unfortunately, no one understood what I was talking about or believed that these problems I'd discovered existed, so I gave up.

When I explained what I saw in network traffic and my WAF logs to an investor and recommended he invest in security, he disregarded my recommendation and told me to write a blog. So, I did. That old security blog is still out there, with traffic from that old WAF. I know a lot more now than I did then, so some of it may not be exactly right, but I did write about some interesting findings. For example, I noticed fake Google search engine bots that were not coming from Google IP addresses. I also saw a lot of malicious traffic coming from specific networks. Some of those networks are still problematic today. However, malware has gotten much sneakier since that time.

I initially didn't know anyone who worked in security. As I continued to research and talk about cybersecurity, boyfriends and co-workers told me I was paranoid. Eventually, I discovered other security researchers and organizations. I read a lot of books and finally got training once I could afford the classes. They were always too expensive, but once I started working for a big company, they paid for some of it, which enabled me to attend and get my certifications and a security master's degree. At about the same time that I started the master's degree, I started the Seattle AWS Architects and Engineers meetup to meet other people using cloud technology and learn more about it.

That is how I got into security — and now more specifically, cloud security. Network traffic can be one of the most reliable indicators that malware has infiltrated your systems. Architecting system communication with malware in mind will make it easier to spot. You can design your network to make it harder for compromises to spread. Don't assume the company hosting your systems knows more about security than you do, or that they're paying attention to your network traffic. That is typically your responsibility unless you have a contract with someone that explicitly states they will do it for you. Looking at network logs is a great place to start for those who want to get into cybersecurity.

By the way, I had no issues at the next hosting provider. However, I eventually moved all my systems to AWS (Amazon Web Services)[19], where I can run virtual computers instead of dealing with physical servers and automate deployments. I now focus primarily on providing security consulting services on major cloud providers like AWS, Azure[20], and Google Cloud Platform (GCP)[21]. Initially, there was no way I was going to move my e-commerce servers to a cloud provider. As I will explain later, over time, AWS improved security processes so much that I believed some companies could reduce cybersecurity risk if they used the platform correctly, combined with the cybersecurity fundamentals you will learn in this book.

---

[19] AWS https://aws.amazon.com/
[20] Azure https://azure.microsoft.com/
[21] Google Cloud Platform https://cloud.google.com/

3
CYBERSECURITY STRATEGY – ASK THE RIGHT QUESTIONS

In a large organization, cybersecurity at the executive level is more about analyzing risk than it is about deciphering network packets. Analyzing risk is always challenging, but the more strategic information executives have, the better decisions they can make. Notice I said *strategic* data – because sometimes too much data creates more problems than it solves. Executives need the right data.

The right data may not be possible to obtain in some organizations at this point, but if executives start asking the right questions, teams will figure out how to get the data. Products and systems will evolve such that they can generate the correct reports that answer the right questions. Producing the right data, in turn, improves cybersecurity outcomes. How will executives know what questions to ask?

Learn the basics of cybersecurity

It's not as hard as you think to learn the top security threats your organization may face if the executives do not receive the information in a way they can understand and take action on it. That is the purpose of this book. From an executive point of view, security is not about understanding network packets, bits, bytes, and assembly language, or reverse engineering malware. A large part of cybersecurity is understanding the macro issues that cause the most breaches and having a way to measure whether you are susceptible to a similar fate — and then doing something about it.

Once you understand what causes the majority of data breaches and how to thwart common attacks, you will be able to ask better questions. These questions will help you quantify the level of cybersecurity risk in your organization more accurately. The answers will help you make more informed cybersecurity decisions. Tracking the right cybersecurity metrics and leveraging automation to prevent mistakes will help your organization close gaps used by attackers to infiltrate systems.

Organizations also need to make sure they meet any legal and regulatory cybersecurity requirements, often called "compliance" by cybersecurity professionals. Compliance involves going through checklists of regulations and making sure the company has implemented all the security requirements on the list. Compliance with security laws and regulations aims to ensure organizations are taking steps to secure their systems.

Although this book mentions compliance-related topics, its primary purpose is to help organizations stop data breaches. Many organizations that pass compliance audits still suffer data breaches, so clearly, compliance is not the answer to that problem. Compliance raises awareness in the minds of people who are not as well informed about security and gets them to do things they might not otherwise do. However, it is not enough to stop a breach. This book covers many of the items in the compliance checklists. More importantly, it provides a different way to view and measure security, focusing less on implementing individual controls in checklists and more on *closing the gaps that allow attackers to gain entry.*

Cybersecurity reports

In some cases, even though you may not notice an attack, and it may not negatively impact your business or your network, attackers may leverage your compromised systems to harm other people and systems. I wrote an article for the online security publication, *Infosecurity*, titled, "People Do What You Inspect, Not What You Expect" (Radichel, People Do What You Inspect, Not What You Expect, 2017). In it, I explain how reports help you inspect what is happening based on metrics, instead of accepting someone's reassurance that everything is OK. This way, you can better quantify and measure whether the risk in your organization is going up or down.

Over time I learned that one of the most important questions to ask before designing a complex financial system is, "What reports do you want the system to generate? Please provide a sample with data." Architecting systems to create reports that answer the right questions generally results in solutions that more accurately solve business problems. That is because the report requirements drive an architecture that supports providing executives the necessary data in a reliable and digestible format. If the system cannot generate the requested report, it is not capturing the correct data or has an architectural flaw. This assertion presumes the business is asking the right questions, and the system creates reliable and accurate data that helps drive better business decisions.

Creating cybersecurity reports will have the following benefits for executives:

- Requiring risk reports will drive the implementation of systems and processes that mitigate top risks instead of buying for buzzwords (i.e. purchasing a product with the latest trendy technology terms in the marketing brochure).

- Cybersecurity reporting can help executives more accurately assess risks that exist in the organization and prioritize work to fix the problems.

- If reports indicate work assigned to fix a security problem is incomplete, liability shifts from the executive to the person that did not do their job.

- Finding people who repeatedly bypass security controls might indicate an insider threat — which otherwise can be challenging to spot.

- Accurate, well-designed reports can help you align cybersecurity spending with risk reduction and increase return on your cybersecurity investments.

Once you start asking questions, your security and IT teams may tell you that it is impossible to provide the answers. They may tell you they need more time or more resources like people, software engineers, or new security products. Your questions will drive investments into things that close security gaps instead of spending money on expensive security products and hoping they work. Existing products may provide value and block *some* attacks, but many do not present the security gaps and risks in your environment as a whole. That is what the questions in this book aim to do. If you can't answer the questions, you may have a security gap.

Security automation

To get accurate reports, you'll need data. Manually collecting the data is going to be inaccurate in the best case, or not even possible in the worst case. How do you solve this? Gather this data from automated processes. Remove humans from the process of generating reports to prevent mistakes and tampering. Eventually, you may even consider automatically fixing security problems identified in reports.

Research has shown that security automation reduces the

expenses incurred as a result of a data breach. Per the Ponemon Institute report (Ponemon Institute, IBM, 2018), as I referenced in chapter 1, without automation, the average cost of a breach goes up from $3.86 million to $4.43 million. Perhaps the mega-breaches costing $350 million would not have been so high if those organizations had automated security. Security automation is not a quick fix, it is an investment and an ongoing process, and it still requires well-trained individuals for best results.

I've written about and been a proponent of security automation for many years, especially as it pertains to cloud security. That's because cloud environments are a big software platform designed for automated deployments and software-driven responses to events. I immediately saw the potential to reduce human error and create transparency around actions that lead to security problems. Cloud providers need to be vetted, of course, but that is a topic for chapter 19 which covers vendor assessments. You don't need the cloud to automate security, but it makes things easier. Check automation capabilities and costs for each vendor before purchasing products and services. I'll dive deeper into automation near the end of the book.

Align objectives — create a security culture

Do you have this problem? Every time I teach a cloud security class, I say, "In some organizations, the development teams got to the cloud first, and now security is trying to catch up after the fact and implement controls. Sometimes developers don't like this so much." Smiles appear on faces. Heads nod; that misalignment increases cybersecurity risk. Security and software teams need to come together to solve problems instead of being at odds with each other, as is the case in many organizations.

Security automation is not just writing software or turning on cloud provider security controls. It requires a deep understanding of networking and security, as well as software architecture and engineering, to create systems that withstand failure. Experienced security professionals understand security threats and risks at a deeper level than most developers. Network security architects know how to design networks that minimize attack surfaces and make it easier to spot malicious traffic. Software engineers understand how to automate and build resilient software systems. QA engineers know how to thoroughly test applications *and infrastructure* (something many companies fail to test adequately, if at all). You need all these skills to design the most effective security automation.

I have a background that includes running companies, security, networking, and software, so I understand what people on all sides are trying to achieve. I believe training and communication would resolve conflicts caused by misaligned objectives. That's why I designed my cloud security class for technical executives, security professionals, IT, DevOps, developers, and QA team members — all together. Instead of sending everyone to separate security classes or showing them a video, get everyone together — not just to learn cloud security, but to discuss and design solutions at the same time. If you can't afford external training, you can set up internal training where these teams work together to provide training to each other and come up with solutions.

I would argue that an organization that complains about a shortage of cybersecurity staff are not leveraging their existing people effectively. Developers are smart. They can learn about security. They can help implement automated security solutions that make security teams more efficient. The more you can automate away simple security problems, the more your security team can avoid burnout and focus on more complex security issues.

Security training can extend to others in the company as well. I recently had a company send their sales staff to my class to learn about cloud security. They will now be able to drive more secure solutions back to product managers and customers and sell cloud security products. Create a security culture by ensuring objectives are aligned, automate as much as possible, and ensure everyone has the training required to avoid mistakes that lead to security problems.

Measuring cyber risk effectively

Here are twenty high-level cybersecurity questions executives can ask their security team. I based these questions on years of researching what causes data breaches, including the time I spent working on a research team for a security vendor that sells firewalls, endpoint security, and wireless security products. I have also written white papers on data breaches. I reference many sources throughout this book that you can read if you want to dive deeper into any of these topics. By asking these questions, you will be able to quantify and measure problems in your organization that could lead to a data breach.

Once you know what is creating the risk, you can work on solutions that reduce potential exposure and losses. If you don't know what all these questions mean, don't worry. I'm going to explain each one in the remaining chapters. For each of these questions, you can drill down into further requirements, issues, and best practices, as the organization matures in its ability to implement secure and automated solutions. I'll also explain at the end how you can leverage these questions to measure risk throughout your company more effectively.

1. How many of our systems are running out-of-date software with known security flaws (otherwise known as CVEs or Common Vulnerabilities and Exposures)?

2. What percentage of our systems are exposed to the Internet?

3. How many systems expose high-risk ports?

4. How many attack paths exist on our network?

5. How much data could an attacker access if any one person's credentials are stolen?

6. What percentage of accounts in all systems the organization uses are integrated into our primary user management system and require MFA (multi-factor authentication)?

7. What percentage of our data is encrypted when stored?

8. What percentage of our network communications are encrypted?

9. How many outstanding findings are there in the results of assessments, penetration tests, or audits?

10. In the event of a security incident or disaster, could we restore our systems from a backup?

11. Do we know who ultimately makes security decisions? Does everyone who makes a security decision understand network, application, and data security?

12. Do we have enforceable security policies in place?

13. Who is generating the most exceptions to security policies — and why?

14. Are security checks built into our deployment systems to prevent vulnerabilities from entering our environment?

15. Do we vet our vendors and require them to follow our security policies?

16. What is the efficacy of the security systems we purchased?

17. Do we have monitoring, incident handling, and response plans in place to identify and manage security incidents?

18. What percentage of our activities are automated to prevent

security gaps and provide security reports?

19. Is the overall risk level within the organization going up or down?

20. How is the threat landscape changing?

I offer these questions as a starting point. The questions, answers, and recommended solutions will differ for each business based on size, industry, and other factors. Use these questions to create cybersecurity reports that help executives quantify risk and prioritize cybersecurity spending appropriately.

4
CVES: SECURITY BUGS THAT BITE

Do you know what CVE-2017–5638 is? It happens to be the unpatched technical vulnerability that allowed attackers to breach Equifax systems[22]. Attackers were able to use this security flaw to gain access to Equifax systems and expose the personal data of 147 million people (Puig, 2019). They attacked a known and published defect in a specific piece of software to gain access to an Equifax server. Once on that server, they used that machine to get to other computers in the company until, ultimately, they were able to access and steal data. The flaw in the software had been published online two months earlier. If Equifax had taken action at that time, the company could have avoided this data breach.

Here is one more example. CVE-2017–0144[23] is the underlying mechanism that facilitated the WannaCry ransomware outbreak (MS-ISAC, 2019), which shut down large companies and hospitals in 2017 (Brandom, 2017). The malware was able to get onto systems using this CVE. It would then encrypt all the files, making

---

[22] NIST details for CVE-2017-5638 https://nvd.nist.gov/vuln/detail/CVE-2017-5638
[23] NIST details for CVE-2017-0144 https://nvd.nist.gov/vuln/detail/CVE-2017-0144

them inaccessible, and then demand a ransom in bitcoins to get them back. This ransomware spreads from computer to computer, organization to organization, automatically (McNeil, 2017). And it is still going! In August 2018, TSMC, a chipmaker that manufactures iPhone chips, said ransomware halted production for an entire day (Kumar, 2019). Although this ransomware shut down hospitals in the U.K., many healthcare organizations have not taken adequate steps to prevent similar attacks. Malwarebytes reports that this is still one of the top five causes of data breaches in healthcare as of April 30, 2019 (Ilascu, Emotet Trojan Is the Most Prevalent Threat in Healthcare Systems, 2019). TechRadar confirmed on January 1, 2020, that WannaCry was still the most prevalent ransomware attack in 2019 (Spadafora, 2020).

What is a CVE?

CVE stands for Common Vulnerabilities and Exposures[24]. CVEs are technology flaws that attackers can use to harm systems in an organization or personal computers and devices. New CVEs discovered by researchers and vendors become part of the list of known CVEs in public databases, so those who use the software can take action to protect themselves. The vulnerabilities include a rating that indicates how critical they are, though this rating is somewhat subjective at times. Executives should ensure their organizations fix security vulnerabilities as soon as possible, starting with the most critical if you cannot fix them all right away.

In 1999, MITRE Corporation launched a CVE List to help organizations track flaws, primarily in software though there have been some hardware-related flaws[25]. The U.S. National Institute of Standards and Technology (NIST) also publishes known CVEs[26]. Another site, CVE Details[27], sometimes has additional

---

[24] CVE: Frequently Asked Questions: https://cve.mitre.org/about/faqs.html
[25] CVE: History https://cve.mitre.org/about/history.html
[26] NIST National Vulnerability Database https://nvd.nist.gov/

information. You can sign up for a newsletter from US-CERT (Community Emergency Response Team)[28], which reports vulnerabilities affecting hardware and software[29].

US-CERT is part of CISA, a component of the US Department of Homeland Security, which works to secure the nation's cybersecurity and communications infrastructure. Countries around the world have CERTs. For example, I had someone in one of my classes from the NZ-CERT, which is the organization that responds to cybersecurity threats in New Zealand[30]. Following these updates helps organizations identify security problems that could affect their systems and fix them before attackers find them.

Organizations can also search for vulnerabilities that affect software running in their environments. The vulnerable software affected in the Equifax Breach is free software available on the Internet (known as open-source software) called Apache Struts[31]. The NIST vulnerability database website and the others mentioned previously have search capabilities to see if any vulnerabilities exist in a particular type of software. Organizations can use this to search for vulnerabilities in the software they run in their organization already or to research third-party software and hardware they are interested in using or purchasing.

How are new vulnerabilities discovered?

Security flaws are sometimes exposed when security researchers test software or hardware. They intentionally attack systems using a variety of techniques, including looking for logic flaws in the code that are the result of faulty programming that doesn't consider all actions an end-user could take on the system. Researchers may also use a technique called fuzzing[32], where they

---

[27] CVE Details https://www.cvedetails.com/
[28] CERT https://en.wikipedia.org/wiki/Computer_emergency_response_team
[29] US-Cert Mailing list https://www.us-cert.gov/mailing-lists-and-feeds
[30] NZ-Cert https://www.cert.govt.nz/
[31] Apache Struts https://struts.apache.org/

intentionally pass a massive amount of bad data into all the places where data is input into the system. If the software does not correctly validate all the data sent into the system, the system could crash. If the researcher can produce a crash, it is an indication that a security flaw may exist that they can exploit to access the system and its data. In some cases, they may discover an exploit known as remote code execution (RCE)[33], which allows them to completely control and run code on the remote system.

Security researchers may also look at malware that has infected systems and use a variety of techniques to reverse engineer that malware. Sometimes, malware tries to obfuscate[34] itself to be sneaky, meaning the attacker makes it harder for tools designed to stop malware to identify it or for security researchers to figure out what it is doing. They do this with something called a packer (Roccia, 2017), or by changing code in text into other formats that humans and security products cannot read (Russo, 2017). Hackers may hide attacks or data in manipulated network traffic (Stødle, 2005). A type of malware known as "fileless malware[35]" runs in the memory of a system, without saving executable files on the infected machine.

Often, researchers will need to open and run malware within tools called disassemblers or debuggers such as IDA[36] or Ghidra[37]. These tools allow the researcher to see the low-level code, called "assembly language[38]," that interacts with the hardware since the source code is often not available. They may also look at the

---

[32] Fuzzing https://www.owasp.org/index.php/Fuzzing
[33] Remote Code Execution https://encyclopedia.kaspersky.com/glossary/remote-code-execution-rce/
[34] What is obfuscation (obfu)? https://searchsoftwarequality.techtarget.com/definition/obfuscation
[35] What is Fileless Malware? https://www.mcafee.com/enterprise/en-us/security-awareness/ransomware/what-is-fileless-malware.html
[36] IDA from Hex-Rays https://www.hex-rays.com/products/ida/
[37] Ghidra from the U.S. NSA (National Security Agency) https://ghidra-sre.org/
[38] Assembly Language https://techterms.com/definition/assembly_language

underlying structure of PDF files, Word documents, or web pages to find nefarious executable code injected into files by attackers. Studying the network activity generated by malware is another useful way to gain insight into malware activity. These are just a few examples of how security researchers inspect and try to reverse engineer malware.

In some cases, vendors discover vulnerabilities in their software internally. Customers or security researchers may also report security problems. A vendor will often provide a fix, known as a patch[39], for the CVE at the same time as the public disclosure. When a vendor makes a patch available that fixes a security problem, customers should install the updated software as soon as possible to prevent attackers from using the vulnerability.

Responsible disclosure

After a researcher finds a vulnerability, he or she may report the findings. Hopefully, they will disclose information in a manner that will not harm others, meaning they don't just put it on a blog post and tell the world the minute they discover it! Doing so might alert malicious actors to the flaw who will then use it against innocent victims. Researchers should first contact the vendor to let them know about the problem and give the vendor a chance to fix it. This process is known as responsible disclosure[40]. If flaws are published before the vendor can fix it, this may allow attackers to break into systems in the meantime.

Unfortunately, some researchers try to report vulnerabilities to vendors, and vendors do not fix the flaws promptly, or they may not fix them at all. In some cases, vendors ignore security researchers, either intentionally or because they do not have a well-defined process for dealing with these reports. In other cases, they may even threaten to sue the researcher or take other

---

[39] Patch to fix software flaws https://en.wikipedia.org/wiki/Patch_(computing)
[40] Responsible Disclosure https://en.wikipedia.org/wiki/Responsible_disclosure

adversarial actions. This reaction causes some security researchers to be apprehensive about telling vendors when they find flaws in products. A better approach is to define and publicize a responsible disclosure program to help researchers and customers report security problems, so the company can quickly resolve them. You can find an example of a responsible disclosure program on the Capital One website:
https://www.capitalone.com/applications/responsible-disclosure/

What motivates security researchers?

Security researchers may have many different motivations for finding and exposing CVEs. First, a security researcher might be genuinely interested in fixing security problems to make the world a better place. As crazy as that sounds, some people do care about keeping the world safe (like me!). Unfortunately, we also all need to make a living to pay our bills and eat, so at some point, a security researcher is generally hoping to make some income from the time they put into security research and finding vulnerabilities.

A security researcher may be hunting for vulnerabilities as part of their job on a research team for a security vendor that creates software to block malware and protect systems. When the researcher uncovers a vulnerability, the company adds new features to products to prevent malware from leveraging the flaw to access systems.

Other companies publish security information to demonstrate security knowledge and share information. Some examples of companies publishing malware research include Google's Project Zero[41] and Cisco's Talos[42]. I worked on a security team for a vendor, and it was one of my favorite jobs. I now continue to research security through my company, 2nd Sight Lab. I publish

---

[41] Google Project Zero blog https://googleprojectzero.blogspot.com/
[42] Cisco Talos blog https://talosintelligence.com/

findings on Twitter and my blog and talk about them at conferences and in classes.

In some cases, a researcher may be interested in gaining some notoriety for finding the flaw. Often, researchers speak at hacker and security conferences like DefCon[43] or BSides[44], where they demonstrate how they broke into systems or software. Many of these researchers are also pentesters (short for penetration testers)[45] hired by companies to try to break into systems. I'll explain more about penetration testing in chapter 14. By proving they were able to exploit systems, they may gain some fame, or perhaps get some more business if they show prowess in hacking into systems.

Another reason researchers look for flaws would be to ask the company for money in return for reporting the vulnerability. Researchers may reach out directly to companies or governments (Barth, 2019) to ask for money when they find programming errors they can use to break into systems. Sometimes they will go through a third party to sell their findings. In that case, the researcher may not know who the other party is that is buying the exploit — and for what purpose — which could be for something malicious. Some companies run bug bounties directly, like Google's Vulnerability Reward Program[46], or through organizations like HackerOne or BugCrowd as a way to allow security researchers to attack systems with permission and report flaws.

Malicious motivations

Of course, malware often exploits CVEs for harmful purposes. The line between security researchers and hackers who attack systems without permission is sometimes blurry. The work tends

---

[43] DefCon https://www.defcon.org/
[44] BSides http://www.securitybsides.com/
[45] Penetration testing https://www.ncsc.gov.uk/guidance/penetration-testing
[46] Google Vulnerability Reward Program
https://www.google.com/about/appsecurity/reward-program/

to be very similar. Consider one of the most popular hacker tools: Metasploit[47]. HD Moore created this tool for pentesters hired by companies to test the security of their systems (Higgens, 2006). Since then, Metasploit has been used for illegal activities as well (Pham, 2015).

Hackers may operate alone or as part of a crime organization that uses exploits to break into systems and make money. In a report on one group called FIN7 (Carr, Goody, Miller, & Vengerik, 2018), FireEye writes:

> On Aug. 1, 2018, the United States District Attorney's Office for the Western District of Washington unsealed indictments and announced the arrests of three individuals within the leadership ranks of a criminal organization that aligns with activity we have tracked since 2015 as FIN7. These malicious actors are members of one of the most prolific financial threat groups of this decade, having carefully crafted attacks targeted at more than 100 organizations.

Many similar groups exist around the world that are tracked by security companies and governments to try to understand their tactics and limit their harmful activities.

A security researcher may also be working for a local or foreign government. Depending on where you live, the word "foreign" has a different context. A security researcher in one country may be considered a criminal hacker in another. Nations have already attacked each other using malware. In some cases, these efforts are initially secret, but eventually, they tend to be exposed.

The book, *Countdown to Zero Day: Stuxnet and the Launch of the World's First Digital Weapon* (Zetter, 2015), explains how the United States attacked and damaged industrial control systems in

---

[47] Metasploit https://www.metasploit.com/

Iranian nuclear facilities when that country was operating outside of an agreement to prevent the proliferation of nuclear material. In five months, 984 centrifuges stopped enriching uranium at an Iranian plant, presumably due to malware known as Stuxnet (Zetter, An Unprecedented Look at Stuxnet, the World's First Digital Weapon, 2014). A USB flash drive delivered the malware to an air-gapped network (one not connected to the Internet).

According to the *New York Times*, President Obama facilitated this use of cyber force (Sanger, 2012). Since that time, Iran has become one of the top cyber threats to the U.S. In June 2019, the Department of Homeland Security wrote a report about how Iran was carrying out cyberattacks on the United States (CISA, 2019). *Forbes* provides more details on the attacks and tactics of this group that security researchers call APT33 or Elfin (Doffman, Secret Iranian Network Behind 'Aggressive' U.S. Cyberattacks Exposed In New Report, 2019). In a recent conflict with the United States, top security experts such as my fellow IANS Faculty member, David Kennedy, warned about retaliation from Iran (Kennedy, Iran's key cybersecurity threat is ransomware: Former NSA hacker, 2020), as noted in the first chapter.

Countries are now employing cyber armies. Sometimes these cyberattacks seem invisible, but at other times they affect people's lives in a more significant way. Israel bombed a building in Gaza alleged to be the base of a Hamas hacking group (Newman, 2019). News organizations reported that Russia is the source of a form of ransomware named NotPetya, which hackers used to take down systems not only in Ukraine but throughout the world, similar to WannaCry (Greenburg, 2018). In 2018, the U.S. government indicted Chinese hackers in a criminal organization associated with the Chinese government (FBI, 2018). In 2020, the U.S. indicted Chinese Military Officials in conjunction with the Equifax breach (Benner, 2020), but Chinese officials denied the accusations (Mozur, 2020).

Zero-day malware

Zero-day malware[48] is malicious software written to attack flaws that security researchers or hackers have discovered but not yet disclosed. Sometimes people refer to these exploits as "zero-days." Bad actors may keep vulnerabilities secret and save them for a special occasion. They want to wait to use the malware for some nefarious purpose, typically something big. The malware may be worth a lot of money in a hacking competition, or the malware developer might sell it to someone who wants to use it on a specific target and objective.

These vulnerabilities are used in rare cases because they are far too valuable. Zero-day malware might allow the attacker to get into a system with proprietary information that they can sell to a competitor for a large sum of money. A government may want to use it for espionage or to defend itself, including as a cyberweapon.

The attackers know the vulnerability will work because no one else knows it exists. There is no mitigation or patch from the vendor. Once the public knows about it and can mitigate the vulnerability in some way, the attackers cannot be sure it will work. The people who created the hardware or software with the security flaw should fix it as soon as they learn about it. While waiting for a fix, customers can do things such as adding firewall restrictions to block access to the insecure application. They may also create rules in specialized network security tools that block network packets with malicious content related to the attack. Security vendors will also create protections in security tools installed on end-user computers.

Although zero-day malware sounds exciting, it is not the cause of most data breaches. Some companies claim that a data breach was

---

[48] What is a zero-day? https://blog.malwarebytes.com/101/2017/04/what-is-a-zero-day/

caused by zero-day malware when, most likely, it wasn't. An attacker is not going to waste this type of exploit, because obtaining zero-day vulnerabilities is time-consuming and expensive. Most of the time, they don't even need to use it. More straightforward ways to attack misconfigured systems exist, so attackers don't need to "burn a zero-day" as the security industry likes to call it. They can use much more basic and well-known software flaws — in other words, CVEs!

5
EXPONENTIAL INCREASES IN CYBER RISK DUE TO INTERNET EXPOSURE

If you think about how breaches occur, there is almost always some Internet exposure involved. It makes sense, then, that reducing Internet exposure reduces risk. Organizations cannot eliminate risk. Of course, a reduction in Internet exposure doesn't completely stop data breaches. Still, systems unnecessarily exposed to anyone on the Internet increases the number of ways an attacker can get into your systems.

The more chances attackers have to break in, the more the odds are in their favor. That's just math. Limiting the access points on your network may not stop every advanced nation-state attack, but it will remove some options. It will also help limit the spread of automated malware and attacks by script kiddies[49] — people who tack together other people's code to attack systems that expose blatant security flaws. Once an attack on a common vulnerability is published and integrated into a tool available on the Internet, anyone who can run it can attack the system even if

---

[49] The Origin of Script Kiddie https://liveoverflow.com/the-origin-of-script-kiddie-hacker-etymology/

they don't know a lot about how the attack works.

Recent trends in cybersecurity have, at times, suggested that network security is overrated in this day and age of cloud and all things connected (Poremba, 2018). If you take a look at who is promoting these ideas, it is often someone who is trying to sell you an identity product, or a product that is devoid of strong network security capabilities. Identity, the ability to prove that someone trying to access your system is who they say they are, is essential. However, network security is especially helpful in blocking attacks at a lower layer in the network stack, before it even gets close to your data or the mechanisms that verify usernames and passwords. Network traffic can also give substantial clues that an attack is underway.

Of course, for things to work, machines and devices need to be able to connect. Organizations can't simply block all network traffic. However, well thought out network architecture can reduce unnecessary risk caused by excessive exposure to the Internet. Proper network architectures can help you see when an attacker is probing your network, or a breach is in progress. Creating secure and effective networks does require additional time and skill. Security is not free, but it will almost always cost less than a data breach. Time invested in a proper network architecture will save your company money in the long run, help reduce the effects of certain types of attacks designed to make your systems inaccessible and may improve application performance.

Defense in depth

Some articles such as one published by *CSO* in 2015 suggest that identity is the new security that will replace firewalls and routers (Grimes, 2015). Some vendors seem to also be pushing this idea that networking is no longer important as long as you have authentication in place. Others I worked with claimed endpoint security (security software you install on your computers, like antivirus software) is better or more important than traditional network monitoring and security controls and would eventually replace them. These types of statements are typically the result of companies and vendors trying to connect to cloud systems from any network location. They miss one of the fundamental premises of cybersecurity: defense in depth. One kind of security control does not replace another. Organizations should have layers of controls that work together to provide security and monitoring at multiple levels.

One of the concepts used to describe traditional networking is called the OSI (Open Systems Interconnection) Model (Shaw, 2018). Without getting too much into the details, network devices split data traversing networks into smaller pieces called packets. Network packets go through various layers on the way out of one network and into another. For example, a packet leaves a computer's network card, and then it may pass through a switch, a router, and a firewall. Generally, each layer adds a network header onto the packet on the way out of a device or network. These headers contain metadata that help a packet reach its intended target. Destination devices remove the corresponding packet headers at each layer. Organizations would be wise to block an attack as soon as it can be identified, rather than to wait until it gets to the authentication portion of an application that exposes sensitive data. Another way to say this is to block the bad traffic at the lowest layer of the stack possible by inspecting and validating it as it passes through different devices on the network.

Network security helps you monitor and block cyber threats before they get anywhere near your application. Even if an attacker steals the usernames and passwords, they can't enter them into a system if the network blocks access to that system. You may have already gotten a sense of the importance of network security from my story on how I got into cybersecurity. I talked about how I identified the breach using network logs. Limiting Internet exposure made it nearly impossible for the malware to function on my server. Let's explore this in more detail.

How a typical breach works

There's a common pattern used by most malware. The first step is to get malware onto a victim machine. Typically, some network traversal is involved. At some point, the malware will then "call home" — meaning it makes a connection back to the attacker's server to let them know it's successfully exploited a victim machine. Often the malware is designed to allow the attacker to send new commands to the compromised machine such as installing additional software or trying to find and attack other computers it can reach on connected networks.

Just as I was able to see suspicious email traffic on my compromised web server, you can look for traffic that indicates malware is sending commands back and forth (calling home). You can block the activity or, at a minimum, identify it on your network. First, if you only allow traffic from networks you trust, you make attacks harder. It will be tougher for the attacker to send malware to the machine or send information back to the attacker's server. Second, this network traffic may be abnormal or suspicious compared to other traffic on your network. Although some networks have massive amounts of traffic, the way they are architected can make any anomalous activity easier to identify.

Botnets — all the infected devices

The attacker's machine that is controlling the victim computer or device is called a command and control server — C&C or C2 server, for short[50]. That C2 server may be manipulating one or many computers, networks, or IoT (Internet of Things) devices.

---

[50] Command and Control [C & C] Server:
https://www.trendmicro.com/vinfo/us/security/definition/command-and-control-server

The victim machines are called bots[51]. Sometimes people instead refer to the software installed on the victim machines as bots. A botnet[52] consists of all the Internet-connected devices controlled by a particular attacker.

The Mirai botnet was one of the most infamous and extensive networks of infected devices (Garrett, 2017). It compromised 65,000 devices in the first 20 hours and, at its peak, reached about 600,000 devices. At one point it nearly took down the Internet. The malware spread fast because it was a worm[53], which means it used automated code to find and attack other devices it could reach on the network. A Rutgers college student developed this botnet with two of his friends. They owe $127,000 in damages and are serving five years of community service as a result. Others have gone to jail for similar cyber-mischief, so they are lucky.

Back when I started learning about cybersecurity, a botnet might have been as simple as a single C2 server or static group of servers. Over time security professionals figured out how to spot attackers on their network by looking for conspicuous traffic in network logs. Firewalls blocked known C2 server network addresses. Attackers got trickier and set up their botnets to connect to changing network addresses and domain names[54], with new types of malware techniques, like fast flux[55], that continuously alter the domain name for a C2 server.

The main point here is that attackers leverage other people's servers to perform attacks and use specialized networks like Tor[56]

---

[51] What is a Botnet? https://usa.kaspersky.com/resource-center/threats/botnet-attacks
[52] Botnet https://en.wikipedia.org/wiki/Botnet
[53] Worm https://en.m.wikipedia.org/wiki/Computer_worm
[54] What is a domain name? https://www.website.com/beginnerguide/domainnames/8/1/what-is-a-domain-name?.ws
[55] Fast Flux https://en.m.wikipedia.org/wiki/Fast_flux
[56] Tor https://www.torproject.org/

that makes it hard to identify the actual source of the attack. That's why attributing the attack to a specific entity is challenging, and hacking back is not advised as I wrote in a blog post on the topic (Radichel, The Problem with Hacking Back: It Might Be Your Network, 2017), because you might attack an innocent victim. It also means that even though you may not be experiencing a data breach, your infected computers might be facilitating a cyberattack.

As a side note, if you decide to use a Tor in an attempt to be anonymous on the Internet, be careful. Just because you install the Tor browser doesn't mean you are always anonymous. Additionally, you may run across some unsavory content. For more information, watch the DefCon 22 presentation by Adrian Crenshaw called *Dropping Docs on Darknets: How People Got Caught* (Crenshaw, 2014).

VPNFilter is a type of malware that evaded detection by residing where people aren't looking. Even if people look at the network traffic on their computer or internal network, they often do not inspect the traffic between that network device and their Internet service provider (the company that provides your Internet access, otherwise known as an ISP). This point is where the VPNFilter malware inserted itself, infecting network devices from manufacturers like NETGEAR, Linksys, TP-Link, and MikroTik (Kirk, 2018) that consumers use to connect to their Internet provider. At the point the FBI seized the domain controlling this malware, it had infected at least 500,000 routers, mostly in Ukraine.

A Russian hacking group called Fancy Bear was purportedly responsible for these infections. This malware would "sniff" network traffic[57], meaning it would inspect the network packets,

---

[57] Wireshark Tutorial
https://searchsecurity.techtarget.com/tip/Wireshark-tutorial-How-to-sniff-network-traffic

looking for credentials and private information. Companies, law enforcement, and other organizations worked together in a coordinated effort to stop the spread of this potentially devastating malware. As mentioned in the article, security experts have long suspected that Russia has used Ukraine to test out new cyberattacks.

It starts with an Internet connection

If you think about how these attacks occur, it all begins with a device connected to the Internet. In many cases, a system must have a vulnerability that the attacker can use to install malware onto the device. I explained how hackers use CVEs to carry out attacks in the last chapter. Software flaws were the root cause of the Equifax breach and Wannacry. However, the initial point of exposure for organizations affected in those breaches was a system exposed to the Internet. What if those systems were not accessible from the Internet, and the attacker could not access them? Even if the CVE was unpatched, the systems could not be compromised if the attacker could not connect to the target machine.

Here's another example showing how network security can help you when it comes to new threats like zero-day malware. I talked about this in a presentation I gave at Microsoft Build with Tanya Janca (Radichel & Janca, Do it Yourself Security Assessment, 2019). Confluence[58] is the name of a product used by a lot of software teams to share information and document their work. The information in this system is almost always information that only people within the organization should access and should not be exposed to the Internet.

Many organizations host this system via a cloud service exposed to the entire Internet. Developers log in over an encrypted connection. They use their username and password to log in

---

[58] Confluence https://www.atlassian.com/software/confluence

(identity). They may even be using MFA. The problem is that when organizations allow their developers to access Confluence via the Internet, so can anyone else. They may not have valid credentials to log into the system. However, attackers can use any newly discovered vulnerability to exploit the exposed server.

And that is what happened. Luckily it was by someone who let the companies know, not an actual attacker.

A security researcher discovered a vulnerability that allowed him to exploit a Confluence system. Then he was able to search for infected systems on the Internet using Google. A tool called Google Dorks, now known as the Google Hacking Database[59], uses this concept of searching for specific keywords and patterns to find all kinds of things exposed to the Internet that shouldn't be, like passwords, encryption keys, and private data. Attackers can also search for error messages and code exposed by systems when search engines visited them. That information may reveal a system running particular software with a known security flaw.

If the Confluence systems had been on private networks, Google wouldn't have been able to reach them and would not have added their information to search engine results. The security researcher wouldn't have been able to reach them. Instead, the systems were exposed and resulted in a blog post from Vignesh C., explaining how he hacked over 50 websites in 6 hours (C, 2019).

The new perimeter

The first aspect of network security I want to explain is perimeter security[60]. That's right — old school, out of favor, forgotten security at the edge of your network. The perimeter means the part of your network, where it touches the Internet. It is what

---

[59] Google Hacking Database https://www.exploit-db.com/google-hacking-database
[60] Perimeter Security Fundamentals http://www.informit.com/articles/article.aspx?p=376256

separates your systems from the rest of the Internet — all the other devices in the world owned by citizens, companies, governments, and hackers. Perimeter security used to be a firewall between your corporate systems in a data center or office building and the Internet. The firewall and other networking equipment defined the rules for what would be allowed in and out of your network.

The difference now is that instead of operating all systems in buildings and on servers you own, the resources you connect to that host your data exist in a distributed configuration on machines maintained by other companies. Your network is a different shape spanning many different locations instead of just one or a few you own. You may not be able to put firewalls in other people's data centers — but you still have a perimeter! If you plan and architect carefully, you can limit access to systems hosting your data to your private network and disallow Internet access except where it is required.

Some of your systems may be in the public cloud on AWS, for example. People may be connecting from your corporate office to the cloud servers. But these distributed systems are still your systems, which you can contain in a private network if you choose. Mechanisms exist to limit all types of cloud solutions to only networks you specify if the cloud provider supports it. I have a full day of networking in my cloud security class explaining how to do that and other essential aspects of network security in the cloud. From an executive point of view, you may not need to know every detail about the network implementation. Still, you can measure the results — how much exposure you have to the Internet — with a simple network question: What is the percentage of our systems that are exposed directly to the Internet?

Why does any of this matter? Because every system you expose to the entire Internet is open for a malicious actor to attack. Within minutes of connecting a device to the Internet, your traffic logs will show connections from devices around the world. These connections may be from attacker-controlled bots and owned by innocent victims that do not realize they are part of a botnet. All these devices are looking for your systems and try to attack them as soon as they are exposed.

Scan, attack, and infected traffic

Attackers are constantly scanning the Internet for machines that are exposed. To prove that statement is correct, you can connect any device to the Internet and look at the network traffic logs about 5 minutes later. In my cloud security class, I have people start a cloud virtual machine, and then look at the traffic. Attackers try to find devices that expose services to the Internet — things like websites or remote administration capabilities. When they find something running that they can reach from the Internet, they can try to attack and get into that system.

Right now, there's a very serious CVE affecting RDP (Remote Desktop Protocol), which allows administrators to make connections to Windows machines from remote locations. As soon as the CVE-2019-0708 became public, security researchers and attackers started publishing code online to use that flaw to break into systems (Goodin, 2019). Soon after, attackers were scanning the Internet seeking machines exposing that CVE so they could attack them and use that flaw to break into networks (Rudis, 2019).

Your options are to update all the systems running the RDP service (which is likely the majority of Windows machines out there) or block Internet access to that machine and the RDP application. Ideally, you want to do both, but you'll need to act fast. A question I ask people when there's a large-scale vulnerability announced that requires upgrading hundreds or thousands of systems is, "Is it faster and easier to update all your system software or block Internet access for that specific flaw?" The answer will depend on your environment. It might be easier to ensure the RDP service is not accessible from the untrusted networks while you work on patching all the systems.

Since scanning the Internet for exposed, vulnerable systems is one of the primary ways attackers find and initiate data breaches, a lot of security researchers do the same, trying to find machines that may be vulnerable to attack. They create websites and publish information about these systems to alert people to the problem. There are so many people scanning the Internet that it creates a lot of unnecessary noise, traffic, and congestion, so if you are thinking about doing this, please refrain. Use existing websites. Only scan the specific systems you own or have explicit permission to test.

Services like Shodan[61] and Censys[62] will let you search for systems exposed to the Internet. Attackers can also find exposed applications without ever checking systems directly by searching on these websites. You can go to Shodan yourself and find out what is open to the Internet on your network. It's an excellent idea to review these sites periodically.

Be aware that your systems may still be exposed, even if you don't find them on these sites. Some cloud providers may be blocking the scanners used by these services in an effort to prevent exposure of information about vulnerable systems on those sites. Blocking the scanners run by these sites is preferable to allowing anyone to search for open ports on your systems in a public database. In some cloud environments, you can run queries to analyze your network exposure, which is more efficient than traditional network scanning and highly accurate. Find the problems yourself, before someone else does.

Some Internet service providers are known for allowing their customers to send any type of traffic they choose, including traffic seeking vulnerabilities on other systems and attack traffic. When I

---

[61] Shodan https://www.shodan.io/
[62] Censys https://censys.io/

started in security, I blogged about all the unwanted traffic in my network logs. I would see traffic pretending to be from an alternate source like fake Google search engine crawlers[63] from non-Google networks, website attacks, and different types of network scans. Certain company names appeared over and over again. Some of the same companies are in the book I mentioned by Brian Krebs called *Spam Nation* (Krebs, 2015).

If you monitor your network and check which companies are sending bad traffic your way, you may notice patterns like this where the same network name appears over and over again. If you want to know how to associate a network address with an organization's name, I wrote about that in a blog post called "Where in The World is That Network Traffic Coming From?" (Radichel, Where in The World is That Network Traffic Coming From?, 2017). Some companies allow a lot of suspicious traffic and websites to reside on their networks. If you determine that nothing good comes from a particular network, you can block it from communicating with yours. For example, a person named Troy Mursch, who goes by the handle @bad_packets on Twitter, has tweeted about malware hosted on a particular web hosting company multiple times (Troy, 2018). If you see repeat offenses from a network or a part of the world that you do not need to connect with for your business, you could consider blocking it altogether.

Just like many people believe Facebook and Twitter should take responsibility for malicious content on their social media platforms (Feiner, 2019), these companies should probably take responsibility to stop criminal activity. This gets tricky because people don't want Internet service providers arbitrarily blocking whatever they want. There is a debate going on about this referred to as Net Neutrality[64]. In some cases, suspicious-looking traffic

---

[63] Search engine crawling
https://www.google.com/search/howsearchworks/crawling-indexing/
[64] Net Neutrality https://en.wikipedia.org/wiki/Net_neutrality

comes from legitimate security testing, but this testing should occur only with prior permission.

Protocols, ports, and the exponential problem

Let's go a bit deeper with some fundamental networking concepts. I'll keep this as simple as possible. Computers and devices on networks send data back and forth using protocols. A protocol[65] is like a language. If one person only speaks Portuguese and another only speaks Swahili, and they are trying to communicate, that's not going to work out so well. For two computers to communicate, they need to send data back and forth using the same protocol. A protocol is a defined set of rules about how the devices will communicate.

Some protocols communicate using ports[66]. Think of a port like a door in a shopping center. There's a door that lets you in and one that lets you out. The doors need to be open for you to get out, just like ports on a network need to be open to let data in or out. If a network administrator doesn't want traffic to go in or out, they can close the ports, just like a shopping center could close their doors.

There are 65,536 ports[67] software can use to make network connections on a device like a computer or Internet-connected camera. Each port has a number starting with "0."[68] Port numbers are usually associated with a particular type of application. Port 25 is typically associated with sending emails. Every port that is running software exposed to the Internet is a potential target because, more than likely, a flaw will be discovered in software using that port to communicate eventually. Attackers are running

---

[65] Common Network Protocols and Their Ports
https://www.interserver.net/tips/kb/common-network-protocols-ports/
[66] Port (computer networking)
https://en.wikipedia.org/wiki/Port_(computer_networking)
[67] 65,535 https://en.wikipedia.org/wiki/65,535
[68] Port 0 https://www.speedguide.net/port.php?port

botnets of hundreds of thousands of infected hosts they can use to scan or attack your Internet-connected systems and ports.

Systems X Ports X Possible Vulnerabilities X Attackers =

Exponential Possibilities

Therein lies the exponential problem. Multiply the number of Internet-accessible ports by all the attackers and their malware-infested devices. Maybe even multiply that by all the different types of potentially vulnerable types of software on each Internet-accessible machine. An operating system, web server software, and specific components of an application running on that web server may all have a CVE at some point. Take one of those variables out of the equation and decrease your risk. As explained, eliminating CVEs is one way to lower risk. Limiting ports exposed to the Internet is another. You can reduce risk by reducing the number of systems directly exposed to the Internet.

Determine the percentage of ports and protocols open to the Internet. Are all those ports and protocols necessary? Also, find out how many systems allow direct Internet access. Can you reduce that number? Of course, some things need to be exposed for systems to function, like a public website that needs to expose port 80 and port 443, but the way applications and networks are architected can limit that exposure. You can access well-designed cloud systems from private networks. If you can't, you might question whether you want to use that vendor or not for highly sensitive data. You can also put protections in front of your Internet-exposed systems and software. Determine the percentage of systems exposed to the Internet and try to reduce that number, which will, in turn, decrease the overall risk.

6
HIGH-RISK PORTS: THE CHINK IN YOUR NETWORK ARMOR

If you've read the book *There and Back Again (The Hobbit)* (Tolkien J. R., 1900) or seen the movie, you may remember how Bilbo Baggins snuck into the lair of Smaug, the dragon. He discovered one bare, unprotected spot in the dragon's underbelly. He told others what he saw, and that weakness was eventually used by Bard to slay the dragon. That small bare patch in the dragon's protective armor is like the administrative port left open on your network. That one hole can provide enough access to take down your organization if it gives access to install malware or take over systems.

Administrators, also called privileged users[69], refers to people with accounts on your systems that can change things that most other people are not allowed to change. It's an elevated level of access that poses a higher risk if the credentials are abused or stolen. For example, network administrators can open and close firewall ports. Opening ports can leave holes that let attackers in your network and data out. A database administrator can

---

[69] Privileged user https://csrc.nist.gov/glossary/term/privileged-user

typically access all your data in the database and change permissions to give other people access. Application and operating system administrators may be able to grant access, install software, and change configurations.

The permissions and actions allowed by administrative accounts pose a severe threat if obtained by attackers. If an attacker gets this privileged access on an operating system like Windows or Linux, they can install any malware they want on your system like ransomware, cryptominers, or malware that steals secrets and data. In a 2019 SANS survey, customers stated that stolen credentials are almost always involved in cloud incidents (Ikeda, 2019 Sans Institute Cloud Security Survey Reveals Top Threats, Which Surprisingly Are Not DDoS Attacks, 2019). Even if attackers obtain credentials, you can make it harder for them to use them by only allowing the network addresses belonging to your organization to access the systems.

Often that administrative access is obtained and abused by attackers and gives them elevated privileges on your systems and network. Potentially they get enough access to grant themselves permissions to additional resources and data or create new resources in cloud environments. They may insert code into existing systems, as was the case in the Target breach (Radichel, Case Study: Critical Controls that Could Have Prevented the Target Breach, 2014). Attackers infiltrated the system and accessed a tool used to install software on the point-of-sale (POS) systems. Leveraging that tool, they were able to quickly deploy the credit card scraping malware to multiple retail store systems. If attackers get administrative access in your environment, you may be in serious trouble.

Remote administrative access

Many times, administrators log into systems remotely. They don't have a computer monitor connected directly to the network equipment, database server, or web server. They will create a connection to the server using some software that allows them to log in from a different location. That's very handy for your administrators. They don't have to drive to the data center; they can work from home. You might even have teams or vendors logging into your systems from different parts of the world from changing network addresses.

In cloud environments like AWS, Azure, or Google Cloud Platform, it is the only way to administer servers. In the cloud, the servers are virtual — meaning they are versions of servers entirely created by software instead of a single piece of hardware for each server. Multiple virtual machines (VMs) can run on one physical hardware server. The only way to access them is to log in over a remote connection since the cloud provider is not going to let you log in to the operating system on a physical server itself (called a hypervisor[70]) because it hosts many different customers' virtual machines.

Your network administrators, database administrators, or developers may think or argue that they need high-risk ports open to the Internet so they can remotely fix problems in systems. They do need remote access in many cases. However, network administrators can set up remote access in a manner that limits the network addresses that can get to the login screen to use these credentials. The network access can be architected with multiple layers of defense, to make it harder for attackers to get to these login screens to use stolen credentials.

Backdoors

Administrators sometimes need remote access for legitimate reasons — administering services and responding to incidents that are causing business problems. In many cases, remote connections are allowed and provided by network and security

---

[70] What is a hypervisor https://www.networkworld.com/article/3243262/what-is-a-hypervisor.html

teams in an authorized manner. In other cases, a person or company might try to add a way to connect remotely without telling anybody. This secret access is called a backdoor[71]. It is a way to get into a system that is not known or intended in the approved implementation of networks and software. The determining factor when deciding if something is or is not a backdoor is whether or not it is unauthorized access.

In some cases, backdoors are intentional. An administrator may create credentials and run a service that allows him or her to access a system at a later time. An administrator may not have malicious intentions but is merely trying to make his or her job easier. In other cases, an individual may have a more nefarious purpose, such as stealing data or harming the organization after they leave the company. Many reports exist that expose backdoors in vendor products. For example, some reports of backdoors appear for Cisco routers (Armansu, 2018). Vodafone found backdoors in Huawei equipment in 2011 and 2012, and reports indicated additional back doors existed in 2019 (Lepido, 2019), but Huawei denies the 2019 claims (BBC, 2019).

Here it becomes tricky — was the backdoor intentional, or was it an accidental inclusion of code with a vulnerability, or credentials leftover from testing? If you look at the list of some of the Cisco backdoors, in some cases they are product vulnerabilities, exploited by hacking organizations. I wouldn't call those backdoors. Those are likely mistakes or oversights during implementation. The same groups attacked and compromised many other products as well, not only Cisco appliances. I would also not consider the case where a customer did not change a published default password to be a backdoor. That would be the responsibility for the customer to change. However, if someone working for a vendor leaves hard-coded user accounts and "test interfaces" accidentally in the code – was it really an accident?

---

[71] Hacker Lexicon: What is a Backdoor? https://www.wired.com/2014/12/hacker-lexicon-backdoor/

It is challenging, if not impossible, to know what the actual motivation was behind the publicly exposed back door in a vendor product. The important thing is for organizations to test products if they have the resources, as I explain in chapter 20, and patch known flaws quickly. Organizations can also monitor network traffic for backdoor activity on the network.

Common administrative services and ports

Here are some common types of software that are used to login to systems remotely to perform administrative actions. This list is an overview for executives lacking some technical details, but it gives you the idea of the type of services you don't want to have exposed to the Internet.

RDP: On Windows, administrators log into remote systems using RDP[72], Remote Desktop Protocol. Microsoft built RDP into Windows. By default, this service runs on port 3389. You can turn it off on Windows systems if it is not required. When you log into a Windows machine remotely, you'll need to put in a username and password just as you would if you were sitting at the computer. The information sent between the administrator machine and the remote server is encrypted as it travels over the Internet.

As explained, a recent CVE in the RDP protocol exists, and Microsoft says over a million machines may be susceptible to this flaw, dubbed BlueKeep. This type of problem can happen to any remote access protocol, so preventing exposure to the Internet can help in these cases. Unfortunately, if you search in Shodan, you'll see that many Windows hosts are, in fact, accessible directly from the Internet.

SSH: Linux runs a service by default on port 22 to allow

---

[72] How to use RDP https://support.microsoft.com/en-us/help/4028379/windows-10-how-to-use-remote-desktop

administrators to log in via Secure Shell (SSH)[73]. Like RDP, this protocol encrypts data sent between the remote administrator and server as it traverses the Internet. SSH, when configured correctly, will also require some form of credentials (username and password or something called an SSH key) to connect to the remote server. An SSH key is simply a long string of characters in a text file. Think of it as a super-long password. An SSH server exposed to the Internet enables attackers to attempt to steal the key or guess the password. If successful, they can get into the system and do anything those credentials are allowed to do.

Telnet: The article mentioned in the section on backdoors accuses the Chinese company, Huawei, of potentially leaving backdoors in telecommunications equipment delivered to Italy. The story was originally published by Bloomberg and later largely dismissed by the security and IT community. The company used telnet[74] to access servers remotely.

Telnet alone, as originally designed, is not encrypted over the Internet. That means when you connect to a remote server using telnet, anyone who can intercept the traffic (which is not hard with a bit of technical training) can read the information going back and forth. A list of software weakness types known as a CWE (Common Weakness Enumeration)[75] documented by Mitre contains this flaw. CWE-319 is Cleartext Transmission of Sensitive Data[76]. Additionally, telnet does not check for authorization when someone tries to connect. It lets anyone connect. That's why security experts say telnet is not secure. You should stop the telnet service and close port 23 used by this service.

Side note: After publishing multiple suspect stories, Bloomberg cybersecurity reporting has been called into question by some

---

[73] SSH https://en.wikipedia.org/wiki/Secure_Shell
[74] Unencrypted Telnet Server https://www.tenable.com/plugins/nessus/42263
[75] CWE List Version 3.4.1 https://cwe.mitre.org/data/index.html
[76] CWE 319 Clear Transmission of Sensitive Data https://cwe.mitre.org/data/definitions/319.html

security professionals in comments on Twitter[77]. Even if the story about Huawei using a backdoor is questionable, that doesn't mean telnet is ok and backdoors don't exist. It just means that Bloomberg appears to have been making unsubstantiated claims in some people's opinions. You will need to decide for yourself. When news articles make claims, always try to find multiple sources before coming to conclusions on the latest cyber-drama. I wait a couple of days before forming an opinion about the exact nature of a newly announced and potentially unsubstantiated threat.

Database Administration: Nearly any database has an administrative port. For example, a Microsoft SQL Server database provides administrative access by default on port 1433[78], and a MySQL database provides access on 3306[79]. Those ports should never be exposed to the Internet in a high-security environment (or preferably ever).

Other high-risk ports

The following services use other high-risk ports I want to mention because they are the underlying cause of numerous attacks, and ensuring these ports are not available on the Internet may help prevent some top reported threats.

SMB: SMB stands for Server Message Block[80]. Windows systems use SMB to connect printers and file shares. However, security professionals have known for a while now that attackers leverage SMB to attack unprotected systems. The EternalBlue exploit initially developed by the NSA, which was stolen and later

---

[77] @malwarejake on Bloomberg stories https://twitter.com/MalwareJake/status/1128663952681046018
[78] SQL Docs: TCP/IP Properties https://docs.microsoft.com/en-us/sql/tools/configuration-manager/tcp-ip-properties-ip-addresses-tab
[79] MySQL Port Reference Tables https://dev.mysql.com/doc/mysql-port-reference/en/mysql-ports-reference-tables.html
[80] Server Message Block https://en.wikipedia.org/wiki/Server_Message_Block

released to the world by a group called the Shadow Brokers in 2017, uses this protocol (Islam, Oppenheim, & Thomas, 2017). That exploit was the basis for WannaCry, and many different types of malware still haunting companies to this day. SMB runs on port 445. Although some internal networks and systems require SMB, attackers should not be able to access this port from the Internet.

NetBIOS: An older protocol similar to SMB that runs on Windows, NetBIOS[81], consists of services that run on ports 137–139. These ports also should never be exposed to the Internet as they have been the source of numerous exploits. If you don't need this service (and many organizations don't, if systems are up to date), shut this service off completely on all systems.

A risk-based approach to locking down your network

Although I'm telling you some of the most problematic administrative and high-risk ports, many others exist that, if exposed to the Internet, could cause similar problems. Additionally, an administrator can reconfigure the services to run on different ports, so for example, SSH could run on port 5000 if an administrator configured it to do so. That's why it's critical to have well-trained security and network staff that know how to find and lock down all these ports and anything related correctly. The security team should be able to understand which services are using every open port on your network, why it's there, and whether or not it is required.

Network administrators will have to do a lot more than what is listed here to create a secure network. Yet, too many organizations have not fixed these fundamental security problems, so this is an excellent place to start. Your rules can be even more fine-grained to limit traffic when you have network administrators and security professionals who understand network engineering. They

---

[81] NetBIOS https://en.wikipedia.org/wiki/NetBIOS

can identify the traffic on your network, reduce unnecessary noise and connections, mitigate threats, and identify security problems quickly.

Locking down your entire network will be much simpler in a small company and exponentially harder in a complex enterprise environment. If you need a place to start, start with the administrative and high-risk ports mentioned above and get those locked down. This risk-based approach is a common strategy in cybersecurity, where the to-do list is longer than the people supporting the organization can reasonably address. Start with the things that are most likely to facilitate an attack and may cause the most damage. This risk-based approach helps you prioritize and eliminate the highest risks in your environment first.

Locking down administrative ports

To lock down administrative ports, but still provide access where needed, companies can do a few different things. One strategy would be only allowing people to access these systems when they are in the office. This approach works for some protocols like SMB. It would also work if a person is in the office or logging into a system in a data center via a private connection, meaning access is only possible from company networks, not the entire Internet.

The problem is that now administrators are working remotely and traveling and need access from any location. Therefore, a different strategy is required because you aren't going to have a private connection from the local coffee shop to your data center (unless you are Starbucks, perhaps). For these use cases, you need a way to protect your remote administration services but still allow people to connect from the Internet. You can do that with a VPN (virtual private network), as I wrote about in a blog post called, "Why use a VPN for remote access in the cloud?" (Radichel, Why use a VPN for remote access in the cloud?, 2018)

A VPN will protect the traffic as it traverses the Internet by encapsulating it in an encrypted tunnel, protecting information related to which system the user is connecting, application data, and credentials in the network traffic. Sometimes people use VPN services from third-party companies. These companies may then be able to see your encrypted traffic, so be very careful when using these services to ensure it is a reputable company. Some people think VPNs are for bypassing firewalls and watching movies in foreign countries, but they have a more critical purpose in a corporate environment.

Remote workers make it difficult to create effective network rules without a VPN. They will have a different network address at every location but must still have administrative access to devices on your private network. As an alternative, network administrators can set up network appliances with VPN capabilities. Users must connect to your VPN and authenticate before they can access systems on your private network. From that point, they will have a specific network address maintained by the company, which can access other resources in your network. Without a VPN, a network administrator has to allow access from any IP address on the Internet if you allow your users to travel and work remotely.

The devices that provide the VPN connection still face attacks because they are exposed to the Internet. However, people who understand networking and security can manage these points of access and monitor them closely. When using a VPN, users must first connect to the VPN before accessing the administrative accounts, which then are only accessible on the private network. These powerful points of access now pose less risk because they are not directly exposed to the Internet, and an attacker must get through multiple layers of defense to access them. This strategy doesn't eliminate every attack that involves administrative credentials, but it does reduce a significant amount of risk.

An even better option would be to allow administrative access only when it is required. An administrator requests access to use a remote administration service, and the systems open the port while they are working to the specific address from which the administrator is connecting. After the administrator finishes working, the request expires, and network devices automatically close the port. I wrote a blog post about opening up the network on AWS to administer servers only while it was required, called "Just-in-time VPN access with an AWS IoT Button," on the *AWS News Blog* (Radichel, Just-in-time VPN access with an AWS IoT button, 2018). In the blog post I explain how to program the button to open up network access when it is required and close it when no longer necessary. Microsoft now offers a similar feature that allows just-in-time access to Azure virtual machines (less the button)[82]. I am hoping for more services like this from other cloud and network device vendors soon.

Locking down cloud administration

Part of locking down cloud administration has to do with usernames and passwords, which will be the topic of chapter 10. However, you can also lock down network access to many cloud consoles where people log in. I talk about different ways to do this in my cloud security class[83]. You may want to ensure there is a way to do this for any cloud providers with whom you choose to do business.

When considering cloud administration, remember to protect all types of access, not just the website where people log in to take actions. Cloud services often allow developers to connect to make programmatic changes using a mechanism called APIs (application programming interfaces)[84]. These automated means

---

[82] Manage virtual machine access using just-in-time
https://docs.microsoft.com/en-us/azure/security-center/security-center-just-in-time
[83] 2nd Sight Lab Cloud Security Training https://2ndsightlab.com/cloud-security-training.html
[84] Application Programming Interface
https://en.wikipedia.org/wiki/Application_programming_interface

of connection enable systems to take actions on each other via programming code, instead of humans typing in a web form and clicking buttons.

Another common type of tool allows administrators to write commands on the local machine they are using. Those commands are then sent over the network to make changes in remote systems. These tools are often called CLIs (Command Line Interfaces)[85]. These types of connections will also access a specific port and network address. The remote systems should be protected from Internet access when possible, especially when working with highly sensitive data and when using administrative credentials.

High-risk network port lockdown

Now you understand that the administrative access is one of the highest-risk and best places to start locking down your network. Additionally, be aware of the ports malware commonly uses to access systems and try to ensure those are not accessible from the Internet unless required. Given that so many companies are falling victim to breaches due to these common problems, it's an excellent place to start reducing your overall risk. You can work with your security team to prioritize which ports you want to see in a cyber risk report as high-risk items. There may be others, depending on your business and the types of systems you use.

---

[85] Command Line Interface https://en.wikipedia.org/wiki/Command-line_interface

7
DATA ACCESS: PROTECT YOUR GOLD

Do you know where the data lives in your organization? If you don't, how do you know if it is exposed or not? If you think you know where it is, do you understand all the ways it can flow in and out of systems that might inadvertently expose it to the Internet or third parties?

The concept of blocking network ports to keep things inside or outside your network presumes you have control over your network perimeter and can track what goes in and out via controlling ports. Sometimes, in this day and age of cloud services, this is easier said than done. Changes in systems and architectures in recent years make managing network access difficult. Some of it has to do with approved third-party access to systems that create paths for data exfiltration[86] (a fancy way to say data extracted from your network in a subversive manner).

The Center for Internet Security publishes a list of the top security controls businesses should implement to maintain a secure environment[87]. That list considers the most common causes of

---

[86] Data Exfiltration https://en.wikipedia.org/wiki/Data_exfiltration
[87] The 20 CIS Controls https://www.cisecurity.org/controls/cis-controls-list/

data breaches and what will stop them. The first two items in the list involve maintaining an inventory of hardware and software assets, which makes a lot of sense. How will you know what systems to patch if you don't know what systems you have and the software running on them? However, I have often wondered: isn't it just as important to know where your data is and where it can flow?

When I give security presentations, I like to say, "Your data is your gold." Businesses derive value, in part, from the data they maintain. Having that data leak may decrease a company's competitive advantage, and along with it, the reason one company is worth more than another. Think about the impact of your competitors knowing your business plans, customers, and intellectual property, not to mention the potential $350-million-dollar price tag of mega-breaches I wrote about in the first chapter.

What are some of the recent causes of data exposure? Of course, I have to mention the rash of AWS S3[88] buckets left open to the Internet[89]. An AWS S3 bucket is a place to store data. Technically it's called "object storage," but to a business executive, it's a way to store files so applications can access and manage them in a cloud environment. Azure[90] and GCP[91] have similar constructs.

During the timeframe I was on the Capital One cloud team, the file transfers to and from the S3 service had to traverse the Internet. I managed the feature requests for Capital One for a while, and one of the things we requested was the ability to restrict access to S3 buckets to our private cloud network. AWS implemented new controls to fulfill that request (originally called S3 endpoints, now network endpoints), which customers can use

---

[88] Amazon Simple Storage Service (S3) https://aws.amazon.com/s3/
[89] S3 bucket breaches in a Google search https://www.google.com/search?q=s3+data+breach&oq=s3+data+breach
[90] Azure – Microsoft's cloud service https://azure.microsoft.com/
[91] Google Cloud Platform https://cloud.google.com/

to prevent any Internet access to a bucket. An organization cannot maintain S3 storage inside a strictly private network (one that only the company can access). However, companies can now prevent traffic to and from an S3 bucket from leaving the Amazon network. They can limit the access to these buckets from their private networks using these endpoint configurations.

I'll explain how the Capital One breach occurred, despite these protections, in chapter 11 but understand that Capital One was doing a much better job than all the companies that had their data directly exposed to the Internet. There is no reason for that with the networking controls that exist now.

People who don't understand and are not thinking about networking won't consider the related exposure risks when they choose a particular solution. Often, it's an executive focused on how something solves their business needs or a developer who is just trying to get something to work. The network and security teams may not even understand how an S3 bucket works or that anyone is using it, let alone that the configuration exposes data to the Internet.

The buckets get exposed in some cases because developers not adequately trained in networking are maintaining Internet access. They change the configuration to open up the bucket and don't fully understand the implications of those actions. In other cases, someone may have initially deployed a secure bucket configuration. Then a person working in operations in a production environment changed it erroneously while responding to a ticket. It could be that malware got into the cloud environment and obtained permissions that allowed it to change the cloud configuration.

Another common configuration problem involves databases exposed directly to the Internet. In the past, network and security teams designed networks to prevent direct access to sensitive data from the Internet. The network architecture and server implementation put those critical databases and data storage servers in a private network that required traversing additional network layers before reaching the data. Developers did not have a choice regarding which server would host the data or in which part of the network.

The recent shift is that now, developers are often responsible for the implementation of cloud environments where networking is easy to change. They sometimes set up databases with direct Internet access. Additionally, some database services from cloud providers only operate over the Internet and are exposed by virtue of how they work. This type of blatant data exposure is especially surprising, given that it is an obvious flaw in system architectures and configuration, but it happens much too often. Some of the most common culprits are Mongo databases (Radichel, Amazon DocumentDB Network Access — Why the VPC?, 2019) and Elasticsearch (Bradbury, 2019). However, attackers have also breached other types of relational databases and cloud storage for the same reason.

Similar to S3 buckets, services like Dropbox, Box, and Google Drive facilitate storage, but a non-technical user in a company often manages access to these services. I was listening to a panel talk about trying to maintain governance for cloud services. A sales executive for a security vendor spoke up and said that he uses Dropbox even though his company does not permit it because it is the only way he can do business and get files to clients. He works for a security company!

Organizations need to understand what people need to be able to do their jobs, so they can facilitate systems that allow what is required while still being able to monitor for unauthorized file transfers. Employees also need security training to understand the repercussions of too much data exposure. Companies need to be aware that these types of storage services have been used by insiders to steal incredibly sensitive data from organizations (Burgess, 2018).

Services that facilitate data flows and data transfers are particularly risky if they are not architected with proper visibility, so a company can monitor where its data is flowing between integrated systems and services. I've helped companies implement cloud infrastructure and applications as a cloud engineer, cloud architect, and Director of SaaS Engineering. I also examined system architecture related to data breaches and for potential acquisitions as Director of Security Strategy and Research for a security vendor. While working on client projects through my company, 2nd Sight Lab, I've had the opportunity to review the system architecture of cloud environments. Due to the way some cloud systems work, it may be challenging for IT and security departments to obtain visibility into data flows between systems. Some companies also do not consider the risk related to these data flows when they are just trying to make things work.

For example, one particular type of application allows companies to quickly transfer data to and from other companies and cloud services by rapidly setting up new connections through a user-friendly console and a few button-clicks. The first problem with this type of system is that the implementation of governance is challenging when people are simply clicking buttons. One application I reviewed had no evidence of change control, and no one was monitoring the logs for suspicious activity. They also were not aware of the steps they should take if a data breach occurs. The risk is high in scenarios like this for a negligent or intentionally malicious change to divert data to the wrong place.

Another problem in this scenario is that two data flows could exist — one that sends data into the service and another that sends data out to some other third party. This type of data flow would never traverse the IT and security monitoring systems the company has in place. IT and security teams may not even know these connections exist.

No one would ever know the data exfiltration occurred. No data loss prevention system, such as a CASB (cloud access security broker)[92], would ever see it if the cloud systems do not send those logs to it. In the case of a security incident, the company would be dependent on the cloud provider to deliver logs for evidence — if they exist, and the cloud provider maintains the chain of custody[93] (proper handling so the logs will be admissible as evidence in a court case).

Another source of many data breaches relates to using connections on websites that blindly send customers to third-party domains or incorporate external code when a webpage is loaded. When a website loads, it may include links to third-party domain names (like https://fonts.google.com/ to get a font to use on the website). Sometimes I open up a web page, and 20 or 30 different connections exist to domains other than the one I am trying to view! These connections seem excessive. News websites are some of the worst offenders when it comes to redirections to third-party web content in my experience.

When a customer opens your web page, and your site is connecting to many other websites, data the customer downloads from or enters into your website could potentially be accessible by these other sites if a vulnerability or misconfiguration exists. The externally hosted website or code could also be serving up malware. The Magecart campaign has reportedly infected over 960 e-commerce stores by injecting malicious code (Gatlan, 2019). The referenced article suggests the problem has something to do with cloud providers. However, it is likely that the attackers are running automated attacks against vulnerable applications customers deployed in these environments, rather than a problem with the cloud provider itself.

Do your developers download third-party code? (They do.) Validate that the code does not contain software vulnerabilities

---

[92] Cloud access security broker (CASB)
https://en.wikipedia.org/wiki/Cloud_access_security_broker
[93] Chain of custody https://en.wikipedia.org/wiki/Chain_of_custody

and serve it up from your domain name and systems. Make sure your site does not expose customer data to external sources that serve up code, advertisements, or even images. One way data is exposed is through misconfiguration of something called CORS (cross-origin resource sharing) (Radichel, Pentesting CORS: Give me all your cookies! OK., 2019) which specifies which third-party websites can access data from your website.

Retrieve the third-party content onto your servers. Validate that it has no vulnerabilities or malware before adding it to your website and presenting it to the customer. Alternatively, proxy the traffic from the third-party site, so it comes from your domain name but originates from their servers. Monitor for suspicious activity as you proxy the traffic to the customers.

As an executive, you don't need to understand all the details of how these particular web technologies work. However, you can ask how many different domains customers are exposed to when they open your website or web application in their browser. Limit those connections to limit data exposure while customers are browsing your site. Additionally, make sure your development staff gets proper security training, so they understand the risks of third-party code, and your security team is involved in designing systems so they can help limit the associated risk.

One other point of data exposure exists when your organization hires external vendors to maintain systems and data. A recent rash of attacks on MSPs, MSSPs, and organizations that develop systems for other companies have exposed data of the customers they support. A *Wall Street Journal* report explains how Chinese hackers breached U.S. Navy contractors (Lubold, 2018). A company named Attunity exposed data of Ford, TD Bank, and Netflix (Heller, 2019). Brian Krebs wrote about the breach of Wipro, India's third-largest IT outsourcing company (Krebs, Experts: Breach at IT Outsourcing Giant Wipro, 2019).

Think about how you monitor network access within your

organization. If your IT or security team sees suspicious actions on your network, they will hopefully take appropriate action. If they see a connection by a vendor you have hired to assist with system maintenance or development, would they consider this activity suspicious? Likely the vendor is connecting over an encrypted channel from a trusted network. Your IT or security team has limited or no visibility into the vendor systems or networks. Companies need to be aware of how well their vendors maintain security within these external systems and networks. Organizations also need to be mindful of what type of data is accessible to the consultants and vendors connecting to their network. Additionally, consider how the vendors are connecting and what can and cannot be monitored.

Companies need to govern how connections to data are established and monitor data transfers for potential loss or exfiltration. Reporting should exist that shows the types of data stored in systems and the intended and possible data flows between those systems to correctly evaluate the risk of loss, modification, or exposure. Organizations need to establish controls related to who can set up new databases, networking, and data connections and with what requirements to help prevent data breaches. Employees — including technical and non-technical personnel — need to understand the risk of data exposure as well via adequate security training.

8
TRUST IS OVERRATED

I admit that I wrote this catchy title to grab people's attention on my blog. Trust is vital in many aspects of life. I recently read a book that Stephen A. Clark, a retired Airforce Major General I met at a security conference, recommended called *The Boys in the Boat* (Brown D. J., 2014). The book is about how a crew team from the University of Washington made it to the 1936 Olympics in Nazi Germany. I don't want to spoil the book for anyone, but it is very powerful and relevant at this moment in time for more reasons than one. Sometimes the things we do in life require a certain amount of trust and working together can take us farther than we can get working alone, as it did for the crew in that boat.

Stephen and I have also had discussions about how a leader of a very large organization can make the right decisions with sometimes less information than they would like to have. At some point, trust does come into the equation when dealing with large teams and cybersecurity because you can't control every single thing people are doing. Otherwise, the organization will never achieve its objectives. That's why I will emphasize training and awareness later in the book. However, as a security professional, the more you learn about the type of attacks that occur, the less likely you will be to blindly trust people, systems, and networks.

Trusting people that you have known well for years and developed a deep bond with is one thing. Trusting people that you don't know is another. I know this all too well. As a child, I had an encounter with an adult neighbor that no child should have to face when my parents sent me off with him on a motorcycle ride in the woods. I tell myself it wasn't good, but it could have been worse.

I didn't tell my parents right away. I was too embarrassed to talk about it in court and cried when my father wanted me to tell the police. My parents never made me go through with it, and that man is still out there. That's one thing I regret in my life, though at the same time, it would have been even more traumatizing to talk to strangers about it. I hope he did not do things to other people, but that thought did not cross my mind as a scared child. I remember when my mom made me return a hammer to that neighbor's house, that I was afraid I would see him. I walked cautiously across the field and gave it to his wife and then ran all the way back home. Now he's very old, and for the most part, I would rather forget it.

I've noticed that a lot of people who work in cybersecurity have similar experiences where someone abused their trust, or at a minimum, they faced a data breach that changed their point of view. They know what is possible because they experienced it or witnessed it. They want to protect people who don't believe bad things can happen to them. Therein lies the conflict in many attempts to achieve a secure environment in some organizations. Some people think bad things can never happen, and other people know they can.

I once had a coworker with children tell me that he hears about all these things happening to children, but he wonders if it occurs as much as people say it does because he's never known anyone that had that experience. I just looked at him and said, "It does."

Someone I know worked with a person who was hosting child pornography at work. He sat right next to the guy and had no idea until law enforcement showed up and took him away. I've known multiple men that have had similar experiences as children with soccer coaches and even family members. If you think these things in the news are all talk, they are not.

We are facing a monumental trust issue around the world right now. People are challenging trusted media sources, claiming the news is fake on all sides (Kirtley, 2019). Computer-generated social media accounts perpetuate falsehoods, myths, and conspiracy theories (Radichel, Are Social Media Bots Influencing You?, 2017). At the same time, propaganda has infiltrated social media and alternative news sources, seeking to create divisions between different groups in the same country and political allies (Thompson, 2018). In January 2020, Twitter shut down an account that was trying to create animosity between Jewish and African Americans (O'Sullivan, 2020).

Reports find that Chinese intelligence services use fake LinkedIn accounts to recruit spies in the United States (Wong E., 2019), France (Samuel, 2018), and Germany (Burgess C., 2017). You can test your ability to tell a real face from a fake one in a photo at http://www.whichfaceisreal.com/. Deepfake videos fool people with computer-generated versions of well-known people that are so convincing they're hard to distinguish from reality. MIT's Center for Advanced Virtual Reality created a deepfake video of Nixon announcing 'the Apollo 11 disaster' (the opposite of the actual outcome) to show just how real these videos can be (Stockler, 2019). Lest anyone think the United States is innocent when it comes to propaganda, the U.S. military used it in Afghanistan by disseminating leaflets that pushed a U.S. agenda, though not quite as effectively as some of the other examples listed here (Lawrence, 2018), and the U.S. commander in Afghanistan later apologized (Mackenzie, 2017). As for trusting the information you receive, it is an excellent idea to validate it via multiple sources, whenever possible.

Although we want to trust people wholeheartedly, and that is what the people that are trying to do their jobs want, a more prudent approach is necessary if you're going to protect your systems and data. My friend, who helped rebuild oil fields in Iraq for the Navy, has a saying which came from his experience and nuclear training in the U.S. military: "Trust but verify." This phrase is often credited to Ronald Regan in his interactions with Russian President Gorbachev in an attempt to end the Cold War (Talbot, 2004). I like this statement because the goal of cybersecurity is not to control every action. However, you can limit access to what is reasonably allowed and monitor for questionable behavior.

Don't be fooled by threats on your internal network

My last few chapters covered network traffic and data flows between your company and the Internet and other entities outside your organization. Often, security professionals call these external sources "untrusted." Now I'm going to explain threats on your internal network, where your systems reside, typically behind a firewall. In the past, security professionals would refer to this environment and the systems in it as "trusted."

CWE-807 addresses the concept of untrusted inputs to software programs: "Without sufficient encryption, integrity checking, or other mechanism, any input that originates from an outsider cannot be trusted."[94] Many network security books cover the topics of trusted and untrusted networks, including *Firewalls and VPN Configurations* (Henmi, Lucas, Singh, & Cantrell, 2006), which states:

> As much as possible, you should define the difference between

---

[94] CWE-807 Reliance on Untrusted Inputs in a Security Decision
https://cwe.mitre.org/data/definitions/807.html

trusted and untrusted networks in your environment; i.e., those networks that can safely transmit sensitive data versus those that are at risk by internal or external attackers.

In theory, communication between the systems that reside inside your network or coming from your applications should be safe. After all, they are your systems managed by your IT team and used by your staff. Unfortunately, this is often not the case. In many breaches, malware breaks into an Internet-connected device and then uses it to connect to another one in the trusted network. The term for this ability to move from one infected machine to another in a network is "pivoting."[95]

How does the malware get onto a system in the first place? Many ways. One of your trusted employees could easily make a mistake and click on a phishing email. Someone could click the wrong link on a website or open a malicious file. Perhaps an attacker was able to obtain a password via brute force (trial and error guessing). The attacker may have infiltrated a legitimate software update process to insert malicious code in place of a valid update or exploited a machine that is running out-of-date software such as a web server or any device connected to the Internet.

Lockheed Martin described the typical attack tactics of cyber adversaries in the seminal paper *Intelligence-Driven Computer Network Defense Informed by Analysis of Adversary Campaigns and Intrusion Kill Chains* (Hutchins, Cloppert, & Amin, 2010). Once the attacker is in one of your systems, the next step will be to scan your internal network for other resources to attack. Often it is easier for an attacker to get into machines on the internal network because the systems trust each other. Attackers can leverage legitimate technologies used by IT departments to traverse your network, looking for exploitable systems. "Living off the land" is a strategy that uses tools that already exist on systems to further an attack (Secureworks Counter Threat Unit Research Team, 2015).

[95] Pivoting https://www.offensive-security.com/metasploit-unleashed/pivoting/

The attacker may be able to jump from system to system until they reach your most sensitive data. At this point, the attacker might attempt to exfiltrate that data. When exiting the network with pilfered data, the attacker may follow the same path back out or use a completely different route.

The Target breach was an excellent and highly sophisticated example of pivoting and stealthy data exfiltration (if I am allowed to use the word "excellent" and "breach" in the same sentence). Please refer to my white paper on this breach for detailed references: *Case Study: Critical Controls that Could Have Prevented the Target Breach* (Radichel, Case Study: Critical Controls that Could Have Prevented the Target Breach, 2014). Hackers were able to obtain 40 million credit cards and personal information of 70 million individuals after breaking into Target's systems.

Attackers first targeted a computer used by an HVAC (heating, ventilation, and air conditioning) vendor. They did not, as some have incorrectly stated, attack the HVAC systems within Target. They were able to get malware onto a machine used by a person who worked at the HVAC company and logged into a vendor management system at Target. Presumably, the attackers knew the HVAC company was a Target vendor since the vendor list existed on a public website.

The attacker obtained credentials to log in to the vendor management system via malware delivered to an employee who clicked a link in a phishing email. With access to the vendor management system, the attacker could search for flaws in that web application and use the vulnerabilities they discovered to break into the machine hosting the vendor management software. From that machine, the attacker pivoted to infiltrate other systems in the Target network. Reports speculate the attacker may have obtained access to the domain controller, which is the machine that controls all the user accounts and their access to other systems on the network. Pentesters and attackers like to call exploiting this type of system, getting "domain admin" (Metcalf,

2018). An attacker with this level of access can pretty much do anything they want since they can set up new accounts and change permissions.

After some pivoting, the attacker was able to get into the system that deployed software updates to the point-of-sale (POS) systems at Target stores. Retail companies use these types of systems to process credit cards transactions, though newer technologies can prevent this type of breach altogether. Before the attack, Microsoft had published a case study about Target using that particular solution (called SCCM or System Center Configuration Manager) to update these POS machines. That document may have given attackers clues that helped them understand exactly how to attack the systems. With access to this deployment system, the attacker inserted malicious code into the deployment process, which then distributed it to the POS systems.

Data needs to be unencrypted for systems to process it. I'll write more about encryption later, but for now, understand that when something is encrypted, it is in a format that someone reading it can't understand. To you and me, it would be a random string of letters and numbers. Once decrypted, it becomes readable text — like this book you're reading. A computer cannot process random letters and numbers as if it were a credit card number. At some point, when data is processed, it needs to be decrypted so a system can read the data to validate it, update it, or query it to find information. This data processing generally happens in the memory of a computer. It was at this point that the attacker's malware scraped and stole the credit card numbers.

Attackers sent commands over the network in a very crafty way. When network administrators are testing whether or not machines can connect on the network, they often use what is called a ping command, or the ICMP protocol[96]. This type of

---

[96] ICMP Protocol
https://en.wikipedia.org/wiki/Internet_Control_Message_Protocol

traffic is common in many networks. Often network administrators or security professionals would ignore it when they see it in the logs because it looks harmless. The attackers were able to control their malware on the internal network by sending commands embedded in specially crafted ICMP network packets that contained extraneous data. The ICMP protocol is supposed to follow a specific format. Most network devices will check that the necessary data points exist but may not be checking for extra data that should not be there. If network monitoring does not look for malformed packets, then this additional data could be tacked onto ICMP packets to send it through the network.

After this point, they sent the stolen data to FTP (file transfer protocol) sites they had set up on other hacked networks in locations like Florida and Brazil. FTP is a way to send files over a network to another remote location. At least some of the owners of the FTP servers were unaware their machines were involved in this attack. This example also shows why attribution (assigning blame for an attack) is hard, and why hacking back might cause problems. It may look like someone is attacking you when, in fact, the owner of the attacking server doesn't know that an attacker is controlling it and using it in attacks.

The Target breach shows how attackers can infiltrate and navigate networks. This method of attacking systems is a common approach in many data breaches, though the tools, technologies, and specific exploits may differ. An attack involves a series of steps from reconnaissance to exploitation to exfiltration. If you trust all the systems to talk to each other in your network (also called a flat network[97]), it gives attackers many opportunities to seek vulnerabilities and sensitive data by scanning and pivoting.

While editing this chapter, two related posts appeared on Twitter. One is a statement I've heard multiple times by people who test for security flaws in organizations, otherwise known as

---

[97] Flat Network https://en.wikipedia.org/wiki/Flat_network

penetration testing. The person stated, "Well-segmented networks have caused me the most headaches when I'm attacking networks. I can't stress how much harder it becomes for me as an attacker."[98] The other was a news article about how segmented networks helped thwart a potentially devastating ransomware attack against the city of Las Vegas (Targett, 2020). I go into more detail in my class on how segmenting networks can both help thwart attackers and help organizations see when an attack is taking place in cloud environments.

The NotPetya malware is another example of how attackers traverse internal networks due to excessive access (Greenburg, 2018). It hit some companies hard, deploying ransomware to many machines very rapidly. In this case, updates from an accounting system vendor in Ukraine distributed the malware. If you have a business, you are presumably using some accounting software. If you install the software on your local computer, it needs to get updates from time to time from the vendor. In the case of the NotPetya malware, the company that provided the accounting software was called MeDoc. Purportedly, Russian hackers got into the MeDoc systems and inserted malware into the software update process. When companies downloaded updates for their accounting systems, they got some bonus software of the evil variety.

Once that software got into the internal network, it quickly spread from machine to machine in an automated way. As explained previously, this type of malware is called a worm. Each device that was subsequently infected had ransomware installed on it. Similar to WannaCry, the ransomware demanded payment in exchange for decrypting the files. WIRED called NotPetya the most devastating cyberattack, and it hit companies like Maersk hard.

In chapter 5 on the exponential risk of Internet-exposed ports, I

[98] @tifkin_ https://twitter.com/tifkin_/status/1205567114653945860

explained that specific ports should never be open to the Internet. One of those is port 445. A protocol named SMB (Server Message Block) typically runs on this port. Some companies do use this port internally for legitimate reasons. However, that port doesn't need to be accessible both from and to every machine on an internal network. Network administrators can construct local networks to only allow traffic to that port from the systems that are supposed to send that traffic. The same goes for every other port — only enable what each host requires for both inbound and outbound connections.

Not only are attackers able to get into internal networks, they often stay there for months before an organization realizes they are present. When I started in the SANS Institute cybersecurity Master's in Information Security Engineering program, the average time to a breach was close to a year. I remember Dr. Eric Cole stating this in class as a statistic from a past *Verizon Data Breach Investigations Report*. The 2013 report states, "In 66% of cases, the breach wasn't discovered for months — or even years" (Verizon, 2013). Organizations in the United States were finding out about compromised data because the FBI was knocking on their doors to tell them someone was selling their data on the dark web.[99]

The dark web is a place where nefarious individuals buy and sell things that probably shouldn't be for sale — like hacking tools and other people's credentials, identity, and credit cards. Search engines do not index these pages, and sometimes they are only accessible if you know the "right" people. You can't get there from your standard web browser and Internet connection. There's an excellent documentary about the dark web and the people like Max Butler,[100] who ran a stolen credit card marketplace on a show called *American Greed*[101] from CNBC. This show is for you if you

---

[99] Dark web https://www.investopedia.com/terms/d/dark-web.asp
[100] Max Butler https://en.m.wikipedia.org/wiki/Max_Butler
[101] American Greed on CNBC https://www.cnbc.com/american-greed

want to watch a real-life hacker story including undercover FBI agents and a hacker who takes out other hackers — and ends up in jail. The whole *American Greed* series fits in nicely with the information in this chapter. It's incredible what people will do for the sake of money — both the people who perform evil deeds and the people who trust them.

The average time for a breach to exist on a company network has gone down significantly, but the time is still months, according to the *2019 Verizon Data Breach Investigations Report* (Verizon, 2019). If hackers have months to live inside a network, they have a great deal of time to steal money and intellectual property, and to monitor communications. To prevent attackers from maintaining this access, you'll want to keep them out in the first place, but chances are one will get in at some point.

For this reason, protect not only your perimeter but also your internal network. You can do that by limiting which systems can talk to each other on the internal network by setting up different network segments for different types of systems that do not need to communicate. Also, turn on the firewalls on your local computer operating system. Windows, Mac, and Linux systems have built-in firewalls. In most cases, two end-user computers, such as new laptops on the same network, never have any business talking to each other. End-user systems rarely need to allow inbound network traffic. Web servers running different applications don't generally need to communicate over the network. You get the idea.

A note for network geeks and those creating network products and protocols: new protocols and equipment that talks in the opposite direction of standard network traffic (a server making a network request to a client) make a network administrator's ability to block and spot malicious activity harder. Protocols and products that work in non-standard ways may bypass security controls, as Google QUIC did upon initial release. You can read more about that in this article, which also tells you how to disable it in your Google Chrome browser: "How Google's QUIC Protocol Impacts Network Security and Reporting" (Liebetrau, 2018). If you block Google QUIC on the network, your browser will still work (Iyengar & Thomson, 2020). If requests are only initiated by end-user machines, never servers initiating requests to user devices, administrators can block all incoming requests. This reduction in allowed traffic cuts the network attack vector virtually in half. Of course, this doesn't eliminate the risk, but it significantly reduces it.

On top of blocking unnecessary traffic and patching your systems, you'll want to turn on logging and monitor your network for suspicious traffic. If you don't have a lot of security or IT staff to do this type of monitoring, various tools can help. On AWS, you can turn on Amazon GuardDuty[102] and receive alerts when suspicious activities occur. Azure[103] and Google[104] have similar services that help you spot malicious traffic. Another tool that can help is Cisco Stealthwatch Cloud[105] — it's designed to be easy to use and can alert you to suspicious behavior in the cloud and on-premises. These are just a few of the tools I've used before. There are plenty of others out there. Most of them will give you a free trial.

Many resources exist that can help you learn how to architect secure networks and monitoring solutions. In my cloud security class[106], I include a full day of material on how to design networks in the cloud that help prevent and identify breaches. Some of this also applies to on-premises environments, even though my primary focus is cloud security. You can design your network to

---

[102] Amazon GuardDuty https://aws.amazon.com/guardduty/
[103] Azure security products https://azure.microsoft.com/en-us/product-categories/security/
[104] Google Security Products https://cloud.google.com/security/products/
[105] Cisco StealthWatch Cloud https://azure.microsoft.com/en-us/product-categories/security/
[106] 2nd Sight Lab Cloud Security Training https://2ndsightlab.com/cloud-security-training.html

make it harder for attackers to infiltrate and pivot and make it easier to spot malicious traffic.

The insider threat

One other sad, but true, fact is that you need to protect your internal network and data from people you hire. Although we would like to trust everyone, the truth is, people will steal things for money or ideological reasons, or do something in retaliation when they are upset. Chapter 10 covers credentials which can help limit the impact of insider threats, but yes, it happens. Organizations should consider policies that limit access when implementing access to sensitive data.

I can't say from first-hand knowledge this is true, but someone in one of my security classes who worked for the NSA said Edward Snowden[107] was a nice guy who asked to borrow someone's credentials to obtain the information he exposed. If you are not familiar with the controversial actions of Edward Snowden, I refer you to the many resources available on that topic, as that is not the primary purpose of mentioning him here, but rather how he obtained classified NSA documents. Another person seeking revenge after his employer fired him deleted £500,000 worth of 'business-critical data' (Corfield, 2019). A network administrator who became annoyed with his employer held the City of San Francisco's network hostage (Kravets, 2008).

Companies should be aware of the insider threat and avoid naïve trust for the sake of not offending employees. If you bring $10,000 in cash to the bank, do you want the bank to trust their employees to deposit the money in the right account? No, you would expect them to have processes and controls to make sure the employees don't put that money in their own pockets. The same type of controls should apply to your data. The processes involving people and sensitive data should take appropriate care to prevent

---

[107] Edward Snowden https://en.m.wikipedia.org/wiki/Edward_Snowden

a rogue employee from stealing the data or harming the organization in some way.

Organizations also need to make sure employees are not stealing sensitive data when they leave your company to go work at another. I heard a story from an anonymous source regarding a company that shall remain nameless. They discovered a CISO trying to exfiltrate large amounts of sensitive data as he was leaving a company. Of all people, you likely would not expect the CISO to undertake such actions. The company found out because they were testing a new security product at the time, which identified large data transfers. That led to the detection of the mass exodus of data and the identification of the perpetrator.

Detecting insider threats is a challenging proposition. Creating proper network controls and monitoring for unusual behaviors will help. I cover monitoring in chapter 21. Some companies specialize in helping to detect insider threats. I spoke on a podcast with Jadee Hansen (@jadeehanson on Twitter), CISO of Code42[108], which tries to help organizations protect trade secrets from insider threats. She mentioned some of the concerns and how to address them in that podcast, *Masters of Data – Security Experts Panel – Second Edition* (Gerchow, George, Radichel, & Hansen, 2019).

Zero trust

Executives who want to reduce risk on internal networks should create security controls that allow data and system access on a need-to-know basis. Employees and systems should receive access required to do their jobs; no more, no less. This concept is referred to as "zero trust." John Kindervag, CTO of Palo Alto Networks, introduced this concept in a Forrester paper, "Build Security into Your Network's DNA: The Zero Trust Network Architecture" (Kindervag, 2010). Avoid the assumption that anything coming from a machine on the local, internal network is safe.

---

[108] Code42 https://www.code42.com/

Organizations should only allow machines on the internal network to communicate on required ports. Use firewalls on individual computers and network segmentation to block and monitor for unnecessary traffic between all the devices on your internal network.

Ask your programmers if they are validating every single input and output for the systems they develop. They should never trust any data coming from any source without proper inspection and verification, even if it comes from the local network. Programmers should be aware of top attacks and understand the need to protect systems from attacks by sources inside as well as outside the organization. Zero trust applies to software and code just as it applies to networks.

When I worked as an architect and director on a SaaS security product, my team had set up endpoints in our cloud environment to test equipment that connected to it without authentication or network controls. They presumed attackers would not be able to find those endpoints. I had to explain to them the concepts in the last few chapters in about 5 minutes. We didn't have a security training budget, and the company wanted us to get the project done fast, so I did as much training as I could. Developers, QA teams, and DevOps engineers often assume nothing will access the things they expose to the Internet. If they aren't worried about Internet connections, they definitely aren't concerned with something on your internal network without proper training and awareness.

At another company where I worked, a certain software system presumed that customer uploads containing sensitive data without encryption would be safe since they were stored and transmitted on internal networks. Others thought it would be OK to download open-source software directly from the Internet into production builds. These things happened at security companies and major corporations. Don't assume your developers know the best security practices or are aware of all possible threats. Without training, they are not thinking about potential sources of an attack on your internal network.

To quantify the risk, ask your security and networking teams how many possible paths an attacker could take through your internal environment. One entry point may be from the Internet via a phishing email to a laptop, and then from there to other laptops. Another may be from a server update process to other systems on the network. Pay special attention to the number of paths that can get to your sensitive data. Then work to reduce the total potential avenues an attacker has to get into and out of your network, and the number of machines any one system can in turn infect.

Defending your systems for the greater good

Before I leave this topic of trust, I want to let people know one other thing about my personal experience mentioned at the beginning of the chapter. Recently, probably due to the #metoo movement, I looked up that old male neighbor and found out he lives in the middle of nowhere. At this time, I don't see the point of pursuing justice. I also do not want to revisit the whole ordeal or play the role of a victim to elicit sympathy or outrage. I do, however, want to raise awareness that these things happen.

The unfortunate thing a lot of people in cybersecurity understand is that child pornography and abuse is more prevalent than most people realize. If we all start defending our networks and taking actions to secure our systems, maybe we can help reduce its prevalence on the Internet, along with that of ransomware and other cyber threats. I ran across these types of images myself when I first started researching security and reported them. I got no response, so I'm not sure what happened with that submission.

Don't allow these people to use your servers and networks to do their dirty work. If you do find something of this nature or any other types of Internet crimes, please report it to the appropriate authorities. If you see something illegal, or something happens to you, the same person might be doing similar things to others. If we all work together, maybe we can make the world a bit better of a place for everyone — including children. Here are some resources where you can report different types of Internet crimes in the U.S.:

U.S. Department of Justice:
https://www.justice.gov/criminal-ceos/report-violations

FBI:
https://www.fbi.gov/investigate/violent-crime/cac

U.S. Government — report crime:
https://www.usa.gov/report-crime

U.S. Government — report fraud:
https://www.usa.gov/stop-scams-frauds

Internet Crime Complaint Center:
https://ic3.gov

CISA — Report Cyber Incidents:
https://www.cisa.gov/reporting-cyber-incidents

9
THE AFTERMATH OF STOLEN AND ABUSED CREDENTIALS

Attackers steal credentials. As history shows us, it is not a matter of *if*, but *when*. I'll talk about ways to help prevent that in the next chapter. First, consider this question: How much damage can an attacker inflict on your company using stolen credentials, and what can you do about it? On my blog, I called this "premeditated damage control."

Blast radius

The term "blast radius"[109] refers to the impact a bomb would have on its surroundings. However, the same concept applies to cybersecurity incidents and the specific vulnerabilities that cause them, including an open network port, CVE, or credential theft. Consider the blast radius in the context of all aspects of your infrastructure and architecture. When an attacker steals credentials, what is the extent of the damage they can do with that access?

---

[109] Blast Radius https://en.wikipedia.org/wiki/Blast_radius

In April 2019, Microsoft reported a breach in which a single set of user credentials enabled an attacker to see information from potentially tens of millions of Microsoft email users (Kerner, 2019). How could this system design be improved? Grant access as needed for the account in question during the time of an incident. Yes, this is harder to do than giving a person or system complete access to all the data. However, secure architectures and processes that protect people's privacy require investment and planning.

A similar problem with overly permissive credentials occurred at Facebook. The company fired a security analyst for using private data to stalk women (Goodin, Facebook security analyst is fired for using private data to stalk women, 2018). How did this analyst have such broad access to personal data? When designing systems, people should have access to data on a need-to-know basis to handle a specific incident. Design systems and processes to give temporary access to solve a problem. If possible, the person granting access should be a different person than the one who is using the access.

These are two examples of cases where organizations created credentials with extensive access. Not thinking through how that access could be misused had negative consequences. In one case, an attacker stole the credentials. In the other, an employee abused credentials he was granted. Either situation can lead to a data breach. I provided examples of how employees misused their access in the last chapter. Let's look at some of the ways attackers steal credentials and what can happen as a result.

Credential stuffing

On January 17th, 2019, Troy Hunt wrote a blog post regarding over 773 million compromised credentials (Hunt, 2019). What is interesting is that the number of unique passwords is much lower than the total number of unique usernames. What does that tell us? Even with some room for error and unrecoverable passwords in the dump, many people are picking the same passwords or reusing identical passwords on different accounts.

Reused passwords enable attackers to take stolen credentials from one breach and attempt to log into and compromise other unrelated systems, otherwise known as credential stuffing[110]. Because people reuse the same password for multiple accounts, attackers can get into other systems beyond the one where they stole the credentials. Dunkin Donuts (Seals, 2019) and Intuit (Gatlan, Tax Returns Exposed in TurboTax Credential Stuffing Attacks, 2019), maker of TurboTax, reported that attackers were able to access customer accounts for this reason.

These compromises were the fault of users who used the same password in multiple places, the vendor who initially lost the passwords, or both, depending on your point of view. Although the company hit by the credential stuffing attack can try to identify the activity, it is sometimes nearly impossible for them to know the owner of the credentials is not the person using them. The whole point of usernames and passwords is to prove who you are. Because you know them, the system gives them access and presumes no one else has those credentials. If someone else gets your credentials, they are effectively you as far as the website or application you log into is concerned. That is the concept of identity[111] — proving you are who you claim to be via a process called authentication[112]. Authentication requires you to provide some information to verify your identity (e.g., a username and password or some other secret that only you have).

The solution to the credential stuffing problem is not preventing the attackers from using the stolen passwords to get into other systems. Attackers should not have been able to obtain them in the first place! Users also should not reuse the same password in many locations. Solutions to these problems include using a

---

[110] Credential Stuffing https://www.owasp.org/index.php/Credential_stuffing
[111] Digital Identity https://en.wikipedia.org/wiki/Digital_identity
[112] Authentication https://en.wikipedia.org/wiki/Authentication

password manager, password-less solutions, biometrics, or MFA (multi-factor authentication), which I'll cover later. For now, let's consider how bad actors obtain credentials and system access.

Phishing

One way that attackers commonly obtain credentials is via Phishing. They send emails with malicious links to unsuspecting users. If the user clicks the link, they may visit a website hosting malicious code or download a file containing malware embedded in it. If the user opens the website or file, the malware can compromise their system. Once the malware is on the system it may be able to read any of the data processed by that system, including credentials in system files or memory.

Many companies run campaigns to test users to see if they click on fake links in emails. This form of security awareness training encourages people to be more cautious when opening their emails. The problem is that even with a substantial amount of training, the chances are good that someone will still click something bad. Phishing emails can be very tricky. Additional protections can help ensure that if and when a phishing attack successfully obtains credentials, the damage is limited.

Mishandled credentials

Google revealed that it had stored plaintext (unencrypted) passwords for 15 years, potentially readable by its employees (O'Donnell, 2019). System design can get very complicated in a hurry. Companies need to have developers and software architects that examine the entire system for data exposure. If an organization is not careful, applications and employees may write credentials to log files, emails, backups, caches, or URLs (links used to access the system). Rogue employees, malware, website attacks, or accidents could all lead to credential exposure.

All the people involved in designing and building systems should be aware of and on the lookout for improper handling of any secret used to access an application or data. A mechanism should be in place for reporting these system implementation errors. Employees who had access to the unencrypted credentials can see them, and any malware that could infiltrate the employee's laptop would potentially have access to them as well (Honig & Sikorski, 2012).

Yahoo and LinkedIn suffered massive breaches that exposed usernames and passwords. The Yahoo breach settlement was resolved just as I was making final edits to this book. Yahoo settled this breach for $117.5 million (Newman, How to Get Your Yahoo Breach Settlement Money, 2020). The LinkedIn breach resulted in a $1.25 million settlement (Fontana, 2015). Even though these companies encrypted the passwords, the attackers were able to figure out what a lot of them were. How did they do it? Let's dive a bit deeper and see how this all works.

Authentication, authorization, and identity

Digital identities represent systems, people, or another external party that wants to access systems, data, locations, or some other resource.[113] When a person or device logs into a system, they prove their identity by providing information only they have or know. Proving who you are is known as authentication.[114] An authentication process might require a username and password, keys (a set of random numbers and letters), a fingerprint, face, or some other secret data. The credentials prove who the person is and, in turn, that they are allowed to access the system. It does not identify what actions the user is allowed to take in that system. Authorization[115] is the term security professionals use for the actions the owner of a set of credentials is permitted to take in a system. A common analogy for authentication is showing your

---

[113] Digital identity https://en.wikipedia.org/wiki/Digital_identity
[114] Authentication https://en.wikipedia.org/wiki/Authentication
[115] Authorization https://en.wikipedia.org/wiki/Authorization

driver's license to prove who you are in the United States. Because you have that driver's license, you are authorized to drive a car on U.S. roads.

A secure system tracks when a user authenticates successfully or unsuccessfully, and when any denied or authorized action occurs, along with the username, time, and date. Each set of credentials should be associated with one identity so that logs can clearly show which user or resource took a specific action. The ability to prove someone did something in a way that the person cannot deny is called "non-repudiation"[116] and is very important when investigating data breaches. Organizations that process credit cards need to comply with PCI DSS (Payment Card Industry Data Security Standards). Requirement 8 of that standard covers this best practice: "Assign a unique ID to each person with computer access" (PCI Security Standards Council, 2018).

If credentials are not shared or are distributed securely, non-repudiation is not possible. An organization may not be able to determine the source of a violation or crime that leveraged those credentials. You also won't have a case that stands up in court if you cannot show without a doubt that the person whom you claim accessed the system inappropriately did so. That's why many cybersecurity standards state that each user should have his or her own set of credentials. This assignment of one person to one set of credentials is also how systems can identify unauthorized users that have accessed the system using stolen usernames and passwords. If the system says you logged in, but you know you didn't, then you know someone has compromised your credentials.

Password hash functions

Systems should store passwords as a hash value, which is a random string of letters and numbers produced by a hash

---

[116] Non-repudiation https://en.wikipedia.org/wiki/Non-repudiation

function.[117] A cryptographic hash is a one-way function, meaning you pass the data through the hashing process. You can't reverse the process to get back the original value. Some people call this one-way encryption,[118] but others debate that term and say it's not encryption because you can't decrypt the data. With a two-way cryptographic function, you encrypt the data with an encryption key.[119] You can then decrypt it to get back the original plain-text value. More on encryption later, but regarding passwords, know that best practices dictate they should be stored as hashes, not using two-way encryption. If someone steals the hash, they cannot reverse it to get back the password.

Note that I am not going to attempt to explain everything about encryption, hashing, and cryptography in an executive-level book. I am generalizing in some areas to make the topics approachable for non-technical readers. If you want to dive into the details, many other books exist on this topic. For those who are sticklers on terminology or wish to understand all the math, I refer you to books like *Applied Cryptography* by Bruce Schneier (Schneier, 1996). For those who do not want to get into the details of the math, I recommend following the best practices recommended by top security organizations and frameworks. For example, OWASP has a *Password Storage Cheat Sheet*.[120]

Password attacks

One thing a hacker may try to do with a hash is to try to guess the password (a method called "brute force"[121]). The term for guessing passwords or somehow reversing the encryption is

---

[117] Hash function https://www.sciencedirect.com/topics/computer-science/hash-function
[118] Encryption https://www.vocabulary.com/dictionary/encryption
[119] Encryption Key https://en.wikipedia.org/wiki/Key_%28cryptography%29
[120] Password Storage Cheat Sheet https://cheatsheetseries.owasp.org/cheatsheets/Password_Storage_Cheat_Sheet.html
[121] Brute Force https://en.wikipedia.org/wiki/Brute-force_attack

"cracking."[122] Tools exist that try to make this process easier. The more complex and lengthier a password is, the longer it will take to crack because the attacker has to guess an exponential set of combinations (length times number of possible values for each character).

Let's do some basic math. If your password is "dog," and you only use lowercase letters from the alphabet (a-z), I'd have to guess 26 times for each possible value times the number of positions (3 in d-o-g) and all the possible combinations. That means if I want to try the letters abc, I'd have to try aaa, aab, aba, baa, abb, bab, abc, acb, cab, cba...and so on. Now, if you add uppercase alphabet letters, 26 turns into 52 — so that's more guesses. A longer password also adds additional positions. I hope you get the idea! These concepts initially led to the idea that passwords should be long and complex. Complex passwords include uppercase and lowercase letters, numbers, and special characters (symbols like !, @, or #).

Often these brute force attempts start by making a word list[123] of commonly used passwords[124] and words or numbers likely to be used by a target. The list is passed into a password cracking tool like John the Ripper.[125] For example, it's baseball season in Seattle, so I might add "Mariners" to my wordlist so I can guess any password with that word in it more quickly. Yes, baseball fans, you might want to change those passwords! OK, let's say you made your password one of the most commonly problematic passwords out there: Summer2020 or whatever month, quarter, or variation of the current date and time. Oh, that's your current password? Sorry, I just told everyone. Go change it now. I'd be

---

[122] Password cracking https://en.wikipedia.org/wiki/Password_cracking
[123] Openwall Wordlists Collection https://www.openwall.com/passwords/wordlists/
[124] List of the most common passwords https://en.wikipedia.org/wiki/List_of_the_most_common_passwords
[125] John the Ripper https://www.openwall.com/john/

able to crack it in seconds because it's one of the first passwords added to any word list for these cracking tools. When I explained this to one of my nephews, he looked at me and said, "I guess I need to go change my password."

When possible, the attacker uses tools that simply look up the password associated with the hash. Here's how it works by breaking it down into three steps:

1. An algorithm is part of a computer program, which is like a formula with inputs and outputs. I pass my password into a standard algorithm that creates a password hash, and the result is some unreadable value. Let's say my password is PurplePopcorn, and the hash of that is X1yZ23AQ4. It's not. I just made that up, but pretend it is for this example. That's the hash of my password.

2. Now the next person comes along and creates the same password, PurplePopcorn, and it goes through the hashing algorithm. What does it turn out to be? X1yZ23AQ4.

3. Unless we do something to mix it up a bit, as I'll explain in a minute, I now have the password for anyone whose password is represented by that hash (X1yZ23AQ4). In other words, when I see that hash, I can just look up the password because I already discovered that hash is associated with the password PurplePopcorn.

Attackers also use something called rainbow tables,[126] which are enormous databases (or a bunch of words in files) with every password and associated hash that they know. Any time a set of credentials is compromised, they search for the values they discovered in these tables to find the corresponding password if they can. It's a lot faster to use a rainbow table than to try to crack the password. Once again, I am oversimplifying how rainbow

---

[126] Rainbow Table https://en.wikipedia.org/wiki/Rainbow_table

tables work. If you want all the technical details, check out the *CISSP Study Guide (Third Edition)* by Eric Conrad, Seth Misenar, and Josh Feldman (Conrad, Misenar, & Feldman, 2015).

Mitigating brute force and rainbow table attacks

How can system implementers mitigate brute force and rainbow table attacks? Use a sufficiently complex hashing function (also known as an algorithm)[127] and a salt.[128] Other factors include password length, complexity (as already explained), and how often a user changes the password. If the user changes the password in the middle of a brute force attack, the attacker has to start over. Some organizations say you don't have to change your passwords as frequently if it is long. However, I still change my passwords regularly. When it comes to stolen passwords, the length of the password doesn't help you. Changing it frequently will.

The topic of password complexity has come up for debate in the past few years due to the way people tend to create complex passwords.[129] Complex passwords are hard to remember, so people replace letters in words with numbers in ways attackers can easily guess. For example, if your password was DOG, you might change the letter 'O' to the number '0' and make the 'G' a lower case: "D0g". Attackers know people do this, so they create variations of common passwords that alter the letters and numbers accordingly. People also tack on the year and an exclamation point at the end. These are still easy to guess passwords. NIST, therefore, changed their recommendations from complex passwords to longer passwords that are easier to remember. You can find all the password recommendations in *NIST 800-63 Digital Identity Guidelines* (NIST, 2017).

---

[127] Hashing Algorithm https://en.wikipedia.org/wiki/Secure_Hash_Algorithms
[128] Cryptographic Salt https://en.wikipedia.org/wiki/Salt_(cryptography)
[129] xkcd comic explaining the problem with complex passwords https://xkcd.com/936/

Hashing Algorithms

What is a hash algorithm? It's a mathematical function. When you have a mathematical function, you provide inputs to the function and get a value as a result. With a cryptographic hash, you pass in some data (a password) and get a resulting value as output (the hash value). The algorithm needs to be sufficiently complex so that someone cannot determine the original value or otherwise break your function. Without going into all the details, a collision[130] is when two different values produce the same hash using a particular hash algorithm. If someone can do that with a hash function, that's called a collision attack,[131] at which point security professionals consider the algorithm broken (i.e. no longer secure).

Which hash algorithm should you use?[132] Some of the most commonly used are MD5, SHA1, and SHA2. At the time of this writing, MD5 and SHA1 are considered broken. If your use case is security related, you need to choose a hash that cannot be broken. If your organization is still using MD5 or SHA1, be aware that NIST (NIST, 2015) and Bruce Schneier (Schneier, MD5 and SHA-1 Still Used in 2018, 2018), one of the world's leading cryptography experts, recommend against it. At the time of the Yahoo! breach, they were still using MD5 (Stockley, 2016). As mentioned, the OWASP (the Open Web Application Standards Project) has some recommendations in their *Password Storage Cheat Sheet*.

The Salt

What exactly is a salt, and why do you need one? It is a random value passed into an algorithm with the password to generate a unique hash. Let's say I use a salt with my password in the example above. I made up these values to illustrate the point.

---

[130] Collision https://en.wikipedia.org/wiki/Collision_(computer_science)
[131] Collision attack https://en.wikipedia.org/wiki/Collision_attack
[132] List of hash functions https://en.wikipedia.org/wiki/List_of_hash_functions

They are not actual hashes that a function would produce.

1. My password (PurplePopcorn) goes through the hashing algorithm along with some random number.

```
PurplePopcorn + 1235678 > Hash > XITMEMMK2
```

2. Another person chooses the same password, and it goes through the hashing algorithm with a different number. That causes the hash function to generate a different result.

```
PurplePopcorn + 4567890 > Hash > BSETY4G72
```

3. Rainbow tables won't work very well because the attacker can't just look up the hash for the password. They would also need to generate a hash for that password with every possible salt. If the salt is random and sufficiently long, that is an exponential number of possibilities.

4. Note that the bad guys can still guess your overused common password by trying to log into the website periodically or using a credential stuffing attack. Seriously. Go change it!

The moral of this example is: make sure your developers are hashing passwords with the most up-to-date recommended algorithm and using a random salt for each hash.

Tokens

Unfortunately, passwords aren't our only source of worry. After a person logs into a system, the application that authenticated the person often returns a value called a "token." This value is generally another (hopefully) sufficiently random string of letters and numbers or some other more specific structure. Instead of passing around the user credentials and checking them each time, the system checks to see if the user has a valid token — often referred to as a session ID.[133] Note that I am intentionally avoiding other forms of authentication tokens for this basic explanation of authentication concepts.

Systems do this for efficiency and to reduce the risk of stolen credentials. The session ID lasts for a certain amount of time, referred to as a session.[134] A session has a start time and an end time. Even if someone obtains the token, it is only usable for a specific length of time (hopefully reasonably short!). The session ID may expire, or an administrator may revoke it in the case of a compromise. The token can no longer be used to access the system. However, the credentials (the username and password used to log in) are still valid. The user can log in again with their credentials, or the system may auto-renew the session with a new token if a user is still actively using the system.

Several mechanisms exist to try to steal IDs and other types of hashes and tokens used to manage a user's session. These tokens are effectively as good as credentials if obtained during the active session (after the start time and before the end time of the session). Sometimes developers pass around and store tokens in ways that allow attackers to obtain these them. Anyone with the token can do whatever the user could do during the active session.

Session tokens should not be present in URLs where they end up in logs or bookmarks. Developers should not store them in insecure cookies (bits of data stored for each site by web browsers like Google Chrome, Firefox, Safari, or Internet Explorer). [135] I've even seen developers, who didn't understand the impact of their choice, use the session ID as the names of files generated by a system that users downloaded from the web application. Anyone with access to those files could then use the token to take action as the logged-in user if the session had not expired. An attacker could obtain the session token anywhere that the file name was

---

[133] Session ID https://en.wikipedia.org/wiki/Session_ID
[134] Session https://en.wikipedia.org/wiki/Session_(computer_science)
[135] Website cookies https://en.wikipedia.org/wiki/HTTP_cookie

logged and displayed in the system for other people to see.

Website vulnerabilities and credential attacks

Cross-Site Scripting (XSS)[136] and Cross-Site Request Forgery (CSRF)[137] are types of web attacks that leverage the permissions of a logged-in user to perform unintended actions (like transferring money from a bank account). Developers should be familiar with the OWASP (Open Web Application Security Project) Top Ten[138] — both current and previous versions, in my opinion — which lists top software flaws in web applications. Developers should also be aware of other types of attacks, such as those outlined by MITRE ATT&CK®[139] and CWEs.[140]

Other attacks involve breaking into a system and using the privileges assigned to that system. Server-Side Request Forgery (SSRF)[141] involves obtaining access to a computer and using the permissions on that machine to obtain resources that the attacker could not otherwise access. Let's say, for example, a web server retrieves data from a database on behalf of authenticated users. An attacker will attempt to use access provided to the web server to obtain data in that database. An SSRF attack was the cause of the Capital One data breach (Radichel, What's in your cloud?, 2019).

Kolby Allen and I presented a trickier example at RSA and AWS re:Invent, showing how stolen credentials found in one system could be used on a completely separate vulnerable system to pull

---

[136] Cross Site Scripting (XSS) https://www.owasp.org/index.php/Cross-site_Scripting_(XSS)
[137] Cross-Site Request Forgery (CSRF) https://www.owasp.org/index.php/Cross-Site_Request_Forgery_(CSRF)
[138] OWASP Top 10 https://www.owasp.org/index.php/Category:OWASP_Top_Ten_Project
[139] MITRE ATT&CK® https://attack.mitre.org/
[140] CWEs https://cwe.mitre.org/community/swa/attacks.html
[141] SSRF https://www.owasp.org/index.php/Server_Side_Request_Forgery

data from a database on a flat network. This presentation explains the importance of both protecting credentials and correctly configuring your network. We talk specifically about AWS in our presentation, called *Red Team vs. Blue Team on AWS* (Allen & Radichel, 2018). However, the concepts apply to any cloud provider and even on-premises systems.

Privilege escalation

If an attacker gets credentials or a token that does not give them much access, the next step is to attempt privilege escalation. The attacker seeks flaws and vulnerabilities that allow a higher level of access than what the stolen credentials have. They may find administrative credentials on the accessed system and then try to crack them. They may also leverage the compromised machine to access other connected systems that have more privileges.

In cloud environments, if attackers have enough permissions via stolen credentials, they can create a new virtual machine with permissions greater than the original credentials they obtained. Then they can connect to the system that has more privileges and do more harm. They may be able to shut down or terminate resources, install cryptominers[142] (software that mines cryptocurrency using your resources that cost you money), or access additional data. They may create backdoor accounts. That way, if you discover and shut down the original credentials, they have a backup way to get into the system.

Another technique an attacker can use to escalate privileges on an operating system like Windows or Linux is called process injection.[143] Operating systems have different processes running with different privileges. An attacker may find a way to inject malware into a running process that has full system access. These

---

[142] Cryptomining https://www.webopedia.com/TERM/C/cryptomining-malware.html
[143] Process injection https://attack.mitre.org/techniques/T1055/

types of attacks are hard to spot since the process they have hijacked looks legitimate.

Most modern operating systems have many mechanisms to prevent this. However, as I learned while obtaining a certification in reverse engineering malware and related research, determined attackers may eventually discover a way in. The attack may come in the form of "file-less malware," which executes in memory only, not from a file on disk, which a person investigating the breach could discover. I hope you are monitoring your network and access logs for suspicious activity, such as many failed logins or repeated access denied error messages.

Premeditated damage control

When designing systems, organizations should not only consider how to protect credentials, but how much damage an attacker could do if an attacker steals a particular set of credentials. In the case of the root credentials of a cloud account, the attacker could delete the entire account. If they obtain credentials from a domain administrator for a company, the attacker could do almost anything they want on a corporate network. Credentials of a database administrator may have unfettered access to all your data.

At some point, it is highly likely that attackers will get credentials of someone in your organization — a computer or a person that leverages credentials to take actions in your environment. This fact is why giving someone too much system access can be especially risky. Not only do you need to worry about the actions people take on purpose, but you also need to consider potential damage if those credentials are stolen and abused. What could an attacker do with one set of credentials? Instead of giving full administrative access to one set of credentials, determine how you can structure access to systems in your organization in a manner that minimizes risk.

Consider the story of Code Spaces (Venezia, 2014). Code Spaces was a company that hosted code and project data for its customers. At some point, an attacker stole their administrative credentials. The attacker demanded money, and Code Spaces refused. The attacker proceeded to delete everything in the account. Code Spaces tried to change the admin password, but the attacker had already created additional credentials. It was no use. I call Code Spaces the "company that got deleted," because after that they went out of business. This sad tale demonstrates why you need to be very careful how much access you give any single set of credentials, and the importance of protecting root credentials.

How much damage can any single set of credentials do in your environment? There's always someone with "the special keys." You know — that person who can fix anything. Allowing someone this almighty access is a risk to your organization. Consider how you might instead construct your credentials and system access to limit the potential damage if an attacker obtains those credentials. Limit broad access to systems and give them only the permissions people require to do their jobs. When setting up cloud environments, lock away the administrative or all-powerful root user. At the very least, make sure your users can't delete your entire cloud account — and your unaltered logs.

Besides attackers stealing credentials, unfortunately, your employees sometimes misuse the access you have granted them. The *2019 Verizon Data Breach Investigations Report* (Verizon, 2019) reported that in multiple incidents, employees used credentials on their way out the door. They attempted to steal data that would give them a competitive advantage at their next job.

You can limit the amount of damage a single set of credentials can do by using the concept of segregation of duties.[144] Give different

---

[144] Segregation of duties
https://www.aicpa.org/interestareas/informationtechnology/resources/value-

people access to different parts of a system and ensure that one individual can't access the system as a whole. As a result, it takes two or more people cooperating to steal sensitive data. Banks do this all the time. Processing a large transaction generally requires two people. A company that wanted to move drug production to Asia split the formulation of the drug into multiple locations. (This presumes no one single government could demand all the facilities to give up the information.)

I don't understand why this concept is not leveraged more widely in IT and software design. However, I have seen some organizations implement it in creative ways. I worked on a project at a company that stored half of a credit card in one system and the half in another. I interviewed one vendor that designed their architecture so it would take a three-party collusion to access data. AWS requires two people to initiate a production deployment based on a presentation I saw by the CISO, Stephen Schmidt. Companies can structure teams to achieve similar objectives when designing cloud systems. The structure needs to support moving fast but simultaneously include checks and balances for critical high-risk functions that could lead to a breach.

One person I know who works in a large company told me the pentesters accessed what I like to call his "special keys" (very powerful credentials). Pentesters are people who test for security flaws, and that is covered in chapter 14. They accessed his computer and then ran a cron job[145] (a scheduled script that runs on a machine) that would periodically pull his AWS credentials off of his laptop. With his access token, they owned the account (or pwned,[146] in gamer and hacker lingo). He asked me, "Who looks for cron jobs on a Mac?" Well, he's lucky it was people hired to intentionally test the system and not someone with more devious objectives!

---

strategy-through-segregation-of-duties.html
[145] Cron job https://en.wikipedia.org/wiki/Cron
[146] pwned https://en.wikipedia.org/wiki/Pwn

And by the way, there's no cheating when it comes to hacking. The defenders have to play by rules. Pentesters can do anything in scope for a pentest. Criminal attackers have no rules to follow. That's how it goes, and that's one of the reasons attacking is easier than defending. Sorry, my friend!

One of the hardest and most important jobs in any company is managing and monitoring credential use and abuse. Tracking all the ways credentials can be compromised is overwhelming. Systems need to be architected correctly. Credential assignment needs to be architected properly as well. The layers and structure of credentials can lead to gaping holes, overly permissive configurations or, in the extreme opposite scenario, an environment where no one can do their job effectively. Certain vendor products try to make credential management easier in large organizations. Some cloud services make it harder because they don't integrate with your internal user management system.

Make sure that the person designing the systems and structure for IAM (identity and access management) at your company understands and can measure the risks associated with stolen credentials. Ask if they can tell you what the maximum potential damage to the organization could be if any single set of credentials fall into the hands of a malicious person. Understand who has risky credentials in your organization. Monitor them closely. If overly permissive credentials exist, work to reduce the risk of exposure in ways that still allow your staff to get things done. They may not be as fast as they would be with unfettered system access. However, they can be efficient enough while at the same time keeping your company out of the headlines as the victim of the next mega-breach.

10
THE PASSWORD PROBLEM

It seems impossible to prevent stolen passwords. What's a system administrator supposed to do when third-party services don't correctly hash passwords and expose databases to the Internet, and when people keep reusing passwords? Fortunately, there are some things you can do to make it harder for attackers to use those credentials if they obtain them.

As explained in the last chapter, attackers use passwords stolen in one data breach to get into other systems because people reuse credentials and create easy to crack passwords. I explained how stronger passwords help prevent data breaches. Now all you need to do is create a different, very long, and hard-to-guess password for all 50 different websites you use that require authentication. So that's just 50 separate long, frequently changing passwords you need to remember. No problem, right?

Some people have told me tricks over the years, like string together four nonsensical words, so the password is lengthy. Use the first letter of every word of the title of a song. For example, "Girls just wanna have fun" would be "Gjwhf" (but that's not a stellar password because it's not very long). You could also use the first letter of some other memorable phrase or sentence. You could try to think of a pattern and change a few characters for each password, but if someone is really after you and figures out the pattern that could backfire. It's probably better than password reuse.

Password managers[147] are applications designed to help people with password fatigue and to make it easier to leverage best practices. You can store all your passwords in a password manager instead of trying to remember them all. The password manager helps you log into websites and applications. Alternatively, the password manager may be able to generate complex passwords for you. Password managers are better than reusing passwords for sure. The purpose of password managers is secure password management, so in theory, it should be safe to store all your passwords in them.

The thing that makes me cautious when it comes to password managers is that now all your passwords are in one place. An attacker who can get into the password manager has all your passwords. When malware gets onto a computer, it can potentially read the values of secrets in memory or exploit a vulnerability in that application. I explained how hackers find security vulnerabilities previously, and CVEs already exist for some versions of password managers. However, a password manager from a reputable vendor is still better than easy-to-crack and reused passwords. If you are interested in using a password manager, many blog posts and articles compare the different available products.

Some companies put their most sensitive passwords (only to be used in case of emergency) in a safe that requires two people to access. One of the considerations is where to put the safe. Is it accessible to people who might steal it and break into it? Is it in a safety deposit box in a bank that is not available outside of

---

[147] Password manager https://en.wikipedia.org/wiki/Password_manager

banking hours? Safes are a valid option, but they come with their own set of challenges.

Other people put passwords on phones. Malware can infect phones as well as computers (Dunham, 2008), but at least you aren't storing them on the system where you log in — or are you? An attacker can break into a phone and steal files just as they would on a computer. Many people use their phones to check email. Click one bad link, and an attacker may have compromised the phone. In one case, a company put part of a password on one person's phone and the rest on another.

No matter how you look at it — passwords are tricky to protect!

Biometrics

An alternative to passwords involves biometrics[148] — letting people log into systems using their fingerprints, faces, eyes, or handprints. When I used to host servers at a facility in Seattle called Internap, I would have to put my hand on a scanner that would verify it was me before letting me in. It was so cool and high-tech at the time! Now, phones and computers have fingerprint scanners and sometimes face readers to let you get into your devices and applications.

If we use our fingerprint, our face, or our eyes to log in, the attacker can't steal those, so we're good, right? Hold on a minute. Think about how a computer validates your fingerprint. You put your finger on the reader, and the reader captures an image or digital replica of your finger. How is that stored? Bits and bytes on a computer or device — just like everything else! An attacker can steal that just like any other type of data.

Let's say you go to a restaurant and have a drink, and someone swipes your fingerprint off of the glass (yep, I've watched too

---

[148] Biometrics https://en.wikipedia.org/wiki/Biometrics

many of those kinds of movies.) Is it possible that the person can now replicate those bits and bytes to trick biometric readers and get into your systems? What if someone steals the bits and bytes representing your fingerprint from some computer system? Can they use it now to log into your accounts? If they can, we have a bigger problem. When an attacker gets your password, you can change it. Security professionals use the term "rotate" for periodic password changes to help prevent attackers from using or cracking them. You can't rotate your fingerprints. Well, technically, maybe you could, but that's not a preferred option if you ask me.

Some have suggested we no longer need password rotation (Spitzner, 2019). Perhaps you are tired of changing passwords, but here's another reason you might want to do so periodically. Sextortion is when an extortionist asks for money in exchange for keeping a sex-related secret (Fazzini, Email sextortion scams are on the rise and they're scary — here's what to do if you get one, 2019). This problem is happening to adults of all ages and even children. For some of these cases, I can't help you. Be cautious on the Internet and with people you don't know and think about what you are doing and how it may be exposed. Sadly, this does happen to innocent people who are just looking for love.

But there's one related campaign going around I can help you with, and it has to do with fake emails. I got one of these fake messages. It claimed to have my password, which it listed in the email, and threatened to expose some nasty secret. Well, I knew it was false on multiple levels. One reason: the password in the email was an old password I haven't used in years. Regularly changing your password can help you spot a fraudulent email like this. What if you are using a fingerprint? You'll never really know if they are lying or telling the truth, in addition to not being able to change it to keep them out.

Systems storing biometric data could do things to protect it using the methods already explained for securely storing passwords.

Storing a hash instead of the actual biometric data might help. I do think biometrics as a second factor is a decent option if a hash can be generated using a piece of device-specific data that is unique and random for the salt. An attacker would need to obtain not only the fingerprint data, but also the device, and the algorithm to generate the hash. The issue remains that if the fingerprint is ever in plaintext at some point in the system as the system is converting it to a hash, malware might be able to access it. Just like with password managers, attackers can steal biometric identifiers while unencrypted in memory.

As a final note on biometrics, be aware that the Chinese government is making use of facial recognition to track and monitor citizens (Mozure, 2019). Nation-state attackers who have your biometric data and licit or illicit access to foreign systems might be able to track people in other countries as well. I hope companies like Delta Airlines, who are starting to use facial recognition, do not force people to use it (Yamanouchi, 2019). Not only could a picture be swiped that can fool some systems (Newman, Hackers Trick Facial-Recognition Logins With Photos From Facebook (What Else?), 2016), but 3-D printer models have tricked these systems (Brewster, 2018), and they make mistakes (Newman, Facial Recognition Has Already Reached Its Breaking Point, 2019).

It is also interesting that the iPhone was one of the first phones to offer facial recognition. Some iPhones assembly occurs in China, and Apple was using parts from China before the U.S. tariffs that exist at the time of this writing (Mihalcik, 2019). Organizations purchasing products that make use of biometric data should consider how it is stored and how it may be accessed. More on supply chain issues in Chapter 19.

Multi-factor authentication (MFA)

What can we do to make it harder for attackers to steal and use our passwords? How can we ever protect ourselves if we want to use a pin or facial recognition? There's one other thing that can help — MFA, which stands for multi-factor authentication.[149] Sometimes it's called 2FA for two-factor authentication. With MFA, even if an attacker gets your password, fingerprint, or pin, they can't log in because MFA requires a second piece of information. Let's look at this in a bit more detail because it's not quite that simple. MFA implementations can be secure or flawed, just like anything else.

You may be familiar with MFA if you have enabled it on your email account or bank account. (Highly recommended!) The typical way MFA works is that when you log in, you receive a number on your phone. You then enter that number into the web application, and it lets you into your account. How does this help? Even if the attacker obtains your password, it's unlikely he or she also compromised your phone unless you are dealing with an advanced and persistent attacker.

An APT (advanced persistent threat)[150] is a type of attacker who is intent on getting your data and is willing to go to great lengths to do it. They often work for nation-states or organized crime rings. Attacks are often narrowly targeted to specific individuals and may take years. The majority of people do not need to worry about this level of targeted attacks, so using a mobile phone for MFA may be OK. However, it is not the best option. We'll start with this example, however, because it is what many people still use, and the only option on some applications.

When you attempt to log in, the system sends a code to an alternate location on a separate device; it's even better if it's on a different network. Sending the information on a separate channel is known as "out-of-band."[151] Using a separate channel helps in

---

[149] Multi-factor authentication https://en.wikipedia.org/wiki/Multi-factor_authentication
[150] Anatomy of an Advanced Persistent Threat https://www.fireeye.com/current-threats/anatomy-of-a-cyberattack.html
[151] Out of band https://en.wikipedia.org/wiki/Out-of-band

scenarios where an attacker is listening to your primary form of communication or has control over your device. For example, during data breach investigations, best practice is to use an out-of-band channel like cell phones, in case the attacker has compromised your corporate network phones.

It is essential to understand this last point because some MFA implementations will send both factors to the same device on the same network. An attacker that can listen on the network may be able to capture all the elements required to log into the system that requires MFA. Malware on your laptop may be able to access both factors if they both exist on a single device. These implementation details make some forms of MFA better than others.

Two factors delivered to the same device on the same network is like someone emailing a username and password in two different messages. That's not going to help if an attacker is reading all your emails! Sending the username via email and the password via a text message over separate networks to two different devices is better. Now the attacker has to obtain access to both to steal the credentials.

MFA traditionally involves something you have (for example, a cell phone) and something you know (like a password). The point about the something you know is that no one has it but you, and no one can steal it out of some system. It only exists in your brain. That's the idea, anyway. Unfortunately, we've gotten to the point where our minds can't hold all the passwords we're supposed to remember. People put passwords on sticky notes or store them in unencrypted files on laptops or cellphones. They may also make passwords that are easy to remember and, therefore, easy to guess.

By requiring something you have, an attacker would need your username and password as well as access to the device you are using as a second factor. If the attacker only has your username and password, they cannot log in. They also need the second piece of the equation, such as a code sent to your phone.

MFA is not perfect, but it helps prevent numerous types of attacks. If an attacker got your password from a dump on Pastebin (a site commonly used to store stolen data),[152] they wouldn't be able to log in without your second factor. Any attack where an attacker got your password alone and tried to use it on a login screen would fail.

Try to ensure that if an attacker accesses one of your devices or your network, they cannot obtain both of the factors involved in MFA. As with anything in security, we make choices based on the risk of loss and potential cost if an undesirable outcome occurs. Although ideal, different channels might not be possible in every circumstance, but whenever possible, try to obtain this level of separation. For example, you log into your bank on your home WiFi network. You then receive a code from your bank over a cellular network via a text message or an application like Google Authenticator for an iPhone[153] or Android.[154]

Password Spraying

MFA can prevent another attack, known as password spraying, that has caused recent breaches.[155] Many systems implement a security mechanism called rate limiting,[156] which locks a user out after a specific number of incorrect login attempts, either permanently or for a set time. To get around this, attackers send

---

[152] Pastebin https://pastebin.com/
[153] Google Authentication for iPhone https://apps.apple.com/us/app/google-authenticator/id388497605
[154] Google Authenticator for Android https://play.google.com/store/apps/details?id=com.google.android.apps.authenticator2&hl=en_US
[155] What is password spraying https://doubleoctopus.com/security-wiki/threats-and-tools/password-spraying/
[156] Rate limiting https://en.wikipedia.org/wiki/Rate_limiting

the same password to many different systems at the same time, instead of sending many different guesses to the same computer. By only guessing once on any particular machine and spreading out the attacks over more extended periods, an attacker won't hit the rate limit and get locked out. With this attack, MFA should still prevent the attackers from accessing the systems when they attempt to log in — unless, of course, a flaw exists in your MFA implementation.

Cybersecurity firm Dragos, which specializes in industrial control system security, witnessed password-spraying campaigns against the U.S. power grid after the U.S. assassination of the Iranian general Qassem Soleimani in early 2020 (Greenberg, 2020). Attackers may have used a password spraying attack in the Citrix breach, and it appears this sophisticated group is targeting many other organizations (O'Flaherty, 2019). Forbes writes, "According to security firm Resecurity, the attacks were perpetrated by an Iranian-linked group known as IRIDIUM, which has hit more than 200 government agencies, oil and gas firms, and technology companies."

During the breach, which went undiscovered for five months, the company was using some form of 2FA. However, the attackers were able to access systems anyway. How could this happen? We don't know all the details about this breach, but let's look at some potential MFA implementation deficiencies that may have contributed to the problem.

MFA caching vulnerability

One of the struggles with MFA implementations is the fact that people get annoyed when they have to enter the second factor over and over again. Some MFA implementations involve a session with a configurable timeout. The person logging in only has to enter the second factor once for the duration of a session. Different systems have varying default timeout lengths — maybe 60 minutes, 8 hours, or 24. When a user checks the box to "keep me signed in," the session may last longer. For example, at the time of this writing, when a user chooses this option when logging into Microsoft's cloud platform, Microsoft Azure AD creates a persistent token. In this case, the user has chosen to *effectively turn off MFA for 180 days* (Microsoft, 2019). That is a very long time for an attacker to try to guess or leverage a stolen password. You can override this default and make it something shorter.

Implementation of some enterprise solutions only requires MFA when someone is on an untrusted network or device. I wrote about that in chapter 8 on zero trust and why trust is overrated when it comes to data breaches. One company I worked at spent a lot of time and energy implementing MFA. After they set it up, I used MFA once and never had to enter the second factor again before I left the company probably over a year later. That is not going to protect you from the attacks I just described.

Fake MFA websites and push notifications

Another type of attack involves tricking a user into entering an MFA token into a fake website. A "researcher" developed a tool with lookalike sites for widely used sites like Amazon.com (Cimpanu, New tool automates phishing attacks that bypass 2FA, 2019). The attacker gets the user to put their MFA credentials into that imposter web site instead of the real one. The user may not notice. The attacker intercepts the MFA code when the user enters it. Train users to be aware this could happen and to be careful to check they are on the correct domain and that the link includes HTTPS at the front.

Google has a solution to that problem that might be a bit easier for most users. Instead of entering a pin, you can install the Gmail mobile application on your phone.[157] When you log into a site that works with your Gmail login, you receive a popup[158] on your

---

[157] Gmail mobile applications https://www.google.com/gmail/about/
[158] Sign in faster with 2-step verification phone prompts

phone asking if you are trying to log in, and you click 'yes.' No number to enter. A company called DUO,[159] purchased by Cisco, has been doing something similar for a while. This option is known as a push notification. It's a user-friendly option compared to other solutions I've used and possibly more secure. It uses two factors on two different networks. If someone is trying to log into your account, you'll get notified on your phone. If you didn't initiate that login, you know someone is trying to get into your account. At this point, you should change your password.

Another way an attacker can get access to MFA-protected systems is called a "SIM swap" attack or "SIM jacking."[160] In this scenario, attackers convince the phone company to switch your phone number over to their own SIM card. Trying to trick someone into doing something so you can get into systems or buildings is called social engineering.[161] Once the attacker has your phone number on their own phone, they can get into your MFA-protected systems if they also have your passwords. Sim jacking has occurred in the U.S. in instances where attackers attempted to steal cryptocurrency (Cimpanu, Wave of SIM swapping attacks hit US cryptocurrency users, 2019). Hopefully, the phone companies are taking action to train staff who work on the phone and in stores to be vigilant. AT&T is currently fighting a lawsuit involving SIM swapping that resulted in stolen cryptocurrency (Osborne, 2019).

To avoid SIM swapping attacks, you can use a device other than your phone for the second factor on some systems. Google offers a Titan security key for this purpose.[162] However, some have complained about the fact that a Chinese company manufactures the device (Novet, 2018). Researchers later exposed a Bluetooth

---

https://support.google.com/accounts/answer/7026266
[159] DUO https://duo.com/
[160] SIM swap scan https://en.wikipedia.org/wiki/SIM_swap_scam
[161] Social Engineering
https://en.wikipedia.org/wiki/Social_engineering_(security)
[162] Google Titan Security Key https://cloud.google.com/titan-security-key/

flaw, and Google replaced some of the keys (Sheridan, 2019). Some systems, including Google, integrate with a similar product called a YubiKey. Yubico manufactures this device in the U.S. and Sweden.[163] To log into a site on your computer, you'll need to plug in the hardware device first.

Hardware devices come with their own set of challenges. What happens when the device is lost? On some platforms like Google, you can register two MFA devices in case you lose one. Unfortunately, some other sites like the AWS cloud console don't have that option at the time of this writing and only allow you to register one device. I hope that changes soon because I submitted a request to the AWS Wishlist for this feature![164]

How will you securely distribute a device to remote users and authorize them on the network? You'll want to make sure only the owner of the account can access the information required to register a new device. I have seen a couple of things I do not recommend. Sometimes registration is performed via a QR (Quick Response) code,[165] which appears on the screen while setting up MFA with Google Authenticator or a similar application. Don't distribute these via a screen share. Only the owner of the account should have access to the QR code used for MFA. Using this method, the person doing the screen share can add that same code to his or her device at the point the QR code is shared on the screen. Non-repudiation is no longer possible if that person can obtain or change the username and password.

Additionally, systems that require a seed for a one-time password[166] or private key[167] should never expose those secrets to anyone but the person whom the secret identifies. Systems prove the person's

---

[163] Yubico YubiKey https://www.yubico.com/products/manufacturing/
[164] AWS Wishlist https://awswishlist.com/
[165] QR code https://en.wikipedia.org/wiki/QR_code
[166] One-time password https://en.wikipedia.org/wiki/One-time_password
[167] Public key cryptography https://en.wikipedia.org/wiki/Public-key_cryptography

identity because they have those secrets. Once multiple people have access to the secrets, you can no longer use them for identity. Applications can automate the generation of private keys, seeds, or other types of secret information on a user's cell phone or computer, for example. That way no one else ever sees or has access to them. If your system administrators or anyone else can get those values, your system design is flawed. Non-repudiation is not possible in this case, and user communications may be at risk of compromise.

Passwordless

Microsoft is pitching a "passwordless[168]" login option for operating systems and online accounts, with various options such as biometrics, pins, or hardware security keys. They store secrets in a TPM (Trusted Platform Module),[169] which is a tamper-resistant hardware component. Sometimes a TPM is implemented only in software. If a TPM lives up to its claim, it is difficult to extract the contents, so an attacker cannot steal your secrets. Of course, TPMs may have security flaws like anything else (Goodin, Millions of high-security crypto keys crippled by newly discovered flaw, 2017).

The idea of getting rid of passwords because people reuse them is intriguing logic, and it sounds appealing. Just make sure, as with all new technology, that you evaluate it carefully before rolling it out to your entire organization. Microsoft offers three passwordless options at the time of this writing: Microsoft Hello for Business, Passwordless sign-in with Microsoft Authenticator, and FIDO2 Security Keys (e.g., a YubiKey) (Microsoft, 2019).

I based the following information on my understanding of these

---

[168] The end of passwords, go passwordless
https://www.microsoft.com/en-us/security/technology/identity-access-management/passwordless
[169] Trusted Platform Module
https://en.wikipedia.org/wiki/Trusted_Platform_Module

MFA options based on the Microsoft website just referenced. Although the technology may change, the purpose of this section is to analyze different MFA solutions in general rather than evaluate a specific implementation. Hopefully, going through this thought process will help you assess any MFA solution you may be considering. If you are considering using these options, you should check with Microsoft to ensure my interpretation is correct.

Windows Hello: If you look at Microsoft's explanation and the diagram for Microsoft Business Hello, there appears to be only one factor. The end-user interacts once with the computer on a single channel. A user only has to know or have one thing to get onto that machine. Microsoft seems to be counting the machine itself as a second factor. In a large corporate environment or at a coffee shop, anyone can walk over to my device if I step away. All they need to get in is my four-digit pin. A four-digit pin is short, and each character only requires guessing one of 10 characters. That's a pretty-easy-to-crack password even if an attacker cannot extract something from a TPM. Windows Hello also faced a security vulnerability at the end of 2019 involving orphaned keys in Active Directory (Stahie, 2019).

Microsoft Authenticator: With Microsoft Authenticator, Microsoft recommends that users back up their credentials to the cloud. I'm not sure how organizations will feel about Microsoft credentials backed up to Apple's iCloud (Microsoft, 2019), but for some, this might be an issue. At least this solution is using multiple out-of-band factors. After receiving a push notification from a separate device, the user enters a pin or uses biometrics to complete the authentication process.

FIDO2 Security Keys: The third option would be to use a FIDO2 security key such as YubiKey. FIDO[170] standards for Fast IDentity Online and is a set of standards from the FIDO Alliance designed

---

[170] Fido Alliance https://fidoalliance.org/

to help companies implement secure authentication solutions. The official definition is as follows: "Based on free and open standards from the FIDO Alliance, FIDO Authentication enables password-only logins to be replaced with secure and fast login experiences across websites and apps."

Take a look at this option on the Microsoft website. At the time of this writing, it requires two factors: the authentication device, such as a YubiKey, and a fingerprint. This option seems like the best solution. Following the FIDO standards, the secrets required to identify a user are in a trusted enclave on the YubiKey device and not accessible to system administrators at Microsoft or on your corporate network. If you have a secure mechanism for distributing the hardware keys, it's difficult for someone to steal the user credentials or impersonate that person.

Now let's think about access to remote computers for a minute. The user is inputting information directly into his or her device. On a laptop configured to use passwordless authentication, Microsoft says the two factors to log in are biometrics or the pin and the device itself. Using the fact that you have access to the machine you are logging into as a factor to access that machine seems a bit like an oxymoron to me. Using something on that device as a factor for website authentication and device-specific information to generate a unique hash does make sense. It then requires the user to have that device to log in to something else.

How does passwordless authentication work when accessing remote computers? Here's where it gets more complicated. As a system administrator at a large company, it is ideal for each person to have a single set of credentials representing their identity for tracking and management. Separate credentials for local and remote access potentially doubles the number of credentials IT departments need to track and monitor.

When accessing a remote computer in a passwordless environment, the person logging in from a remote location is not sitting at the machine. They can't input their biometrics directly into that piece of hardware. Will the biometrics be stored in memory and passed over to the remote equipment? Will the biometric hash be passed around the network? Are they stored in the cloud? These are potential points of exposure for biometric data used to identify a particular individual. Organizations have already reported breaches of biometric data (Doffman, New Data Breach Has Exposed Millions Of Fingerprint And Facial Recognition Records: Repor, 2019).

It appears this was still a work in progress at the time passwordless was released, based on some discussions I have read. I'm not going to attempt to explain how to implement Microsoft RDP using passwordless authentication here in layman's terms. It involves a key storage provider (KSP) (Microsoft, 2019). I find the AWS documentation on KSPs easier to understand if you want to read more about this topic (AWS, 2020). It involves PKI (public key infrastructure), which can be challenging to manage for IT administrators, even though it may be more straightforward for end-users.[171] Trying to use passwordless solutions for remote access presents complexity and new challenges that need to be carefully evaluated by experienced security professionals.

Analyzing authentication solutions

I have performed technical due diligence on authentication systems for mergers and acquisitions (M & A). There are many considerations involved in making sure credentials cannot be compromised. One of your best bets is to use industry-backed standards when choosing solutions. Also, make sure you think through the potential attacks on any system — otherwise known as threat modeling.[172] Test out new solutions in your environment

---

[171] Public Key Infrastructure https://en.wikipedia.org/wiki/Public_key_infrastructure
[172] Threat Modeling https://en.wikipedia.org/wiki/Threat_model

on a small scale before rolling them out to your entire organization. Don't forget about cloud environments, remote workers, and devices like printers and IoT devices that may require authentication.

If a flaw exists in your architecture or implementation, leveraging segregation limits what is exposed by a single set of credentials. Lock down your network to limit which devices can access sensitive data. Logging and monitoring failed access attempts help organizations spot abuse. But on top of that, MFA and changing passwords frequently can help. Keep an eye on the passwordless option and choose a solution that provides the right level of security and management that aligns with risk and the cost of data loss.

11
ENCRYPTION AT REST

Encryption is a mechanism for turning sensitive data into something unreadable and unusable.[173] Even if someone can see or access the data, it is of no use to that person. They can't read it or know what it says. The phrase, "encryption at rest," refers to encrypting data before storing it — wherever that may be. You can encrypt data stored in a database, in a file, or new types of cloud storage like AWS S3 buckets or Azure Blob Storage (which is similar to AWS S3). [174] Typically, some software passes your data into an encryption algorithm along with a bunch of letters and numbers called a key. The output will be your data in an encrypted format.

A simple encryption example using OpenSSL

Let's see what this looks like via a simple example. Let's say I want to encrypt the following text:

```
Cybersecurity all the things
```

---

[173] Encryption
https://www.oxfordlearnersdictionaries.com/us/definition/english/encryption
[174] Azure Blog Storage https://azure.microsoft.com/en-us/services/storage/blobs/

That combination of characters, in computer-speak, is called a string. It's a set of characters, treated differently by programming languages than pure numbers. If I want to encrypt that data, I have some options. Here are a few:

- I could encrypt only the string.

- I could save the string in a file like Microsoft Word, notepad, or text edit, and encrypt the whole file.

- I could store the file on my operating system (Windows, Linux, or Macintosh, for example) and then enable the feature to encrypt my entire hard drive. Some operating systems and laptops can do this, but you have to turn it on. Now every file on my hard drive is protected. Maybe.

- I could store the file on a cloud service that encrypts everything for me, so I don't have to think about it. Maybe.

Let's look at these options in a bit more detail.

The following example is for demonstration purposes only, not a recommendation of how you should encrypt files in production systems hosting sensitive data. I am attempting to show readers who don't usually do the encryption themselves what it looks like using a basic example. I'm using a program called OpenSSL,[175] which comes pre-installed on Macintosh computers. You can run these commands yourself using the Terminal app.

First, I type this command to create an encryption key:

```
openssl genrsa -out key.txt 2048
```

After typing that command, I get output like this:

---

[175] OpenSSL https://www.openssl.org/

```
Generating RSA private key, 2048 bit long modulus
......................+++
..................................................
..................................................
..................................................
.................................................+++
e is 65537 (0x10001)
```

The command generates a key and stores it in the file "key.txt." If I open and look at the file, here's what I see:

```
-----BEGIN RSA PRIVATE KEY-----
MIIEpAIBAAKCAQEA044nqaLRzh7OyB0YqWgZcOwc0gXGCGypet1U/+kuBcsDDzQH
YFjFHmeAUT+xVX8ivKZdTVqS5vRu3u2cjROwKOhGr5fovR8Aokl34YC6qLoBy/1P
ORbDZCoBDeTJSSLcoDXKqT00t34UaEUneH1BJYP41jQTyo+q2GH5b+JqoVxtaiC7
Pixhwn+59TSgizLGzWGFw63BLQnzitUgVOCGPRDB2L8813bm4ul5pNm3qzJNQGf34
ojqTWelue4qypvf7PheUTV0Y8cIy/tkXJpEirKOyXEbUZ8mQBMgIChNGV1aBLNKS
8V398RiZ6EdYlq3vL1M0EJAW601+uI18Ngl91wIDAQABAoIBAQCPkQoTkd4lrjyQ
CObgODgDrQhF8wsYTn2ZVrjHTrwfzEyQNbPHy5ZB8uVevgWfSr8NHS12QEAvIbRX
7xJtnu3OZQsLQOD97xskBw2m6BBETq7HeLItwOfqgqLihd+flVv6EWcuAM5Us+gv
dra5iu76AZxieobvOR2U6LA5IINSasXaOvVnSexkicRmXJ8afgdmQ+sDYbqrUCqu
hQ6/HH/mFClCVRYKBXqCC5XcuHofps609tF/xi0BleLbBT9Nt8ch2Pt4sh7IwBs5
s/8W/VVvYdGwJ16rQ+xEfL2VzGnlfhplV9hbT2XJIcRGvl7yeItTLr81QKiwyzDj
kJy0DXghAoGBAPN+5xwFFlcD9NRSIb35pkhr4olJzPEyoaqb8MN5wbUFJ0WbKgMZ
f8QXwONjRCzEG2Px+sU6rJNc38ijmvcCO977gZahAIr8x8FetBksR40KCYkK5vQl
+2kz2xqThlisALY7gfxpQwvHFFWyadvxAS+Or+46KAtRNTMvNuEm9xARAoGBAN5r
WZTlLaqmeEnASRqx7/J7+k7PDUQbJ4kC4ObcowhdtxtNsEbMAubaLA9nblaFe/1s
/WnOpbRg4Hpiy22BYvBKtnhtsqaQlP/et5gMvSbigRrdVo7Yfrz6Nqr3Vor4kF9N
VEMY0EcsDRaOaZSJw+Zivnk+p6ZhGuGgbzYTqJdnAoGAaVTWKLrSpSWi/U3iJsod
8moo/vab3yLl6GW4yvaaovHtwSCUFe8r4+namQLR9QOITb3ZmwP8r2qXq7WKTZv7
xkPKFRzknTsoNi//fHw5H3veEBhVO/xKO4IhH+f9vo/5ZttrKYNna2rdEw0w2eHx
f2+MQ2OI+wxQFSoxdUhjy+ECgYEA1Gk4+BWWcy7gGa7lIfVk7fKwrarXRH+aViLF
njSADnFReWXMPxB+hPE+usdQfJimPPRlXzLW1VjfiIHpPP8f+dOgR4qb3q6dXW7Z
bwBbdFNEcN+IloqzHs7mfogPwlB3sEwteJat8gqDxVLkSdL3n4IV3byUZzS9clTA
YKiNjWkCgYBRyCWV+V9Vk0pCum1FCk2tuOzGGPodpCsDcqyb8NV37CUgR5qpc5RU
NlQOWV9JE+V7K6Bvhk21WAFNMKGjtzky08oLVLiOZPDmnCX/QiDOXTXFeL4amtsP
pnWHP8a25+jlRVHn0TjASdW9gYjszRecyp3GFomO6yjtH6vrq0lapg==
-----END RSA PRIVATE KEY-----
```

Note that you should never, ever, share your private key like I just did! As you can see, a key is simply a long string of random characters in a specific format that works with a particular type of encryption method, called an algorithm.

Let's say I want to encrypt my string using my key. To encrypt my string above, I type this command:

```
echo "Cybersecurity all the things" | openssl
rsautl -inkey key.txt -encrypt > encrypted-
```

```
string.bin
```

Now I have a new file in my directory called "encrypted-string.bin." The > character above tells the command to write the output to a file called encrypted-string.bin. If I try to open that file, I'll see a lot of meaningless characters. The output looks different depending on what you use to open it. This encrypted file is in a format called binary. A text editor can't decipher it and produces gibberish if you try to open it. And that's what we want when we encrypt files! In theory, if I encrypted this file with a secret key you didn't know, you could never read my secret file.

If I have the secret key and I want to get the data back, I can pass in the key and my encrypted file to the encryption algorithm using this command:

```
openssl rsautl -inkey key.txt -decrypt < encrypted-string.bin
```

Magic! And I get back my text. Actually, it has to do with math and cryptography,[176] not magic. As mentioned earlier, you can read books like *Applied Cryptography*, by Bruce Schneier, for more information (Schneier, Applied Cryptography, 1996).

The encryption fallacy

So, if I encrypt my data, no one else can read it, right?

Think about that for a minute — I'll wait. Is it true that no one can read your encrypted data under any circumstances?

No one else can see my data — unless they have my key. What if I publish my key on a blog anyone can read? What if I put it in a public source code repository for anyone to download? What if I store my key right next to the encrypted file on my laptop? If malware gets onto my computer, the attacker can run the

---

[176] Cryptography https://en.wikipedia.org/wiki/Cryptography

command I just ran and decrypt my data.

What do I need to do to protect my encrypted data? I'd need to store my key somewhere separate and secure. I'd also need to make sure the attacker couldn't get into the memory on my machine at the same time the data was being encrypted or decrypted. Otherwise, the attacker might get the key or the data at that point. Attackers stole credit card data from systems by capturing it as it was processed in plain text in memory on the systems that processed the transactions at Target stores (Radichel, Case Study: Critical Controls that Could Have Prevented the Target Breach, 2014).

I also need to make sure no logs are storing my data or key in a manner that can be useful to attackers. Additionally, I'll need to use an appropriate encryption algorithm and ensure my chosen software uses proper techniques to encrypt the data. If you use an insecure algorithm (similar to using an insecure hashing function), an attacker may be able to crack your encryption and get the data that way. Improper programming leads to flaws that can leak data as well.

When encrypting a file, the same complications apply. I could copy my string and paste it into a file and then save the file. Then I run a command to encrypt the entire file instead of my one string. If I have many strings, I can put them all in the file, and then I can encrypt them all at once. The output is longer, so it is harder to guess — for reasons discussed in chapter 9 on hashing, where I introduced encryption. A new problem results from storing all the data in one file with a single key. If an attacker gets that one key and file, they can access all my data. In cybersecurity, it seems like we are always trading one problem for another and trying to choose the best option for the scenario at hand to reduce the risk.

At any rate, you can see that although encryption may be hard to break, other factors may still expose the data if we are not careful. Encrypting information is one thing; leveraging encryption in a way that truly protects all your data is another. Someone can tell you that all your data is encrypted. However, if they are not doing it carefully, that encryption could be meaningless.

What about encrypting your entire hard drive? Operating systems and the hardware they run on have improved in ways that allow you to encrypt data on your hard drive automatically. You can enable encryption options within your operating system to try to prevent someone from reading the data on a stolen laptop. In some implementations, your key may be stored very securely by the hardware on your computer so no one can get at it. That sounds perfect! Now all your data is protected. You don't need to worry about managing an encryption key, assuming you trust the hardware and software vendors to build it all securely. Problem solved, right?

Sort of. If your hard drive is encrypted and your stolen computer is not running, everything is fine. But what happens when you are working in the coffee shop, and your computer is running? You are editing one of your encrypted documents when you step away to get your favorite half-caff-mochachina-macchiato-soy-vanilla-extra-frothy-fru-fru drink. Someone swipes your running laptop while you are not looking. If you didn't lock the screen with a screen saver that requires your password to unlock, anyone who has access to the machine could open and read that file, including malware.

Now you can see that encryption helps, but it's essential to understand in which scenarios. Key management is critical, as is understanding how and when your encrypted data might be vulnerable to an attack. It's also crucial to train your employees to lock their computers when they step away. Better yet, if they're doing work at a coffee shop, they can take their computers with them when they get up to avoid theft altogether!

At one place I worked, if you walked away from your computer without locking it, someone might pull a prank as a little reminder that you forgot something. The office was full of pranksters. "I" once invited our entire development team out for drinks at happy hour — on me. Needless to say, I had to renege as someone sent that email on my behalf. One of my favorite pranks was the guy who changed someone's spell checker to type the word "bananas" every time the person typed, "the." She didn't know what was going on and had to call the help desk to try to explain. I can only imagine how that call sounded. It still makes me laugh out loud as I'm typing this. That's evil.

Encryption and the Capital One breach

How about letting the cloud do your encrypting for you? Some cloud providers tell you that they encrypt all your data for you. They use the best encryption algorithms and go to great lengths to protect encryption keys. Their best practices in the cloud make it easier for you. What could go wrong in this scenario? It's perfect! Almost.

An attacker could get access to data in the cloud when it's unencrypted in memory the same way they could in the scenario I mentioned with your laptop in the coffee shop. An attacker can also get access to any files that a machine they compromise can access. They can decrypt anything the device has permission to decrypt.

Let's look at the Capital One breach I wrote about on my blog (Radichel, What's in your cloud?, 2019). Capital One has many people doing the right things. They had policies that enforced encryption on S3 buckets when I was there. They created policies on AWS that rejected file uploads that contained unencrypted files. I don't know if they still do that, but it is an excellent policy, and I always recommend it in my classes. I was fortunate enough to attend a dinner with Werner Vogels, CTO of Amazon, one year at re:Invent with some other CTOs. At this event, he said he liked Capital One's decision to create a policy to encrypt everything.

If you think about it, why spend time figuring out what you should and should not encrypt? It's possible to encrypt everything in the cloud. The cost of encryption is likely less than the expense of being out of compliance with regulations or having data at rest stolen in an unencrypted format. In the Capital One breach, the stolen data was presumably encrypted. What went wrong?

I cannot say exactly what happened in the Capital One breach because I did not work there at the time of the breach. However, this is my guess as to what went wrong based on my analysis of the news reports. Even if the scenario was slightly different, it is entirely possible. I did talk to some people who were familiar with the configuration who said this explanation is fairly accurate, so we can learn from this example.

The problem was likely that the attacker effectively had access to the encryption key by breaching a system that had permission to decrypt the files. The attacker may not have had the key material (the characters making up the key itself, as I demonstrated in my simple example). However, the attacker could decrypt the data because the architecture of the system granted virtual server access to all the files and permission use the encryption key. Capital One called it a misconfiguration. I think it may have been a bit more complicated than that. Let's walk through what happened, as far as we can tell.

Obtaining access to a system and using its permissions to retrieve resources that would otherwise be unavailable is known as Server Side Request Forgery[177] or an SSRF attack. The attacker presumably gained access to a machine connected to the Internet via a flaw in some firewall software running on a machine. The attacker could then run commands on the device. When those commands executed, they leveraged the permissions of that machine to access and decrypt the stolen files.

---

[177] Server Side Request Forgery https://owasp.org/www-community/attacks/Server_Side_Request_Forgery

Even though the files were encrypted, it didn't stop the breach. What may have helped? AWS has mechanisms for creating more restrictive policies on encryption keys. As I wrote about in my blog post, other architectural changes would have also limited access to the data and made it harder to obtain. However, this chapter is about encryption so we will stick to that topic for now.

One positive thing was that Capital One used another technique to protect U.S. Social Security Numbers. Tokenization replaces a sensitive piece of information with placeholder data instead of the secret information. When the data is processed, if that value is required, it can be retrieved using that token. Capital One had tokenized the social security numbers, so those were not exposed. Unfortunately for our friends to the north, the system didn't tokenize the Canadian IDs. It is important to understand all the sensitive data that exists in your systems.

Is encryption useless? No! At least not yet. The issue here is that a lot of compliance frameworks and cybersecurity best practices tell organizations to encrypt data. However, when best practices say you should encrypt data, they don't say how in enough detail. In each case, organizations should perform threat modeling to understand when data is encrypted, unencrypted, and who can decrypt it. They don't always emphasize the need to protect encryption keys adequately or how to architect systems to prevent data loss even when encryption is in use.

The fundamental problem is that encryption needs to be implemented correctly to be useful. In some cases, people aren't adequately trained or don't understand the risk associated with how they handle keys and architect systems. Companies do not always employ adequate threat modeling. When organizations encrypt data, they need to know how to do it correctly and consider the big picture of the overall security architecture, not just the fact that "everything is encrypted."

Encryption in the Cloud

It's much easier to ensure all your data is encrypted at some basic level when cloud providers may encrypt everything, like Google.[178] However, as noted, you should do some threat modeling to determine how and when that helps you. When encryption is not turned on everywhere by default, it may be simpler for you to turn it on in a cloud environment than it is on-premises. You can check a box in the AWS console to turn it on for an S3 bucket[179] or a virtual machine. Cloud providers also allow you to use encryption keys you create and maintain yourself in some cases. Understanding where the key exists in that case, where the encryption occurs, and who has access to it becomes an important consideration. In my class, we discuss the pros and cons of the various options on AWS, Google, and Azure.

Cloud providers offer automation that can help protect encryption keys and prevent mistakes. Compared to the things some companies do on-premises, they are likely much better off using these cloud options. Many of the technical staff within companies do not understand encryption even to the level explained in this book, which is not very technical. Even if they do, encryption key management is extremely challenging. The problem is, any time you hand over your encryption keys to someone else, some level of trust exists that the other entity will not misuse your keys or the data.

Establish trust by looking at the track record of the cloud provider. Have they experienced many breaches? It's easy to search the news in Google to find out which cloud providers have exposed customer data and which ones have not. Review the

---

[178] Encryption at Rest on Google Cloud
https://cloud.google.com/security/encryption-at-rest/
[179] How Do I Add Encryption to an S3 Object
https://docs.aws.amazon.com/AmazonS3/latest/user-guide/add-object-encryption.html

cloud provider data to understand their cybersecurity practices.[180] Assessments and audits help with the things we can't see when trusting a cloud provider. I explain more about vendor assessments in chapter 19. In the end, the cloud provider is bound by contracts to do what they say they do and not view your data. That includes protecting it from misuse by its employees. If a cloud provider does something to lose that trust, they will most definitely be out of business very quickly. It is in their best interest to maintain the trust of their customers.

Handing over encryption to another organization involves trusting that organization with your data. Anytime you give up your encryption keys to another party, they can decrypt and read your data. You are trusting their promises not to do so. Trust seems to be harder and harder to come by these days. I worked for a company that recorded meetings without telling people, which I find highly unethical. I wondered, after that, if they had tapped my office, but I had nothing to hide, so I didn't care.

You want to trust your employers, government, and vendors to do the right thing. You don't expect them to spy on you. Unfortunately, that is just not always the case. No revelation demonstrates this more clearly than the story that came to light in early 2020. Since the 1940s, the CIA had spied on countries around the world by selling them machines designed to encrypt data. They created weak encryption algorithms that allowed them to crack the data and reveal the communications (Miller, 2020). How can any vendor be trusted in light of this revelation?

One of my friends was an Air Force pilot for 24 years. He flew planes in seven conflicts, served two tours in Iraq, and four in Afghanistan. Here is his take on governments reading encrypted data:

---

[180] Amazon Web Services: Overview of Security Processes
https://d1.awsstatic.com/whitepapers/Security/AWS_Security_Whitepaper.pdf

How is the government supposed to protect the citizens of America without spying on the bad guys? I am in favor of the NSA, CIA, and FBI having the ability to read people's email, text, and listen to voice messages. When I was fighting in Afghanistan, there were countless times that U.S. soldiers were protected from harm due to this capability. I don't care what the government reads of mine because I don't break laws.

Someone I used to work with on the Capital One cloud team recently asked, how can you ever trust your vendors after hearing a story like that? My take is, at some point, any technology, including encryption or devices to protect networks, may be broken. Buy security products and services from countries and companies you trust. As for the companies and countries who are breaking into the communications, "with great power comes great responsibility." This capability should be used to protect people, not to steal corporate or military secrets or for political gain. People within those organizations should keep each other in check to ensure they are not overstepping bounds and using these capabilities for personal or organizational gain. As Google used to say, before they took this motto out of their mission statement, "Don't be evil."[181]

One of my students told me a story. He said when reports revealed that the NSA was intercepting Google's and Yahoo's private network communications (Gallagher, How the NSA's MUSCULAR tapped Google's and Yahoo's private networks, 2013), Google went the extra mile and encrypted all data on their internal networks (Gallagher, Googlers say "F*** you" to NSA, company encrypts internal network, 2013). He said they then sent a cake to the agency with the words, "Not today, NSA." Hopefully, now you can trust that the NSA is not reading your data if you use Google products and services. Instead, you have to trust Google. The NSA can't help you if any crimes are occurring on Google's network or in their systems. The same is true with

---

[181] Don't be evil https://time.com/4060575/alphabet-google-dont-be-evil/

any company you trust to protect you from Government spying by encrypting your data.

How can companies combat problems related to vendors reading and misusing their data? Chapter 20 covers security product assessment and testing to determine if they have security flaws. In the case of these encryption devices, the U.S. government still had to capture the data. Secure networking would help prevent them from accessing the machines and traffic traversing private networks. However, any attackers can intercept the data as it traverses the Internet. The other thing companies can do is avoid putting all the data in one cloud service or location.

Segregate data, so it is harder to steal, by storing it in different locations. The Pentagon in the U.S. chose the opposite approach when they limited their cloud contract to one vendor. They awarded this $10B contract named "Jedi" to Microsoft. However, Amazon is challenging the contract in court, and a judge just ordered a suspension (Gaus, 2020). Technologies like PGP (Pretty Good Privacy) work with a public and a private key. If you use this to encrypt your email before you send it into cloud systems, for example, you are the only one with that key. Defense in depth is still one of your best strategies to make it harder to access your data.

Even if you believe the cloud provider will do its part correctly, you still must understand how to implement your part of the security architecture. The idea that you share responsibility in the cloud with the cloud provider is known as the Shared Responsibility Model[182]. AWS first introduced this concept, and most other cloud providers have adopted something similar. This shared responsibility applies to all security controls in the cloud, not just encryption.[183]

---

[182] Shared Responsibility Model https://aws.amazon.com/compliance/shared-responsibility-model/
[183] AWS Cryptography Services

AWS and other cloud providers help you protect your encryption keys by tying the ability to access them to authorization via authentication. Major cloud platforms allow you to create technical policies that require people or resources to have appropriate permissions to use a particular key to encrypt or decrypt data. It's better than having a key that anyone on the planet can use, but you'll still need to think through the entire threat model. You have shifted the problem of protecting the key to safeguarding credentials that can access the key. Think about what they can access, should they be exposed.

Hardware security module (HSM)

In an on-premises environment, large companies sometimes use something called a hardware security module (HSM) to protect keys.[184] A file can be copied and transferred off the network. When embedding the key in a tamper-resistant hardware device, the encryption key is a bit harder to access. Hardware-based encryption may also be faster and offer performance benefits. HSMs are technically the most secure option for storing keys according to many security professionals. However, HSMs come with a whole slew of complexity and management issues that may make them hard to implement in some environments. I'm not going to get into that here. Although security professionals consider them one of the most secure ways to protect encryption keys, other factors sometimes make them a less than ideal choice.

You can get an HSM in the cloud from the three major cloud providers — AWS,[185] Azure,[186] and Google.[187] When considering these solutions, security professionals look at whether the devices are dedicated or shared and whether they are hardware or

---

https://docs.aws.amazon.com/crypto/latest/userguide/crypto-ug.pdf
[184] Hardware Security Module
https://en.wikipedia.org/wiki/Hardware_security_module
[185] AWS HSM https://aws.amazon.com/cloudhsm/
[186] Azure HSM https://azure.microsoft.com/en-us/services/azure-dedicated-hsm/
[187] Google Cloud HSM https://cloud.google.com/hsm/

software implementations. The problems hardware HSMs cause in cloud environments involve limited scalability, latency, and disaster recovery problems. As a result, cloud providers came up with alternative approaches that are more automated and work better with cloud architectures.

Many companies do use these automated methods instead of traditional dedicated HSMs. They are, in some cases, FIPS-compliant for those who require it. FIPS (Federal Information Processing Standards)[188] were established by NIST to establish requirements for secure systems. When thinking about how encryption keys are stored and used, it's important to look at the big picture to determine what the actual threat vectors are and how to prevent breaches. So far, using these automated mechanisms for key storage has proven to be robust — if appropriately used within the broader security architecture.

Encryption algorithms for encryption at rest

The other element that affects an attacker's ability to decrypt the data is the selected algorithm. As with a hashing function, you can think of an algorithm for encrypting data at rest as a formula. You pass in some inputs — the data and a key — and the output is encrypted data. If the attacker doesn't have the key, he or she still may be able to crack the data if the algorithm is weak. When implementing encryption, developers need to use the right mode with some algorithms. I go into more detail on different types of encryption in my class. The main point is to make sure you and your vendors are using the correct and recommended algorithm and key size for whatever type of encryption you are implementing. Some algorithms — such as DES, Triple DES, and MD5 — have been cracked or demonstrated to have weaknesses and are no longer recommended (NIST, 2019).

---

[188] Federal Information Processing Standards
https://en.wikipedia.org/wiki/Federal_Information_Processing_Standards

The movie *The Imitation Game* (Tyldum, 2014), although maybe not precisely accurate, is a fascinating show. The film presents the story of how Alan Turing[189] and his staff cracked the German encryption code (algorithm) called Enigma,[190] to effectively end the Second World War. Why would breaking the code end the war?

What if your enemy knows everything you are going to do before you do it?

We count on encryption in many ways to protect our data and communications. As computers have gotten faster and faster, encryption algorithms that used to take years to break may take minutes. Scientists are warning that with the rise of quantum computing, today's encryption algorithms may become obsolete. Forward-looking individuals working on or with cryptography may want to think about new ways to protect our data before that time comes. Organizations protecting communications might want to invest research dollars in this area. Some people are already working on quantum encryption algorithms.

Encryption algorithms are hard to create correctly, and the general rule is don't try to create your own. Usually, it involves many different people and years of review before the industry deems it secure. Various attempts to protect data using encryption failed due to logic errors such as splitting a piece of data in half and encrypting each half separately. The longer value is harder to crack than two short values. Another company failed to randomize the values used in the encryption process. Additionally, developers store keys in places that are easy to reverse engineer in software licenses, DRM (digital rights

---

[189] Alan Turing https://en.wikipedia.org/wiki/Alan_Turing
[190] Enigma https://en.wikipedia.org/wiki/Cryptanalysis_of_the_Enigma

management) solutions, and IoT devices.

All these complications and considerations lead me to my final points about encryption at rest. What should you do?

Encrypt everything. It still helps. That's why one of the items on my list of questions to ask security teams is — what is the percentage of data encrypted at rest? Even better would be to ensure proper encryption implementation, but we need to start somewhere.

Think very carefully about key management. You'll likely want to include some form of authentication. Refer to the preceding chapters 9 and 10 on credentials and authentication.

Train staff to use encryption properly. People making decisions about encryption need to understand the threat vectors, perform threat modeling, and implement all aspects of encryption correctly.

Leverage segregation of duties. Separate the people who manage encryption keys from the people and systems that use them. Amazon CTO, Werner Vogels, suggests separating the people from the data. All the things I wrote about in chapter 9 on the aftermath of stolen credentials apply to encryption key management. How much data is exposed when a single key is stolen or accessed?

Encryption keys are like passwords. They provide access to your data. Consider how much data will be exposed if someone obtains access to a key. The longer the better, just like a password. However, different algorithms work effectively with varying lengths, so the size of the key is relative to the length typically used with a specific algorithm. Key length and the algorithm used will depend on many factors. Explaining all that is beyond the scope of this chapter. Just like a password, it's an excellent habit to change your encryption keys regularly, otherwise known as "key rotation." That is sometimes easier said than done, but if an attacker is trying to guess or obtain your key, frequent changes make it harder.

Remember: if you lose your key, you lose your data. For those bitcoin owners out there, hopefully, you understand that bitcoin is a form of encryption. Your bitcoin is a key, which is a password to your money. If anyone gets your key, they get your money. If you lose your key, you can't get your money back. The same is true in corporate environments. How will you prevent your encryption key from being lost? If it is, do you have a secure fallback mechanism to access the data?

Hopefully, that helps explain encryption at a very high level. If you want to protect your data, encryption is one of the many tools that can help you. We architect security to use all the tools together in ways that make it harder to get at the data. When leveraging encryption, system developers and architects need to consider many factors and must implement encryption carefully and correctly for it to do its job. But in the end, encryption is still a critical part of your overall security plan, and you should use it as much as possible and follow best practices.

12
ENCRYPTION ON WIRED AND WIRELESS NETWORKS

When two systems send data back and forth, they need to send data to the right location and speak the same language. As data moves across the network, it should be encrypted so people cannot intercept and view the data as it flows through different types of network equipment. Encrypting data as it traverses the network from one machine to another is known as encryption in transit. Encrypting the data from the starting machine to the destination machine so only the sender and recipient can read it is known as end-to-end encryption.[191]

All the machines on the network can access your data!

The chapters on networking introduced the concepts of ports and protocols. When data traverses a network, it uses different protocols, sometimes called the network stack or protocol stack[192]. I wrote about protocols like RDP, SSH, and HTTP. These protocols are used in the highest layer of the stack, layer 7, also known as

---

[191] End to end encryption https://en.wikipedia.org/wiki/End-to-end_encryption
[192] Protocol stack https://en.wikipedia.org/wiki/Protocol_stack

the Application Layer[193]. Your operating system on your computer typically handles the processing of this layer of the stack for things like web page requests and connecting to remote computers.

At a very high level, when your computer sends a request to a website to retrieve a web page, the request is passed to a device called a router on your local network. The router knows how to get your request from the local network to the correct web server, usually via the Internet. When network devices route your request over the Internet, it typically passes through network equipment owned and maintained by different people and organizations. If devices transmit your data as plain text (unencrypted), then hardware or software on any of those devices could read your data. Someone could also try to insert a rogue device to view the traffic as it traverses the network.

Different protocols handle the transmission of data as it passes through the network, and networking equipment forwards it along. Protocols like the Internet Protocol (IP), Transmission Control Protocol (TCP), and User Datagram Protocol (UDP) wrap the data in things called packet headers or protocol headers as it passes through different types of network equipment. The information in these headers ensures the data makes it to the right place. When the data reaches its final destination, the payload (the data in each packet less the headers) is reassembled and processed or stored by the target machine.

When evaluating encryption in transit solutions, it is vital to understand how much of the packet information is encrypted. Are all the layers and packet headers encrypted, or only the layer with the payload? Which protocols encrypt data? Some do, and some don't. Many different protocols exist on your network for different types of technology and different networking layers. IoT devices, networking equipment, and web servers all use different

---

[193] Application Layer https://en.wikipedia.org/wiki/Application_layer

protocols to send and receive data and facilitate communications. When you want to send your data wirelessly to a TV to play a video, that transmission of data uses a different protocol than the one your laptop uses to visit a website. Although some of the data in transit may be encrypted, the attacker may be accessing it by a different protocol or from some part of the communication that is unencrypted.

Attackers may also get access to your data as it traverses the Internet if they can trick your computer into believing that the attacker's computer is the router. Then when you send a request, it goes to the attacker's machine instead of the correct router. The attacker then forwards it to the router. As the packets pass through the attacker's device, any unencrypted traffic may be read by the attacker as you make web requests.

YOUR COMPUTER >> ATTACKER >> YOUR ROUTER

The attacker may also trick the user into clicking on and accepting an invalid encryption certificate, which then also allows the attacker to read encrypted data. The name for this type of packet rerouting and snooping is called a Man-in-the-Middle attack, or MITM. The attacker machine sits between two legitimate sources spying on the data going back and forth. This same approach is used by pentesters when inspecting traffic that is encrypted in transit between a web browser and a website to try to see if they can exploit website vulnerabilities during a penetration test. In this case, the testers are performing an MITM attack on themselves so they can inspect their own data, which would be otherwise encrypted.

When IoT (Internet of things) devices exchange data, they may use other types of protocols like Bluetooth, Zigbee, or MQTT. These protocols are designed to be light and fast for small devices.

Even though these protocols aren't flowing over your typical network router, this data in transit still needs to be encrypted. Criminals can buy devices that intercept this type of wireless traffic and read or manipulate it. I watched someone use one of these tools to hijack transmissions between a key fob and a car lock at DefCon. If you also connect these devices to your wireless and wired networks, attackers could potentially route traffic between the two different types of networks to hide nefarious activity. Authenticating and encrypting traffic between IoT devices helps prevent rogue devices on these IoT networks from spying on communications or using them to carry out attacks.

The same precautions apply to cellular communications and WiFi networks. Different pentesting and attacker tools and devices intercept this type of traffic when attackers find vulnerabilities and poorly designed networks. Older WiFi routers operate like a network device called a hub[194] that sends data for every device to every other device on the network. Wired networks communicate via devices called a switch[195] that only sends data to the target destination. Some newer WiFi devices try to prevent sniffing by acting more like a switch. One device used to intercept traffic on WiFi networks is called a WiFi pineapple.[196]

Consider how much of your data is exposed when using different types of encryption that operate at different layers in a network. As packets traverse a network, different types of devices add data to the packet as they pass through. This additional data, referred to as packet headers, tells network devices how to route your traffic to the correct destination. If you use an IPSEC[197] VPN (Virtual Private Network), it encapsulates the entire packet — all headers and data — in an encrypted tunnel (Bartlett & Inamdar, 2016).

---

[194] Hub https://en.wikipedia.org/wiki/Ethernet_hub
[195] Switch https://en.wikipedia.org/wiki/Network_switch
[196] WiFi Pineapple https://shop.hak5.org/products/wifi-pineapple
[197] IPSEC https://en.wikipedia.org/wiki/IPsec

With other types of encryption protocols and implementations, only the payload (the data only and not the headers) is encrypted, and some of the information included in the headers is still exposed. Sometimes, only traffic from your web browser gets encrypted. Other types of traffic coming from different applications on your computer might transmit outside the encrypted channel. Additionally, some companies implement what is known as a split VPN tunnel,[198] where some data is encrypted, and other data is not. They may do this because processing the encrypted data is slower than processing unencrypted data. Encrypting all the data may overload network devices that don't have the processing power to encrypt all the data fast enough.

Exposing any data, like domain names that identify systems to which your computer is connecting, may provide the attacker with useful information. Any exposed packet headers could be manipulated by an attacker to include commands sent to malware or to exfiltrate data. Attackers can still see and manipulate some of the packet headers if the solution only encrypts the payload. Your computer uses many protocols to communicate. SSL and TLS do not encrypt all those protocols in most cases. If you use an IPSEC VPN, most protocols flow through an encrypted, authenticated tunnel as it traverses the Internet. Some local network protocols do not traverse the Internet, so those have no reason to go through the VPN. Therefore, you might want to also consider how an attack might leverage those to exfiltrate data.

These aspects of network communications show that it's essential not only to encrypt data. You also need to understand how much and what data may still be exposed, which depends on the encryption implementation. Unfortunately, that's not the only thing you need to worry about when implementing encryption in transit.

---

[198] Split Tunneling https://en.wikipedia.org/wiki/Split_tunneling

The Apple Watch mystery

This story is a slight diversion from the encryption topic. However, it shows you data you expect to be encrypted may follow a different path than expected. It also provides further explanation as to how traffic flowing through an encrypted VPN tunnel might end up reaching the Internet another way.

As I was writing this book, I had a Macintosh computer that I only use for work connected to a specific WiFi network. I also have an Apple phone and an Apple Watch. Suddenly, my WiFi hotspot indicated that a second device had connected. I had not authorized any other devices to connect. Upon further inspection, the watch had connected to the hotspot — without my specific permission or authorization! It's one thing to enable all your devices to connect magically to one another if you find it convenient and choose to do so. It's another when they do it without your consent.

I never set up WiFi on my watch, nor did I want it connecting to WiFi networks. I never authorized any access from my work laptop to or from my watch or my phone. I never authorized Apple to send my WiFi connection data from this laptop to their iCloud service or any other Apple location. I did not have any connections activated and never have, between the computer and the Apple Watch, or the phone. Bluetooth was disabled on the laptop. I never entered the WiFi password into the Apple Watch. I had recently reset it and was not even aware that WiFi was enabled on the watch.

When I posted this on Twitter, people provided answers like, "The watch connected to the hotspot via WiFi from the phone." They didn't read the fact that the phone had WiFi disabled on the phone (which is usually the case), and the watch had no access to the computer connected to WiFi and never has. The watch had WiFi enabled but would not be able to connect until it received my password from somewhere. They also assumed I connected my devices to iCloud, which I never authorize when I set up Apple devices. Neither the phone nor the watch was able to connect to the laptop, so they could not get the password through it.

This story demonstrates how understanding cloud systems and network protocols is helpful. It is also an excellent example to explain why companies need to think through where and how devices connect and where their data flows. Companies should think about where their sensitive data and credentials exist in transit, at rest, and what protects them from spying eyes. Cloud systems send your data around in ways you might not expect and without your knowledge. It is in your best interest to understand how and when this is happening to protect systems and data. Make sure they are not sending data to locations you did not authorize. Be especially careful with data that you do not want to leave your network. I like to say that *if a network path exists, data will flow there.*

Simplistic answers exist that often don't make sense when you dive into the details. Be wary when vendors do this to you when trying to sell you a product. Some people might tend to think these issues are beyond their comprehension. I don't think so. Let's look at connections that existed at the time of the event or in the past. At that moment, I had Bluetooth enabled on my phone and my watch. Those two devices could connect. I had once connected the phone to the WiFi hotspot to download a software update and then turned WiFi off after. I typically have WiFi disabled on my phone, and it was disabled at that moment. This past connection had never triggered the watch to connect to the hotspot. Perhaps I had Bluetooth disabled when updating the phone, which is common.

The phone could connect to the Internet using its cellular connection. The watch does not have a cellular connection or any way to get to the Internet that I explicitly enabled. It can only get data from the phone (I think), so any data sent to the watch from the Internet had to go through the phone. Bluetooth was disabled on the laptop. Therefore, the phone and watch had no way to connect to the laptop directly; Unless disabling Bluetooth is broken. I joked on Twitter that in that case, Apple owes me a large bug bounty! Of course, if that were true, I would responsibly disclose it. I do not know that to be the case and have not had time to look into it. I presume disabling Bluetooth is working properly at this point.

How did the watch get the WiFi connection information, and what triggered it to connect? *In my opinion, it should not have based on my settings and what I authorized.* Let's walk through the available connections that would have made this possible. I don't have time to investigate this thoroughly, but here is what I think happened.

I needed to update some software on the laptop. I logged into my Apple account to do so. I only intended to download and update software, not to send anything to the cloud. It was shortly after this point that the watch connected. I did not have any feature that I know of enabled that allows Apple to send my WiFi details to the cloud from my laptop. Apparently, when I connected to the Apple network to update the software, my WiFi password went up into the cloud. From there, my phone retrieved it (again, without my consent) via the cellular network. From that point, the phone pushed the WiFi connection information to the watch. The Watch then connected to the hotspot.

Laptop (WiFi) > iCloud (Cellular) > Phone (Bluetooth) > Watch (WiFi)

This functionality is somewhat disturbing to me because I did not knowingly enable any such options. I also did not explicitly allow Apple to send my WiFi connection information and password to the cloud. I would never do that. In fact, I recently went through some setup options, and I thought I had disabled a feature like that. Many people are not security nerds like me handling sensitive customer data on their laptops. They don't mind all their devices connecting to random hotspots. I, on the other hand, am very concerned about putting customer data at risk when I'm working for them. Therefore, I did *not* want my Apple Watch or any other device I had not explicitly authorized connected to my work network or laptop.

What is the problem here for organizations trying to maintain security on their networks? Chances are employees using work computers log into their Apple accounts. Their work computers likely connect to corporate WiFi. If this functionality is enabled, that WiFi connection information may be going to the Apple cloud. Additionally, most people like the fact that their devices connect automatically or don't even know this is happening, so have not disabled it. Any device where the person previously logged in with their Apple account potentially obtains the WiFi connection information. Note that I was not logged into my Apple account on my phone when this event occurred.

How did I resolve the problem? My case is pretty simple. Rather than spending a lot of time investigating the software and networking involved, I blocked the traffic on the network. I turned off WiFi on the Apple Watch and blocked it on the hotspot. This example demonstrates how companies can leverage networking when trying to protect data when other options fail or have vulnerabilities. If I only relied on authentication, I would have fewer options. Instead, I simply block the connections on the network.

I will also review all the settings to ensure my Apple products are not sending my WiFi password to their cloud. If I allowed Apple to send my WiFi password to their cloud, I would want details about how they protect that information with encryption in transit and at rest. I would want to know if their employees potentially have access to that data. I also am guessing that for the price consumers pay, security is not as high as it would be for business solutions. iCloud has experienced breaches in the past (Lewis, 2014). Additionally, reports indicate that Apple is not encrypting data end to end with data backed up to iCloud (Lopez, 2020). Although I like cloud solutions for some purposes, having my WiFi password stored or transmitted through the Apple cloud is simply not necessary. I prefer to eliminate that particular risk.

Protect your private keys

Asymmetric encryption, also known as public-key cryptography, leverages a public and private key to encrypt the data instead of one key shared between both parties.[199] The private key needs to be protected because it identifies the owner and also ensures encrypted communications to and from the entity are secure. If anyone else gets access to the private key, communications are compromised. A private key can be created automatically on a device. No one manufacturing the device ever needs to see the private key. Ideally, any process that exchanges keys, data, or handles encryption should not expose private keys to any person or device other than the one identified by that key.

When you set up encryption in transit for your website, you have to generate a private and public key to get what is known as a TLS[200] (formerly SSL[201]) certificate. Protect the private keys for your TLS certificates carefully. Do not let anyone check them into your source control system where you maintain your source code, for example. Store secrets like encryption keys securely, typically in a secure vault designed to store secrets where authorized users and applications can retrieve the secrets when required.

Different people may have the responsibility to manage

---

[199] Public Key Cryptography https://en.wikipedia.org/wiki/Public-key_cryptography
[200] TLS https://en.wikipedia.org/wiki/Transport_Layer_Security
[201] Pulbic key certificate https://en.wikipedia.org/wiki/Public_key_certificate

encryption keys and the applications that use them. The people managing any of your encryption keys should have security training, so they understand how to handle and manage these keys properly. Companies like Venafi offer products that help with the management of encryption keys and automated solutions for on-premises and cloud environments.

When using cloud services like AWS, the whole process of getting and renewing TLS certificates can be automated. No one managing encryption can access the private key, depending on how you architect your deployment systems, networks, and operational access to your cloud accounts. Of course, you are trusting the cloud provider in that case, so you should ask them who on their side can access the keys. Check audits and assessments for third-party verification that prove the cloud provider implements encryption. Include encryption requirements in contracts.

Trusted platform modules

When generating encryption keys for an IoT device, a TPM can store private keys presumably more securely on your computers, servers, and IoT devices. As described earlier, a TPM is typically hardware manufactured into the device to store keys. However, virtual software TPMs also exist. Generally, security professionals consider hardware to be more secure. In the end, even the hardware TPMs interact with software that may have a vulnerability. A code library developed by a German TPM chipmaker named Infineon had a vulnerability that existed for five years before anyone discovered it. The flaw allowed attackers to calculate a private key for a corresponding public key, making encryption by those chipsets completely ineffective (Goodin, Millions of high-security crypto keys crippled by newly discovered flaw, 2017).

A file can be stolen and transferred. Something built into the hardware, not so much. Additionally, hardware that segregates sensitive data on a device from other operations should help protect those secrets. If someone tries to tamper with or remove data from a TPM, it should prevent that. Sometimes the documentation on how it does that is not very detailed.

Additionally, not all TPMs do this, according to Wikipedia, at the time of this writing.[202] The keys should never leave the TPM. Of course, you don't want to trust the acronym TPM blindly; look for independent third-party verification of the implementation by a trusted source who understands the technology. Some vendors use TPM as a marketing term, but the implementation is flawed. Do your homework if you are in a high-security environment.

Hardware has connections on circuit boards that can also transmit data in unexpected ways. A student in my class who formerly worked for the U.S. Department of Defense suggested that hardware flaws are on the rise and will be a primary threat vector in the future. How can you protect yourself from hardware flaws? Hire hardware experts, if you can. Likely many businesses don't keep this expertise on staff. Alternatively, read reviews, third-party reports, and audits, and monitor network traffic coming out of those devices for suspicious behavior. If you have access and expertise, you can monitor system memory for secrets exposed in places they should not be and other anomalous system behavior.

IPv4 vs. IPv6

With the rise of SaaS (software as a service),[203] in many cases, IoT vendors are sending data to the cloud. Additionally, devices often need to connect back to manufacturers to get software updates. You should understand how those devices authenticate and encrypt your credentials or authentication data in transit. A MAC (Media Access Control)[204] address is an identifier consisting of

---

[202] Trusted Platform Module https://en.wikipedia.org/wiki/Trusted_Platform_Module
[203] SaaS https://en.wikipedia.org/wiki/Software_as_a_service

numbers and letters associated with the network card in your devices. It identifies a specific network interface (how a machine connects to the network),[205] and thereby the device that contains the network card.

Some companies use weak mechanisms to identify and authenticate a device, such as verifying a MAC address. This data may not be encrypted in transit over the network, thereby allowing an attacker to impersonate one of your devices. The MAC address exists in clear text on internal networks when using the most common protocol used for network communications — IPv4.[206]

On the newer version of the same protocol, IPv6,[207] your MAC address traverses the Internet, not only the local network. It may appear in clear text in network traffic traversing devices run by other organizations. If your vendors leverage a MAC address to identify a device, this is not considered secure in the first place (Perrin, 2008). It's even worse on an IPv6 network where the MAC address routes over the Internet and untrusted devices.

Companies offering IoT or other devices require a means to authenticate devices that connect back to manufacturer's systems for updates, logging, and other functionality. An attacker may be able to spoof an IoT device using a MAC address for identification and authentication to access the SaaS or manufacturer network. By impersonating the IoT device, the attacker may obtain access to sensitive data. An intermediary could pretend to have your MAC address and communicate with the device manufacturer's systems and then trick your device into connecting to the attacker instead of the manufacturer. The attacker may be able to steal your sensitive data in the process.

---

[204] MAC address https://en.wikipedia.org/wiki/MAC_address
[205] Network interface https://en.wikipedia.org/wiki/Network_interface
[206] IPv4 https://en.wikipedia.org/wiki/IPv4
[207] IPv6 https://en.wikipedia.org/wiki/IPv6

A MAC address is just one example of authenticating using unencrypted credentials or means of identification. When implementing authentication for remote devices, ensure the authentication information is encrypted correctly, and any encryption keys used in the process are protected.

Cellular communications

Cellular networks have traditionally used a protocol called SS7 (Signaling System Number 7).[208] Some telecommunications companies are updating their networks to use protocols like IP and TCP (the protocols used when you are browsing the web from your computer). If your voice and data communications from your cell phone are not encrypted, anyone with access to those SS7 or other cellular networks could listen to your conversations.

In theory, it's harder for people to get access to those SS7 and other telecom networks, so your communications are harder to tap. However, it can happen, and far too many people underestimate the reach of governments, spies, and organized crime. Governments and organized crime groups may offer insiders a significant amount of money to capture sensitive data. One report talks about how a vulnerability on phones could provide access to SS7 networks (Cimpanu, Simjacker attack exploited in the wild to track users for at least two years, 2019). Positive Technologies produced a report called *Primary Security Threats for SS7 Cellular Networks* in 2017, which shows attacks that were possible at that time (Positive Technology, 2016).

The first step to securing your communications involves your cellular provider. When is the last time a company took steps to vet their cellular provider? Did you ask them how they secure their networks, vet employees, segregate duties, and separate employees from cellular communications? The other problem is

---

[208] SS7 https://en.wikipedia.org/wiki/Signalling_System_No._7

when you travel to other countries or areas where the cell provider partners with other companies to provide service. Then you are at the mercy of whatever network to which your phone is connected. You can turn off roaming on your phone, but that limits communications.

I have heard FBI agents and security professionals say they use burner phones in other countries. These are phones you use once and throw away. Unfortunately, now even burner phones are at risk. An article by *Help Net Security* explains how attackers target burner phones with malicious updates, radiofrequency hacking, physical software installations by customs agents, and fake cell towers. Burner phones may also be infected by other well-known attacks like targeting hotel WiFi or creating a look-alike hotspot (known as an evil maid attack) (Campbell, 2020). People can buy cell towers and other devices to intercept and listen in on traffic. If you connect your device to a WiFi network, all the prior information about WiFi applies to any data transmitted via that network.

The next thing you need to worry about is your device. Who manufactured your phone? What hardware and software did they put into it? If you use the phone and the default software to send messages, are they encrypted? What vulnerabilities could expose your communications? The hardware and software on your device provide the encryption on cellular networks. Ideally, that hardware or software securely encrypts your text messages and calls when sending them over the network. Otherwise, anyone in the cellular network can read them. Criminals have also offered to sell access to SS7 networks on underground spyware networks in 2017 (Newman, Fixing the Cell Network Flaw That Lets Hackers Drain Bank Accounts, 2017).

A mechanism needs to exist for each device involved in the communication to obtain the appropriate keys to perform encryption. Software on each device needs to be able to handle this key exchange securely. If you send an iMessage between two

Apple devices, the traffic is encrypted. [209] You will notice that the message is blue when sent as an iMessage. If you send a standard text message from an iPhone to an Android device, Apple doesn't have control of the Android software and sends the message in cleartext. The message is green on your iPhone in that case.

Applications like Signal[210] and WhatsApp are designed to send and receive secure, encrypted communications, regardless of what phone or network you are using. Bruce Schneier[211] is a renowned encryption expert and endorses Signal on the product home page at the time of this writing. It is in use by multiple governments. Anyone can download this application and use it for free. Both people involved in the communication need to use these applications for end-to-end encryption. Additionally, beware of limitations, as discussed in this Wired article: "Encrypted Messaging isn't Perfect" (Foote, 2018). You still have to trust the other person not to expose the data, and the application could have security flaws, as has been the case for Signal (Dunn, 2018) and WhatsApp (Wong J. C., 2019). It's important to keep these applications up to date with the latest software patches.

Algorithms

Just as with encryption at rest, encryption in transit needs to use a secure algorithm. For example, when you are using your web browser to visit a website, you may see HTTPS:// in the address bar. If you went to the 2nd Sight Lab website in your browser, it would look like this:

https://2ndSightLab.com

If the URL only started with HTTP, that would mean the traffic is not encrypted, unless you encrypt it on your end with a VPN or some other type of encryption technology.

---

[209] iMessage https://en.wikipedia.org/wiki/IMessage
[210] Signal https://signal.org/
[211] Bruce Schneier blog https://www.schneier.com/

When you see the HTTPS prefix on an address, it means that the browser is encrypting the traffic it is sending to the web server. However, seeing HTTPS in the web browser address bar doesn't tell you the version of the protocol used to encrypt the data. Websites used to use a protocol called SSL (Secure Socket Layer), and different versions of SSL exist. SSL evolved into a new standard. Now websites should be using TLS (Transport Layer Security) and preferably the most recent version of TLS. Older versions of SSL and TLS are subject to attacks like Heartbleed, Beast, and Poodle, which disclose data. Major browsers are going to stop allowing older versions of TLS with these flaws in 2020.

When you visit a website that is serving an HTTPS page, your browser negotiates with the web server to find a compatible encryption protocol and version. Attackers figured out how to manipulate this process in various ways to trick browsers into using an older protocol when the configuration on a web server does not correctly implement encryption. Once the communications are flowing over an older protocol, attackers can use whatever attacks exist for that protocol. In most browsers and on some servers, you can change the settings to disallow old encryption protocols. Many cloud providers offer a setting for this in their services. Make sure you are using the most up-to-date version of TLS possible.

SSL originally came about when e-commerce was new, and people were looking for a way to trust vendors and perform transactions online. When you want to encrypt traffic to and from your website, you needed to obtain something called an SSL (now TLS) certificate from a third party. The certificate from the third party, known as a certificate authority (CA) is designed to validate that your website certificate and the connection is legitimate. It also provides encryption in transit.

You'll have to go through various steps to get and install a certificate. In the past, those steps involved a lot of manual actions. This request process includes generating a private key, which needs to be maintained securely. Then you exchange information with a public certificate authority to get a public certificate validated by them, and you install that on your web server. People can look at your certificate information when they go to your website and see the vendor who issued the certificate.

Anyone who has had the pleasure of manually configuring SSL and TLS certificates can tell you it is tedious and was even more so in the past. Over the years, some companies like DigiCert have simplified the process, but it still takes several steps. I used to write blog posts to remind myself how to get and install TLS certificates since I only did it once or twice per year.

After you get a certificate and install it, you have to remember to renew it when it expires. Companies have experienced hours of downtime as they tried to figure out why systems were suddenly failing, only to find out it was due to an expired SSL or TLS certificate. In some cases, the company lost thousands or millions of dollars while systems were down. Make sure you monitor certificates for expirations or automate the renewal process.

Sometimes developers don't use TLS for encryption in transit. They instead encrypt data with algorithms intended for encryption at rest. Then the encrypted data is sent via an unencrypted network channel. These solutions only encrypt the payload. Using protocols not designed for encryption in transit also lacks some of the server validation provided by TLS. How do you know you are sending the data to the correct recipient? TLS provides some of this validation if configured properly.

The other problem with the transmission of data by protocols not designed for encryption in transit is that they do not have a way to transmit a symmetric key securely. Symmetric encryption uses the same key to both encrypt and decrypt data. It is more efficient than asymmetric encryption for large amounts of data. Typically, when encrypting large files or data in a database, systems use symmetric encryption. The sender and receiver need a secure method to exchange the shared key.

Without going into all the details, TLS solves this key-sharing problem with a combination of asymmetric and symmetric encryption. First, two hosts that need to communicate securely use public and private keys to encrypt and exchange a shared symmetric key. After that point, the two sides have the shared key to encrypt and decrypt larger volumes of data using symmetric encryption. Protocols like TLS facilitate key exchange over networks because cryptographers designed them specifically for encryption in transit and to solve these types of problems.

Additional details exist surrounding the proper implementation of encryption, so you'll want to make sure your developers receive adequate training. Different software libraries manage encryption in transit, and some are more secure than others. As a result of the rash of various SSL vulnerabilities like Heartbleed[212] and POODLE,[213] AWS created their own TLS library called s2n[214] to use on their platform. It's open-source software, which allows anyone to inspect and use the code. Using secure libraries from trusted sources that have been implemented by people with relevant expertise helps ensure you have a more secure solution.

When using cloud platforms like AWS, Azure, and Google, organizations may give some encryption responsibilities to the cloud provider. At this time, you can request a TLS certificate from AWS directly and associate it with AWS resources. It is possible to automate the entire process, though it takes a bit of effort. Once you have a certificate installed, it renews automatically. You can also manage the process of getting a certificate yourself on any of these platforms.

On the one hand, having the cloud provider manage your TLS

---

[212] Heartbleed http://heartbleed.com/
[213] POODLE https://en.wikipedia.org/wiki/POODLE
[214] s2n https://aws.amazon.com/blogs/security/introducing-s2n-a-new-open-source-tls-implementation/

certificate potentially exposes your private key to that vendor. This point is where proper vendor assessments become essential. Ensure that you understand how the vendor manages private keys and that you can trust the vendor. Review how they hire, monitor, and vet employees and what access they have to your encryption keys. Review third-party audits or directly assess the vendor yourself if you can.

On the other hand, you may find the cloud provider does a better job of managing keys than you. They may automate everything such that no human ever has access to the keys. The automation and standardization offer security benefits as well. I perform cloud penetration tests. When I discover a company is using an AWS TLS certificate, I know testing TLS likely won't turn up any significant problems. I still check, but since the configuration is automated and standardized, it's probably ok.

I do find companies aren't enforcing the latest version of TLS in CDN (Content delivery network)[215] configurations. However, that part of the setup is the customer's responsibility. CDNs serve website content, software downloads, and other application functionality from servers located closer to the end-users around the world. Amazon's CDN is called CloudFront, and you may have heard of others like Akamai or Cloudflare. Customers need to understand where and how data is encrypted as it passes through these types of services and what might be exposed.

Termination

When considering encryption in transit, understand where the encryption terminates. For example, a load balancer in front of several web servers tries to distribute the load to optimize your website performance. Sometimes the encryption terminates at the load balancer. The traffic between the load balancer and the web

---

[215] Content delivery network
https://en.wikipedia.org/wiki/Content_delivery_network

server is unencrypted. Is that ok? There are legitimate reasons for doing this. However, now anyone who can access the traffic between your load balancer and the web server can sniff and view it. How much do you trust your cloud provider? Have you asked them who can access that data and how?

Browser >[encrypted] > Load Balancer > [unencrypted] > Web Server

What about traffic flows between different servers on your internal network? Should that be encrypted? Who might access it on the network? How about network traffic between APIs (application programming interfaces) and containers that encapsulate different applications on a single operating system? What about serverless[216] functions that connect to databases in cloud environments? These functions allow developers to run code without configuring a machine or operating system. Do you know all the places where data is encrypted and unencrypted as it flows through your networks and over the Internet?

Any time data is sent from one device or computer resource to another, it may be exposed. Organizations first need to understand what data they have, where it is stored, and where it flows, as I explained previously. Remember to protect voice and IoT communications as well as traditional networking between computers. Understand whether the traffic to systems within your internal network between servers, network devices, databases, functions, and containers is encrypted or not. Try to encrypt as much as possible. The risk associated with plaintext data depends on the sensitivity and value of the data. Ensure your teams implement encryption in transit everywhere possible and according to best practices to prevent interception, downgraded encryption algorithms, and compromised encryption keys.

---

[216] Serverless computing https://en.wikipedia.org/wiki/Serverless_computing

13
THE RIGHT CYBERSECURITY TRAINING

Think for a minute about how companies make cybersecurity decisions that ultimately lead to a data breach — or not. Leaders need to understand the big picture and have accurate information to make effective decisions at a macro level. They need to be able to communicate cyber-directives to staff. Then they need to be able to count on the people they employ to make the right individual decisions that align with stated business objectives and organizational risk posture. It only takes one mistake to facilitate the next cyber breach. How can leaders mitigate this risk when it is dependent on so many individual decisions and so many data points?

Teach your team to make decisions that help prevent and detect data breaches

Based on the rise in data breaches, having the security teams making recommendations and telling people what they did wrong after the fact isn't working. As I explain in chapter 16, which covers security policies, it has not worked for years.

As companies move to the cloud, sometimes a shift in authority to make security-related decisions moves from people with years of experience to those lacking similar qualifications. Based on breach statistics and the root cause of a large percentage of breaches, this approach may also contribute to the problem. When I started writing this book, 2019 was on track to be the worst year to date for cyber breaches, according to some reports, with over 4.1 billion records exposed in the first half of the year (Winder, Data Breaches Expose 4.1 Billion Records In First Six Months Of 2019, 2019). Many of these breaches were the result of simple misconfigurations (Radichel, Amazon DocumentDB Network Access — Why the VPC?, 2019).

Does that mean we should take away responsibility? Not necessarily. In my opinion, the problem is two-fold. First, the people making the decisions lack training. Secondly, appropriate governance does not exist in some cases to prevent accidental configuration mistakes. This chapter covers training. Chapters 16 and 22 explain how to prevent mistakes by having appropriate policies and leveraging security automation. Chapter 23 explains how to monitor for mistakes that can lead to a data breach.

How can we turn this statistic around? Don't blame the CISO.

First, we need to understand who is responsible for the decisions that are causing these breaches. Is it the security team? In almost every case, no.

Most of these massive data breaches are the result of misconfigurations implemented by teams outside the security department. It is highly likely that the security team had no input or visibility into many of the choices that led to the breach, based on personal experience. When it comes to SaaS (Security as a Service) cloud solutions, often, a business unit signs up for the application, and the security team finds out after the fact. In other cases, the security team assesses the SaaS application before signing a contract but then has no say in how the applications are implemented and maintained after that point. Sometimes executive leadership approves application architectures with significant security flaws against cybersecurity recommendations and best practices. Everyone involved in making security-related decisions is, in part, responsible for any data breach resulting from those judgment calls.

I presume most people are not making these mistakes intentionally and with a complete understanding of the potential consequences. Generally, people in an organization do not want to be responsible for the next massive data breach on the front page of the news. The problem is that those making decisions that increase the risk do not understand how their actions contribute to the chances the organization will experience a breach. They may also be facing pressures within the organization from managers and executives within the organization who want them to hurry up and get things done. Organizational constraints or duties sometimes override best practices even when the person is aware of the risk.

For these reasons, every level of the organization requires training to improve cybersecurity decision-making and actions across the board. When developers understand security, they implement secure solutions from the start. When management understands cybersecurity and the potential cost of a mistake, they are less apt to pressure teams to build for blatantly insecure systems. The training needs to be impactful and focused on the right information that makes a difference when it comes to stopping breaches. Watching security awareness videos helps, but is not enough, based on the number of these I have watched and the statistics at the beginning of the chapter.

Most breaches are the result of fundamental security flaws. These are not complex decisions. Attackers are exploiting very simple misconfigurations, not leveraging zero-day malware, in the majority of breaches (Verizon, 2019). Knowing cybersecurity fundamentals helps decision-makers when it comes to making decisions about system implementation. Additionally, by understanding what causes breaches, decision-makers can implement better monitoring, metrics, and alerting procedures to help spot gaps and mitigate cybersecurity risks. Organizations can spot security problems faster if those responsible for implementing systems build them in ways that facilitate appropriate visibility. Those monitoring systems need to understand how to detect the movements and actions of attackers.

The training your cyber defenders need

What is the first thing someone does when they join the military? They don't go into battle. They go through basic training. Everyone in the military learns the necessary skills to be a good soldier. Every individual in the military needs to do their part in the face of an attack. Individual soldiers take orders, but also, every individual needs to have the appropriate skills and must know what to do to have a capable military that can win battles. Sharing similar training experiences helps reinforce collective knowledge and skills.

Anyone who makes decisions that impact system configuration and implementation is part of your cyber army. These are the people who are making the decisions that keep systems secure — or change them in ways that increase attack vectors and create vulnerabilities. These are the people writing code, designing the architecture, and approving system changes that end up in your production environment. These are the people who decide what to monitor and how to react when alerted to abnormalities in your system logs.

Organizations need to do more than say cybersecurity is a priority. They need to train people in the organization so that their employees know what to do and why it matters when it comes to implementing security controls and monitoring systems. If a breach or disaster occurs, employees need to be prepared to handle the incident appropriately.

What do executives need to know?

Businesspeople say security people need to understand the business objectives for the company to make money. Security teams do need to learn to explain "How" and sometimes a more understandable and detailed "Why" instead of "No," but this isn't the biggest issue, in my opinion. I've worked at all levels of companies, in startups to Fortune 150 to running my software consulting and web application hosting company. Business objectives almost always trump security in my experience.

I feel that the more significant gap is due to people who don't understand the impact of their decisions and influence on cybersecurity risk. Even if they do understand, it is not clear what they can do to balance business objectives and cyber risk in a way that reduces breaches. This gap in understanding may be, in part, due to challenges cybersecurity teams experience when trying to explain risks. It also may have to do with explanations without tangible solutions. I hope this book helps close the gap and provide some concrete steps executives can take to reduce the chances of a data breach within their organization.

The question is, who is making the security decisions that lead to data breaches, and why? The breach statistics I just shared indicate that somewhere, a breakdown in decision-making exists. Analysis of recent breaches suggests that the decisions involved were a blatant disregard or misunderstanding of best practices, rather than well-intentioned analysis gone wrong. Chances are, the people involved lacked training.

I have also experienced another phenomenon in organizations where I worked, and I expect it has contributed to some breaches. In some cases, it seems like people were facing organizational pressures from above that led them to choose unwisely for the sake of bonuses or even continued employment. I have experienced this kind of pressure and gotten in trouble for pushing for more secure solutions. I'm sure it affected my bonuses, and even my employment altogether. Sometimes, middle-level executives receive pressure from top-level executives to approve projects. Employees don't want to tell bosses things they don't want to hear. Avoidance of delivering bad news can lead to less than ideal security decisions.

In other cases, organizations aren't investing enough into the right kind of security monitoring with well-trained staff to help them quickly find and stop breaches. Although you can buy cybersecurity products that include artificial intelligence and machine learning to help alert your organization to security problems, someone needs to monitor and tune these systems. The people assigned to monitor systems require the capability to decipher the logs and take appropriate actions.

Another problem is that often, businesses don't have a sufficient way to measure overall cybersecurity risk. This problem stems, in part, from systems that do not report security metrics effectively, as I explain in chapter 23. Building systems that report accurate cybersecurity metrics costs time and money, but it is a pay-now-or-pay-later scenario. An investment in systems that help report accurate cybersecurity statistics helps companies prevent breaches and respond to threats more quickly.

Trying to explain cybersecurity to executives in five minutes when the pressure is on to get a project done or during a security incident is not the best approach. You are already taking steps to learn security by reading this book. Provide dedicated time to those you manage so they too can learn security fundamentals and, in turn, make better risk decisions. Training everyone within the organization to make better security decisions from the ground up leads to fewer escalations and conflicts between developers, project and product managers, and security teams. More importantly, it helps prevent data breaches at the point where people make crucial decisions that allow vulnerabilities to infiltrate systems.

What do developers need to know?

Often a developer is focusing on making something work, not system security. A developer is thinking, "I put an asterisk (*) in my CORS configuration, and I stopped getting that pesky error message. Cool," rather than, "Hmm, I wonder why that CORS configuration is there and what it's supposed to do." Hint: a secure CORS (Cross-Origin Resource Sharing) configuration protects websites from attacks facilitated by third-party content that attempts to steal cookies and cause users to take unwanted actions without their knowledge (Radichel, Pentesting CORS: Give me all your cookies! OK., 2019). I have run across misconfigured CORS policies in many penetration tests because people didn't understand what it was or why it even exists. A team I managed implemented this very "fix," which I hope they have reconfigured by now. I left that team before getting that issue resolved.

When it comes to secure implementations, many developers try to do the right thing, but sometimes you don't know what you don't know. For example, developers may implement encryption but do not understand how implementation choices in modes, algorithms, configuration, and architectural decisions may render that encryption useless. Many people making cybersecurity-related decisions don't know how breaches happen, who the threat actors are, how malware works, the cyber kill chain, threat modeling, incident handling, or why specific traditional security architectures exist. They don't know that how they create and manage logs and build systems may facilitate a breach or exponentially increase the cost when one occurs. In some cloud implementations, security teams have no visibility into the logs. The business and development teams responsible for maintaining those systems are focused on building and leveraging data, not threat hunting, security monitoring, or incident handling.

Some developers and people managing software systems still

have never heard of OWASP (the Open Web Application Security Project).[217] Some know it in name only. Also, some people think the only thing developers need to know is the OWASP Top 10. However, many developers are responsible for IAM (identity and access management) and networking in cloud environments. They also need to understand how breaches occur to create secure architectures. Developers, DevOps teams, and unfortunately, some software architects, are frequently at odds with security teams over architectural decisions that lead to data breaches. Often this stems from the fact that they don't understand why the security team wants them to make the requested changes. Developers need basic security training to understand not just individual security flaws, but an overall discussion of risk, top threats, how breaches occur, how malware works, threat modeling, security architecture, and how to *think about security*.

What does the security team need to know?

Many companies have a security team — in some cases, an elite security team that has in-depth cybersecurity knowledge. This team understands how attackers are going to get into your system. They know why and how systems need to be locked down to reduce your attack surface and attack vector. Often, they are overworked, understaffed, and facing constant pressure from the rest of the organization to lighten up on their security restrictions.

Many security teams still believe that the use of cloud systems is inherently flawed because someone else outside of the organization might be able to see their data. The cloud does bring about new security concerns, but also new opportunities to automate governance, incident handling, and response. As I wrote about previously, the Ponemon Institute reports that automation can reduce the average cost of a data breach. A cloud environment may enable an organization to implement applications more

---

[217] OWASP https://owasp.com

securely than they do internally (Ponemon Institute, IBM, 2018) Reduction in cybersecurity risk depends on the current practices of the organization internally, the proper vetting of the cloud provider, and the implementation of secure configuration by the customer.

In this brave new world of cloud, security teams need to understand that *some* cloud platforms offer benefits that can enhance the security of their organization. They provide a fully automated platform where almost every action is possible via software. Leveraging this automation capability can help companies respond faster to security threats. These platforms offer practically unlimited storage for security logs and fine-grained controls to implement zero-trust security models more easily than with traditional on-premises technologies. Security teams can write code or work with their developers to implement self-defending systems and automated incident handling and response (Radichel, Case Study: Critical Controls that Could Have Prevented the Target Breach, 2014). If you don't want to give up encryption keys to the cloud provider, you can still implement security automation in an on-premises environment.

Security teams need the training to understand new types of services, configurations, data processing resources, and logs in cloud systems to be able to monitor them effectively. They need to understand how to evaluate new solutions, like SaaS cloud solutions, to determine if it increases risk or reduces liability in the case of a data breach. Finally, security teams need to understand how their development teams are leveraging automation to deploy systems faster via DevOps,[218] DevSecOps (Radichel, My History of DevSecOps, 2019), and other new software development processes so they can get preventative security checks in place earlier in the development lifecycle and deployment pipeline.

---

[218] DevOps https://en.wikipedia.org/wiki/DevOps

As already mentioned, security teams need to understand and support business objectives. Sometimes security teams are focused on doing things the way they have always done in the past. When Jeff Bezos started a company to sell books online, I remember everyone said the banks would never approve online transactions due to the risk. E-commerce gave rise to SSL, and now TLS. When someone told me packet capture in the cloud was not possible, I wrote a white paper showing how it was (Radichel, Packet Capture on AWS, 2017). In June of 2019, AWS introduced VPC Traffic Mirroring to help solve this problem.[219]

With developers and security professionals working together to solve security problems in more automated ways, we can do more to improve security and reduce data breaches. However, developers often do not have the in-depth knowledge security professionals have, as they have not invested as much time into that educational area. Security professionals can help produce solutions devoid of security flaws by leveraging years of experience and thorough knowledge of security attacks. Security teams need to learn more about how developers work, and what they are doing so they can enlist their help to come up with better security solutions — especially in cloud environments. Developers think creatively about how to solve problems and have the knowledge to write software to create automated solutions that can reduce problems (if architected and implemented correctly).

What should your cybersecurity training cover?

Many different types of cybersecurity training exist. I've obtained relevant certifications in all the areas mentioned below. I also study data breaches and what causes them. You'll want to focus your training dollars on classes that develop an understanding of security that leads to improved decisions at the point of system implementation, monitoring, and incident response. You also may

---

[219] VPC Traffic Mirroring – Capture & Inspect Network Traffic
https://aws.amazon.com/blogs/aws/new-vpc-traffic-mirroring/

need people with particular skillsets for different job functions. Here are some of the types of training available and how they can help your team:

Bootcamp and broad-based security classes: These types of classes give broad, high-level knowledge of many different security topics. They explain security threats, cyber risks, and how to deal with them at a more general level. These classes may cover risk management and an introduction to many different security topics.

Security Awareness: Most companies offer security awareness training that teaches people how to spot phishing attacks and fake SSL/TLS certificates. They educate end-users of applications to be aware of and watch out for security threats that may target non-technical as well as technical individuals when using software programs, email, and websites.

Application Security: Some security training focuses on application security. These classes may focus on teaching the OWASP Top 10 or how to secure applications written in a specific software language. These classes have a very narrow and deep focus. They generally do not cover other fundamental cybersecurity concepts mentioned here and focus specifically on software development mistakes and writing secure application-level code.

Penetration testing: These types of classes are suitable for individuals who want to work as penetration testers and red team members. Lessons may involve pentesting websites, applications, cloud environments, network equipment, exploit writing, social engineering, and fuzzing. Learning how to attack systems is fun. However, a lot of penetration testing classes and CTF (capture the flag) contests teach skills in a piecemeal manner that shows different types of attacks rather than how to protect systems holistically.

Intrusion detection and monitoring: Some classes focus on intrusion detection and monitoring — what do you need to look for in the logs to spot a security incident? How do you decipher network packets and packet headers? How should you configure and set up your SIEM, IDS, IPS, and other log analysis tools? These classes may teach students how to correlate different logs to piece together the timeline of an attack and determine how it occurred.

Incident response: Learn the process for dealing with a cybersecurity incident. Typically, this involves capturing data off infected disks and from memory, as well as other logs in a way that is admissible in court. Then the IR team needs to investigate the data (sometimes retrieving deleted files) to determine what happened and restore systems. This class will involve correlating events and determining the timeline and cause of attacks. It also will cover issues like preparation, communication and dealing with law enforcement.

Infrastructure and operating system security: These classes cover how to configure infrastructure such as networking and operating systems. Different operating systems have different settings and options that IT and DevOps teams need to set up securely. Network devices, load balancers, and storage all need to be implemented with security in mind. These classes may cover managing enterprise environments, software update processes, password management, and related topics.

Reverse engineering malware: Some classes cover reverse engineering malware, including website code, network behavior, bytecode, and assembly language. Students may learn how to analyze infected Word, PDF, and other documents. Instruction may cover reverse engineering tools like disassemblers, decompilers, hex editors, and debuggers. This class is most appropriate for someone who wants to work at companies that sell products that help companies defend against malware. Larger companies may also have security professionals on staff with reverse engineering skills. Cyber law enforcement professionals, pentesters, and incident handlers may also benefit from reverse engineering classes.

Auditing and Compliance: Some classes cover topics like auditing and compliance. These classes teach people how to perform those specific jobs and help companies stay in line with regulations that apply to their industry. Auditing classes focus on specific skills required by auditors that follow industry-standard auditing practices to assess whether companies meet industry regulations or follow best practices.

Security Architecture: This type of class teaches people how to apply individual security controls holistically to a system or enterprise. Students learn to create secure architectures that reduce attack vectors and attack surface. Security architecture considers cost, performance, compliance, deployments, logging and monitoring systems, disaster recovery, and business continuity. Students learn to design architectures that are more difficult to infiltrate and exfiltrate using the principle of defense in depth. Security architecture focuses on closing gaps and mitigating the risks in your environment that may lead to a breach, hopefully in an automated and metric-driven fashion.

Red team/Blue Team: Some classes include both attack (penetration testing) and defense methodologies, so people understand how the attackers are getting in and how to defend against those attacks. These classes may include aspects of all the other classes already mentioned.

Specialized classes: Some classes focus on a particular industry or solution, such as my cloud security class, which covers top cloud computing security concerns, architectures, and services. It also covers security fundamentals and most of the topics above at a high-level, but in the context of how they apply in a cloud environment. Other specialized classes cover virtualization, industrial control systems, or other vendor or industry-specific information.

Which class is right for you and your team?

The class that is right for you and your team depends on your objectives and what problem you are trying to solve. You may need to send different people to different classes. People may need a broad understanding of security, or very specialized knowledge to perform a particular function within your organization. Sending a team to training together that spans different job functions within the organization can promote cooperation, communication, and teamwork. Hopefully, the above summary helps you pick a class that helps improve the security knowledge overall within your organization, thereby informing better cybersecurity decisions. Each decision will either increase or decrease your cybersecurity risk. Better decisions reduce overall risk.

14
TESTING YOUR CYBERSECURITY

How do you know your security controls are working? How do you know someone hasn't made a configuration error, or that your team has the knowledge to implement security controls effectively? How can you evaluate whether systems are devoid of security flaws? Besides understanding the answers to those questions, organizations may require security control testing to obtain new customers or comply with industry or government regulations.

Organizations should periodically validate that their efforts to implement cybersecurity are working using penetration tests, audits, or assessments. Although your teams may be working diligently to implement secure systems, gaps may exist due to lack of training or knowledge of cybersecurity threats, or mistakes. The other risk is that an insider may be intentionally misconfiguring systems. Having a separate internal team or third party test your systems can help you find gaps and misconfigurations you might not otherwise discover. Additionally, sometimes, just having a person with a different perspective analyze the systems helps find things that your team may otherwise miss.

Companies can test systems for cybersecurity weaknesses using different levels of validation and testing. Penetration tests, assessments, and audits all involve activities to validate security. The evaluators provide a report back to the company on the findings — and hopefully also the mitigations (things you can do to fix the problems they found). You have various options for testing the effectiveness of your cybersecurity controls.

Cybersecurity audits

A cybersecurity audit tests a set of controls to see if and how the company has implemented them. The controls may be defined externally by a particular standard, or the auditors may extrapolate a set of controls for the audit from those standards or internal policies. ISACA (the Information Systems Audit and Control Association) defines a cybersecurity audit as follows (ISACA, 2019):

> The objective of a cyber security audit is to provide management with an assessment of an organization's cyber security policies and procedures and their operating effectiveness. Additionally, cyber security audits identify internal control and regulatory deficiencies that could put the organization at risk.

For example, do you encrypt data at rest? Do you protect and rotate the encryption key? An audit may or may not get into the details as to whether or not a control is effective. They often tell you if you have the control — yes or no — based on interviews and reviewing system reports. Some may go farther into testing systems, but sometimes auditors are not given direct access to the systems themselves. The other point to keep in mind is that auditors do not have time to check everything, so they typically select sample systems to evaluate. The process by which auditors select systems, processes, or teams to evaluate hopefully helps find some of the riskiest systems in your organization. They may base these selections on the type of data stored and known potential mismanagement.

Sometimes auditors hire a subject matter expert (SME)[220] to come in and provide technical expertise to help formulate the questions and controls the auditors then inspect and test. For example, as a SME on an audit, I helped a company evaluate some of their SaaS (software as a service) systems. The company wanted to know how well they were protecting their data that employees put into third-party systems. Since they were unfamiliar with cloud technologies, they wanted someone who could explain the technology and risks and find potential weaknesses they might have otherwise missed.

Auditors follow industry-standard best practices for their profession, though each company may implement its audits in different ways. There are different types of audits, as well. Sarbanes-Oxley,[221] which includes a cybersecurity component, is an example of an audit mandated by regulations in the United States. Other countries have their own cybersecurity regulations companies must follow. Companies may also perform internal operational inspections[222] to see if people are implementing cybersecurity best practices and following internal policies.

Cybersecurity risk assessments

Cybersecurity risk assessments are similar to audits but may go a step farther to try to determine the effectiveness of security controls and the impact of the risk. Instead of just asking if a company implements encryption, an assessment may look at whether the implementation and overall architecture of systems prevent breaches. As already explained, just having encryption doesn't prevent someone from reading your data. Organizations

---

[220] Subject Matter Expert https://en.wikipedia.org/wiki/Subject-matter_expert
[221] Sarbanes Oxley https://searchcio.techtarget.com/definition/Sarbanes-Oxley-Act
[222] Operational Audit https://en.wikipedia.org/wiki/Operational_auditing

need to understand how and when the data may reside in an unencrypted state, such as while a system is processing it in memory, and who might be able to access it at that point. Additionally, if keys are not protected or decryption permissions are too broad, the encryption does no good.

NIST (National Institute of Standards and Technology) characterizes a risk assessment as follows (NIST, 2012):

> The purpose of risk assessments is to inform decision-makers and support risk responses by identifying: (i) relevant threats to organizations or threats directed through organizations against other organizations; (ii) vulnerabilities both internal and external to organizations;(iii) impact (i.e., harm) to organizations that may occur given the potential for threats exploiting vulnerabilities; and (iv) likelihood
>
> that harm will occur.

Some cybersecurity assessment frameworks offer mechanisms for testing controls that are in place. Testing to see whether the control is in place and working is better than simply checking a box or asking open-ended questions where people say a control exists. For example, the Center for Internet Security (CIS)[223] offers benchmarks[224] for securing many different types of technologies. Each recommended best practice generally includes tests to determine if the control is in place or not. Although complete analysis of controls, risks, and security gaps still requires humans, evaluation using measurable and, better yet, automated tests help improve the effectiveness of audits and assessments.

A specific compliance requirement mandated by a particular industry or government organization may require an assessment. An assessor may be certified to perform a certain type of assessment related to compliance with a particular standard such

---

[223] Center for Internet Security (CIS) https://www.cisecurity.org/
[224] CIS Benchmarks https://www.cisecurity.org/cis-benchmarks/

as the Payment Card Industry (PCI) compliance standard mandated and administered by the Payment Card Industry Security Standards Council.[225] Organizations that accept credit cards as a form of payment must maintain compliance to continue to do so.

Other types of assessments may have other non-compliance related objectives. For example, an evaluation of the use of cloud systems can look for security gaps or assess on-premises architecture to look for security flaws. Some companies specialize in the analysis of cryptography implementations or industry-specific requirements such as health care systems (e.g. HIPAA[226]) or critical infrastructure like power plants (e.g. NERC[227]). Assessments may involve interviewing people, reviewing documentation, architecture and code reviews, evaluating system reporting, or running scans on systems to find vulnerabilities, among other things. The goal, as always, should be to try to find security gaps in your environment.

Penetration tests or pentesting

Penetration tests, sometimes called pentests or pen tests, involve intentional attacks to try to break into systems or show that an attacker could access sensitive data. This type of testing originated in the U.S. government. Security researchers started researching how attackers might exploit systems. The government started hiring what they called "tiger teams"[228] to break into systems to discover flaws. If the teams could break into the systems, then the government would know what to fix by patching systems or taking other measures to prevent the threat from occurring.

---

[225] PCI Security Standards Council https://www.pcisecuritystandards.org/
[226] Health Insurance Portability and Accountability Act
https://en.wikipedia.org/wiki/Health_Insurance_Portability_and_Accountability_Act
[227] North American Electric Reliability Corporation
https://en.wikipedia.org/wiki/North_American_Electric_Reliability_Corporation
[228] Tiger Teams https://en.wikipedia.org/wiki/Tiger_team

The primary difference between the penetration test and audits or assessments is the fact that the pentester is attempting to exploit system vulnerabilities instead of just showing that they exist. Instead of only scanning systems, a pentest tries to demonstrate how an attacker can compromise a system. They may illustrate how an attacker could pivot and get to other systems or exfiltrate data. A pentester may expose different types of vulnerabilities that allow an attacker to obtain administrative user credentials to get into systems or let one customer get into another customer's data.

An organization can get many different types of penetration tests at varying price points. Penetration testers operate in various ways to provide value to customers. Some companies may only perform a scan of systems and report vulnerabilities. These scans are generally the least expensive types of "pentest," though, in reality, it's an assessment, not a pentest. I have had companies approach me for a pentest after they tried to obtain SOC 2 (Service Organization Control) compliance with these types of pentests. The auditor instructed them to improve the quality of their pentests before they could meet the SOC2 requirements.[229]

I'm not going to get into the details of what SOC2 is, and as already explained, compliance is not the primary goal of this book. Just know there are different levels of penetration tests, and auditors may hold organizations to a higher standard if trying to achieve compliance with a regulated or industry standard. Although basic scanning services are not full-fledged pentests, they are a starting point for companies who are not taking any security scanning actions at this time or are new to penetration testing. Performing these scans in advance of a penetration test and fixing those vulnerabilities helps avoid lengthy reports with fundamental security flaws classified as high-risk findings on future tests.

---

[229] SSAE16 https://en.wikipedia.org/wiki/SSAE_16

Red teams

Some people also use a term called "red team"[230] interchangeably with penetration testers, but most security professionals distinguish between the two. The Army defines red teaming as a "structured, iterative process executed by trained, educated and practiced team members that provides commanders an independent capability to continuously challenge plans, operations, concepts, organizations and capabilities in the context of the operational environment and from our partners' and adversaries' perspectives."(U.S. Army, 2005)

The exact definition of a red team is another one of those terms often debated. I leave it to someone else to articulate or argue the difference between red team activities and penetration testing. For our purposes in this book, we are concerned with having someone test your security controls. Red teams are similar to penetration testers in that they exploit systems, though they may have additional functions or objectives. Sometimes the red team tries to be stealthy so as not to be discovered while carrying out a test to see whether the defenders notice them. They may carry out a test to achieve a particular mission. In contrast, a pentester may be trying to find all the vulnerabilities they can in your systems in the allotted time.

I am only speculating here based on statements made by other security professionals who discuss and debate such topics online. Likely companies that offer red team services charge more, hence the attempt for some companies to rebrand themselves as red teams. They are performing more work than someone who scans your systems and gives you a canned report. The service is more valuable than a simple scan, hence the higher cost. Still, a penetration test that provides a great deal of coverage also has significant value. Depending on your objectives, you may be more interested in finding as many vulnerabilities as possible, rather

---

[230] red team https://en.wikipedia.org/wiki/Red_team

than having a team achieve a specific mission or objective or testing your team's ability to spot an attack in progress.

Bug bounties

Some companies are leveraging bug bounties[231] in place of, or in addition to penetration tests. A bug bounty is a way for a company to allow security professionals to try to break into their systems and pay for individual findings. Sometimes companies run bug bounties themselves, like the Google Vulnerability Reward Program,[232] and allow security testers and researchers to submit the bugs to an internal team. Sometimes organizations get help running bug bounties from other companies such as Bugcrowd and HackerOne.

Benefits of a bug bounty program include the ability to have many different penetration testers and security researchers attack systems. The cost of individual findings could be lower than a full-fledged pentest. Penetration tests performed by the same people year after year may be missing new types of attacks. Each penetration tester may look at the system in a new way or try to find different things based on his or her personal experience and expertise. Running a bug bounty opens up your systems to many different individuals with diverse backgrounds and skills.

One downside of bug bounties is that you are opening up systems to unknown individuals who may have nefarious motives. They may not tell you about all their findings, and save something for another purpose, such as hacking competitions or selling it to someone who pays more. A recent hacking competition in Chengdu, China, called the Tianfu Cup exposed many zero-day software flaws in software like popular web browsers, mobile phone operating systems, and the underlying software for some

---

[231] Bug Bounty Program https://en.wikipedia.org/wiki/Bug_bounty_program
[232] Google Vulnerability Reward Program
https://www.google.com/about/appsecurity/reward-program/

cloud platforms (Cimpanu, Chrome, Edge, Safari hacked at elite Chinese hacking contest, 2019). Other security researchers I follow on Twitter[233] speculated that researchers save up vulnerabilities they find for these competitions. They also do not submit everything they brought to a competition if they can't get the top prize.

Many security researchers complain that some large organizations do not offer bug bounties or do not pay enough (Clover, 2017). Lack of market-rate payments leads them to invest less time into researching and reporting vulnerabilities to those companies. Some may also sell and expose vulnerabilities in other forums. Those with lower ethical standards may sell vulnerabilities on forums designed for such purposes — and sometimes the buyer is unknown. I just saw a Twitter post with a link to an ad selling credentials of an employee at a large Forex trading company. I'm not linking to that here for obvious reasons.

If you are going to offer a bug bounty, offer enough money to make it worth people's time. Doing so encourages researchers and testers to invest time and inform you of vulnerabilities — before someone else sells them to an unsavory character. Ideally, governments stop these sales, but it's difficult if the malicious actor is in another country. As we've seen, governments may also be *involved* in the transactions. As you can see from the prizes in hacking competitions, vulnerabilities can be worth a lot of money. Some zero-day bugs have gone for hundreds of thousands, even millions, of dollars (Marczak & Scott-Railton, 2016).

Another issue with bug bounties is that often, the people who participate in them don't make enough to earn a living if they do it full time. Often you hear about the people who make substantial amounts of money on bug bounties. They are few and far between. I do know someone who received $18,000 for a bug he reported to Google. However, it appears that bug bounty income

---

[233] @teriradichel https://twitter.com/teriradichel

was not sustainable because he eventually returned to his day job. The higher-skilled individuals want a guaranteed payout. Based on comments I've seen on Twitter and presentations at conferences, some security researchers use bug bounties to test out new exploits for penetration tests. Most perform testing in their spare time or implement automated mechanisms to find elusive exploits with high payouts.

One thing people who participate in bug bounties do is scan systems to find low-hanging fruit quickly. Then they drop out. The problem for a security researcher investing a significant amount of time into these bug bounties is that at the same time, another person could be reporting the same bug. Whoever gets there first gets the payout in most cases. That means a person could spend a great deal of time working on a bug and, in the end, get paid nothing. Some companies running bug bounties have reported they start with a lower payout to catch the small problems and then increase the payout over time. George Gerchow, CISO of Sumo Logic, told me they use a bug bounty and are very happy with the results using this approach.

Whether or not you offer a bug bounty, you should have an effective way for people to report vulnerabilities to your company. Even if you do not have a bug bounty, security researchers may contact your company to report a vulnerability and request money in exchange for their findings. You need to be ready for this so you can handle the report effectively. Be aware that once you pay someone for a finding, they might continue to search for bugs on your system and request payments for their services. If you do not pay, or threaten to sue the researcher, this could have adverse consequences.

Security testing tactics

When you hire someone to test your security, the first thing you need to do is specify what type of tests you want. If you are requesting an audit or an assessment, testers only perform manual reviews, interviews, or scans in most cases. However, when you are hiring someone to attempt to break into your organization, you need to specify what types of testing you allow or require. What is more important than whether you get a red team engagement, a penetration test, or a bug bounty is that you get the services you require to determine the security of systems to the level you desire. Testing may include the following, and sometimes companies and testers specialize in one particular aspect of an overall test.

Social engineering: One of my favorite examples of social engineering is in the talk *Spies Among Us* (Winkler, 2017). Ira Winkler explains how he used social engineering to steal plans for a nuclear reactor. Watch the video of his presentation, and you understand just how vulnerable humans are in the realm of security processes and procedures. Edward Snowden used social engineering to obtain credentials, as I explained earlier.

Physical penetration testing: This type of physical testing involves trying to break into buildings and facilities in person. Testing could include bypassing security controls like walls, locks, cameras, and alarms. Deviant Ollam explains this in a talk called *I'll Let Myself in: Tactics of Physical Pen Testers* (Ollam, 2017). (Warning: strong language for those that don't like that sort of thing, but for those making related security decisions — you need to know about these vulnerabilities.)

Network and wireless penetration testing: Network penetration testing may involve things like using network scanning tools and testing network equipment. For example, a network penetration tester may try to alter network packets or leverage flaws in protocols used by network equipment. Some types of wireless penetration testing require specialized equipment to intercept Bluetooth, Zigbee,[234] and other wireless protocols.[235] Car and door

---

[234] Zigbee https://en.wikipedia.org/wiki/Zigbee
[235] The Complete List of Wireless IoT Network Protocols https://www.link-

locks, sensors, and other IoT devices use these protocols.

Application penetration testing: Application penetration testing may involve testing web and compiled applications installed on computers, virtual machines, IoT, mobile devices, and other specialized equipment or vehicles for security flaws. Advanced penetration testers may leverage fuzzing, logic evaluation, and reverse engineering skills in addition to things like scanning for CVEs and OWASP Top 10 security flaws on web applications.

Cloud penetration testing: Cloud penetration testing involves testing cloud-specific security controls and seeking architecture flaws that an attacker could exploit. This type of test often includes some web application penetration testing. Cloud penetration testing can help determine if your company is vulnerable to misconfigurations, such as those that caused the Capital One cloud breach. Those performing cloud pentests need to continuously confirm that they are only attacking the systems of their client, due to the changing nature of cloud resources.

Regardless of the terminology or category you use to define your penetration test, make sure whomever you hire tests your most critical systems. If you are only trying to maintain compliance, the test might involve a different set of systems and types of attacks to meet whatever the compliance standard requires. Also, make sure the person performing the test has the capabilities you require to perform an effective test.

Evaluating the evaluator

As explained earlier, script kiddies use tools without understanding the details of how they work. When a particular penetration testing tool fails, the tester needs to figure out how to solve the problem. For example, many websites are using newer technologies that make it hard for a commonly used web

---

labs.com/blog/complete-list-IoT-network-protocols

penetration testing tool called Burp Suite[236] to capture all the links in the site. When I noticed that happening, I had to come up with another way to obtain this information. Tools are incredibly helpful, and I expect that updates are coming to resolve the issue. However, this is the type of problem experienced testers who have software, IT, and advanced training can resolve — they realize when something is not working and come up with a new solution.

Are certifications necessary? Certifications are certainly not a requirement, nor do they guarantee the person doing the work is highly skilled. In some cases, people cheat or are good at taking tests, but not good at doing the work outside of the testing environment. Sometimes tests are no longer aligned with top vulnerabilities and modern mechanisms for attacking and securing systems. Some people are too busy to find the time to take tests as they already have produced enough visible work to obtain industry acknowledgment of their skills. They do not need a certificate to prove their knowledge. However, certification shows that someone put in the time and effort and was able to pass a test that indicates they know the subject at hand.

Companies that process credit cards must be PCI (Payment Card Industry)[237] compliant, meaning they follow certain industry standard cybersecurity practices. Larger companies must have an assessor review their systems and networks to prove they are meeting the requirements. PCI version 3.2.1 compliance security controls and processes, section 11.3 requires an annual penetration test (PCI Security Standards Council, 2018). The PCI Security Standards Council offers a document called "Penetration Testing Guidance," which recommends some certifications — three of which your author has at the time of this writing. We'll see how many of these I maintain because they are expensive and time-consuming to obtain. I saw a Twitter post and comments by

---

[236] Burp Suite https://portswigger.net/burp
[237] Payment card industry https://en.wikipedia.org/wiki/Payment_card_industry

security professionals while writing this book that mocked one of the certifications (not one I have). People said the questions were not relevant or accurate. Although certifications are helpful, they are not perfect. They still demonstrate that someone took the time to learn and prove their knowledge so they can help if you are not sure about someone's qualifications.

Contracts

Before starting an engagement with an external company, both parties should sign a contract. With internal and external pentesters, each side needs to understand how pentests work, the scope, and possible outcomes. Allowing the tester to perform a broad array of tests provides more system coverage to find as many security problems as possible. An inspection also could potentially lead to system downtime because security testing involves sending malicious inputs to systems. If your developers have not adequately accounted for those inputs, systems might go offline.

Customers and pentesters alike want to have confidentiality clauses in agreements. Organizations do not want vulnerabilities disclosed to third parties. Testers may have proprietary tools, report formats, and methods they want to keep confidential. One of the things customers should check for in a security testing agreement that includes scanning or exploits is the appropriate level of insurance exists and reasonable care is taken in the testing process. The contract should define the scope, process, and methods of testing. A C-Level executive (CEO, CISO, CTO, or someone of equivalent authority) should sign the contract.

A recent case demonstrates something that can go wrong on a penetration test when the scope of the test is not clear, and the person who authorized the test lacked the proper authority. A pair of physical penetration testers broke into a courthouse in Iowa. They had the appropriate documentation (or at least documentation that had worked countless times before). They broke into one of the buildings. Unfortunately, the person authorizing the test may not have legally had permission to add that building to the scope of the test. Other problems may have been political rivalry within the Iowa government and judges that were unfamiliar with how penetration testing works.

Initially, the penetration testers landed in jail. Later some of the charges were reduced or dropped, but not all of them. Once a penetration tester has a criminal record, it may be hard for them to find jobs or continue in their line of work. That's why it's always crucial to obtain appropriate permission and make sure the scope and methods of testing are clearly defined.

You can read more about this story in these two articles: "Check the scope: Pen-testers nabbed, jailed in Iowa courthouse break-in attempt" (Gallagher, 2019) and "Iowa paid a security firm to break into a courthouse, then arrested employees when they succeeded" (Fazzini, Iowa paid a security firm to break into a courthouse, then arrested employees when they succeeded, 2019). A judge has since dropped the charges, thankfully (Krebs, Iowa Prosecutors Drop Charges Against Men Hired to Test Their Security, 2020).

Contracts should define the scope of the penetration test, the process used to carry it out, and who will be involved. The scope may include the type of tests, timeframe, and other details to ensure both parties understand what the pentesters are allowed to test, when, and how. Credentials need to be exchanged securely, and organizations may want on-going communication throughout the test. I explain these topics in more detail and describe what you might expect from a penetration test report on my cloud security blog (Radichel, Effective Security Testing, 2019). I have multiple posts on the topic of pentesting.

The assessment, audit, bug bounty, or pentest report

At the end of a security evaluation, or when a security researcher finds a bug in a bug bounty program, the security tester, auditor, or assessor gives you a report. Mission accomplished. You're done, right? Not quite!

Now you have some work to do. Undoubtedly, your report will have at least a few findings. What can you expect? Reports usually have an overview of the discoveries, calling out high-risk issues you should look into right away. Next, the report provides a summary of all the findings, followed by a complete list, details, and mitigations. The report will end with a summary and possibly an appendix with additional information.

The test should describe the scope, including what the pentester did and did not test. During some engagements, I discovered domain names I suspected should be in scope even though they were not. I contacted the customer to confirm whether or not they wanted to add these endpoints to the test scope. I noted that in the report. In other cases, bugs or other issues prevented testing certain aspects of the system. I also explain what I could and could not test in my reports if this occurs.

The findings

Now your job is to evaluate the findings, and for each one, determine your course of action. You have options as to how to address the results in the report. You may not fix every single one. Here are some strategies for dealing with the findings:

Fix: You may opt to take steps to correct the issue. If it is a simple code flaw, for example, you might assign a developer the task of fixing that flaw in the system. Sometimes the fix involves changing a process or training people. It may also include re-architecting systems. Some vulnerabilities may prove to require complex changes that increase the risk of downtime or other errors or takes a long time to implement.

Mitigate: Instead of fixing the finding, you may decide to mitigate it by blocking access to it, for example. In some cases, an organization may have additional information that the pentester did not know that results in a finding becoming a non-issue. Be careful with this one. Sometimes mitigating factors can be flawed as well, so whenever possible, fix the discovery. In some cases, it may be too costly or take too much time, so the company chooses this route.

Accept the risk: An organization may decide the cost to fix is more than the potential loss if an attacker exploits the vulnerability. The other reason a company may accept the risk is that the vulnerability is complicated to utilize, and it is unlikely an attacker would do it. Additionally, the vulnerability might only expose data that is already public.

Evaluate the risk and assign the work

If you get a report from a security test or audit and talk about it, but then never fix the problems, you are increasing your risk. Now multiple people know the vulnerability exists. Who had access to the report? Was it transmitted securely in every case? Where is it backed up? Make sure you have stored the document securely — but more importantly, make sure you mitigate any high-risk issues as quickly as possible.

When you request a penetration test, audit, or assessment, the report may produce work items unaccounted for in existing schedules. Be prepared to adjust schedules. Developers may need to set aside an existing project to have the time to fix the security vulnerabilities. The security team or IT department may require a reprieve from other duties to focus on an important security finding.

Make sure the person assigned to fix the problem has adequate security training to understand it fully and address it appropriately. Too many times, I have seen managers who don't understand the implications of security (or other) challenges. They assign work to someone who did not have the background to implement an accurate or sufficient solution. If you are not sure, have someone with more experience review their work before it is released. Hopefully, the report includes steps to reproduce the issue for most of the findings, so repeat the steps and verify the fix.

Be warned, however, that sometimes fixing the exact finding does not fix the entire problem. For example, on a penetration test, I reported a flaw in an XSS filter that was causing an XSS vulnerability on a website (XSS is one of the OWASP Top 10 website flaws — and I'm not going to explain it in detail here because I hope you can see my point regardless).[238] I included the links to the web pages on which I found the vulnerability. If the company only fixed the pages that I reported, instead of the underlying problem, any new pages added to the site would have the same issue. The XSS filter, which was supposed to *prevent* the type of vulnerability it caused, needed to be fixed or replaced. When I retested the site, I found the same vulnerability. I don't know why it still existed. The second time around, I tried to explain the issue with the underlying software library in more detail in case I had not explained it well enough the first time.

Address the root cause

Be prepared to provide funding or resources for other types of problems as well. While assisting with an audit, one of the observations was that the security team was too small to handle the additional work to use a security tool the company purchased. The result could be that the company needs to hire more people so the security team can effectively use that tool to mitigate threats. In another case, a company had software developers that were unfamiliar with the OWASP Top 10, cloud, or security best practices. Security training may be required to resolve these issues. Alternatively, responsibility for security decisions could be shifted to people with appropriate experience and training.

---

[238] XSS https://www.owasp.org/index.php/Cross-site_Scripting_(XSS)

What else might findings uncover? An audit or assessment may expose that people have too much system access, and this creates a risk for the company. An organization may need to determine if they want to accept that risk or restructure teams, permissions, or architecture of deployment systems to resolve this issue. This change is not easy because people generally do not like it when you remove their access to things they could do before. Include appropriate communication and explanations as to why the organization is implementing the changes in the roll-out plan.

Finally, executives should prepare to hear— and better yet, ask — what is blocking people from implementing cybersecurity best practices. The answer may be a lack of executive support or political issues within the company that make it hard for them to do their jobs. The organization may not be incentivizing, motivating, or training people adequately. It could be that the organization processes, workflows, or managers do not prioritize their assigned tasks in alignment with the organization's security objectives. Sometimes too many competing objectives may exist. Fixing these issues is the responsibility of the executives who have the authority to restructure organizations, define workflows, and set priorities. Often executives think that everyone is implementing systems securely. However, the reality (speaking from experience!) is far from it for the reasons I just mentioned. Sometimes employees don't tell executives things they think their leaders don't want to hear.

Measure the results

Don't wait for your next audit, assessment, or pentest report to find out if the vulnerabilities still exist. Track findings and measure whether the risk is going up or down within your organization. That is what the 20 questions in this book are all about: finding ways to quantify the risk by measuring cybersecurity gaps within your organization over time.

I have heard many penetration testers talk about how they come back year after year and perform a test — and the same problems appear on the report. Why is this? It could be that no one ever addressed the prior findings. After you read a security test report, how do you track that the specific vulnerabilities exist or not, month after month, year after year? Do you know if and when they were fixed, and by whom? Waiting a whole year to find out a vulnerability still exists is a long time for an attacker to find it!

15
PREPARING FOR CYBERSECURITY DISASTERS

Sure, you've heard it a hundred times before if you have spent any length of time in IT, security, or dealing with systems and data. *Back it up.* Make a copy in case something goes wrong so you can restore it all.

Backups are not simple

It sounds simple, but it's not. Creating adequate backups and the ability to restore systems efficiently requires forethought and planning, threat modeling, access management, encryption, and lifecycle management. Backup and recovery routines should be run by those who pay excellent attention to details. The one day your backups fail could be the day you need them. Who is monitoring and testing your backups?

I tell this story in my cloud security class sometimes as it applies to contracts, but it also applies to backups. I hired a company to do my server backups for one of my prior companies, Radical Software, Inc., a long time ago. I was new to running a business and new to managing vendors or systems. At some point, one of the Linux systems failed. I asked the company to restore it. They said, "Oh, we were only backing up the Windows systems." *What?* My contract specified backups. Nowhere in the contract did it state only to back up the Windows systems. I was so fortunate that my customer had a copy of their software in another location and did not sue me. Then I, in turn, would have to try to figure out what to do about the contract with my vendor.

This experience teaches some excellent lessons. Contracts are essential when it comes to vendor management. Don't make assumptions. Make sure it is in the contract. These assumptions also apply to the soundness of your backups. Even if you pay someone else to perform system backups, you want to take steps to ensure the backups exist and can be restored when you need them. Your organization should verify the implementation of backup systems like anything else.

Ransomware and backups

Some ransomware attacks also teach lessons about backing up data. Ransomware is malware that attackers get onto a system. Once installed, it starts encrypting all the files. As explained, encryption makes your files unreadable. The ransomware leaves a note telling the owner of the files how to pay a ransom, usually in bitcoins or some other form of cryptocurrency, to get the data back to a readable state.

Paying the attackers gives them more incentive to keep spreading ransomware. Also, the attackers do not always restore the files once payment is received. Insurance companies do not always cover the costs, and the number of ransomware attacks insurance companies pay out on is resulting in higher rates for everyone. Databreaches.net reports that in some cases, insurance rates have increased as much as 25 percent (Ikeda, Ransomware Attacks Are Causing Cyber Insurance Rates to Go Through the Roof; Premiums up as Much as 25 Percent, 2020).

If you thought ransomware was going away, it's not. The Dutch government sent out a warning about three types of ransomware affecting over 1800 businesses (Ilascu, Dutch Govt Warns of 3 Ransomware Infecting 1,800 Businesses, 2019). Brian Krebs wrote about how ransomware cut off nursing homes from medical records (Krebs, 110 Nursing Homes Cut Off from Health Records in Ransomware Attack, 2019). Ransomware recently infected a company hosting online applications for over 440,000 customers (Cimpanu, Major ASP.NET hosting provider infected by ransomware, 2019). These are just a few examples.

Having backups is a part of an overall strategy for protecting your systems against ransomware. If someone clicks a malicious link, opens a malicious attachment, or a system exposed to the Internet is compromised, you can say no thanks to the ransom if you have a way to restore your systems in the required time. Instead of paying the attackers, eradicate the malware, ensure that it cannot return by fixing the vulnerability that let it in, and restore the system and data. This process helps ensure you can avoid paying the toll. However, the solution is not as simple as it sounds.

Sometimes ransomware spreads from one machine to another, using a tactic called pivoting. The ransomware might even do this automatically and spread around the world by infecting one device from another infected device, as it did in the case of WannaCry. Other times it spreads internally within a company, as the NotPetya ransomware did. When the malware spreads, it could affect your backup systems if the network and credentials do not adequately segregate them from other systems. A sophisticated attacker might even target backup systems to take them out.

Additionally, in the Brian Krebs article I just referenced, he writes in the comments (Krebs, 110 Nursing Homes Cut Off from Health Records in Ransomware Attack, 2019):

> In nearly every story I've written about ransomware, the victim had a backup system of some kind. And nearly every story,

some readers comment that if they only had backups…

While there are ways of backing up key data that make it far more difficult for ransomware to fiddle with, the mindset that enables that kind of preparation assumes the target is also doing things like actively and continuously monitoring for intrusions. And those organizations are few and far between. Also, keep in mind that these ransomware purveyors usually don't pull the trigger until they've done what they need to do to escalate their privileges within the target to the point where they can do what the target's administrators can do, and that includes managing the backup procedures.

A better strategy is to prevent the ransomware in the first place, using the strategies in this book. Also, note that just having backups may not be enough. In some cyberattacks involving ransomware, the backups got encrypted along with everything else, because the attackers had access to the backups on the network from systems they had compromised. If attackers have administrative credentials, they can do anything the administrators can do, including encrypting backup files.

Disaster recovery strategies

What do you need to consider when it comes to backups? Disaster recovery (DR) and business continuity planning (BCP) are broad topics with many considerations, some of which are specific to your particular organization. You need to invest the appropriate amount of time and money to ensure your business maintains operations at an acceptable level so you can minimize losses and stay in business.

Businesses come up with objectives they want to meet in the event of a disaster to ensure they can maintain operations to the desired level. The organization then architects and deploys mechanisms to make sure they can meet those target objectives. Industry-standard metrics related to disaster recovery and business continuity include:

Recovery time objective (RTO):[239] the time systems can be in the recovery phase. For example, from the point the disaster hits, the system can be down 5 hours max.

Recovery point objective (RPO):[240] the point in time after an outage to which recovery processes need to restore data. For example, the systems recovery processes must restore systems to a point where only 5 minutes of transactions were lost.

Business continuity planning (BCP):[241] defines a set of plans for how an organization maintains operations in the event of a disruption.

Using these principles, architect backup systems and outline business processes to ensure your business remains operational in the event of a disaster. From an executive viewpoint, here are some of the most critical questions related to backups and disaster recovery you should ask:

Do we have disaster recovery and business continuity plans?

Find out if your organization has plans if you are not sure. If you are a top executive in the company, you should be involved in defining and carrying out these plans in the event of a disaster. Sometimes contracts require vendors to have DR and BCP plans.

When is the last time we tested our backups and failover?

Just having a backup process doesn't mean it works. You don't want to find this out the day you need the backups, as I did.

---

[239] Recovery Time Objective https://csrc.nist.gov/glossary/term/Recovery-Time-Objective
[240] Recovery Point Objective https://csrc.nist.gov/glossary/term/Recovery-Point-Objective
[241] Business Continuity Planning https://csrc.nist.gov/glossary/term/business-continuity-plan

Lesson learned! Test your backups the same way you are (hopefully) testing your website functionality and web application security.

Were they tested by someone very detail-oriented and separate from the people who implemented the backups?

Just like editing your written material, the person who created the backups might not notice their own mistakes. Sometimes, no matter how many times I read over something I have written, I don't see my typos. Then I read it later or have someone else read it, and the mistakes become apparent.

The same could be the case for the person who implemented your backups. They think they did everything correctly but didn't notice their own mistakes. Alternatively, the people who implemented the backups may not want to expose or admit mistakes. Worse, you could have an insider threat in your organization. Who tested the backups? Does this process have appropriate segregation of duties so different teams implement and validate different aspects of the system? Is the person responsible for testing detail-oriented and well-versed in testing and quality assurance?

How were the backups tested?

Did someone only check that files exist in a backup system, or did they fully restore the system? How critical the data and uptime are to your business dictates the level of testing required. At one large financial company where I worked, an exercise occurred every few months to completely fail over all operations from one physical data center to another. This process took many hours but not more than a day. Invariably systems broke, and processes failed, which led to improvements and verification of the backups, failover, and recovery process.

How long did the recovery take?

Some companies, like Netflix, test failover by terminating systems in production and validating that the system recovers automatically. Automation is much easier on a cloud platform like AWS, which is designed for this purpose from the ground up. Netflix can failover from one AWS region (a geographical location where AWS has data centers) to another in under 10 minutes (Kosewski, Ramanujam, Behnam, Blohowiak, & Probst, 2018). Proper architecture and planning help ensure your backups are available when needed, and recovery processes can meet the required objectives.

Were the systems tested, and was the data integrity validated?

Make sure that failover testing does not only involve executing the recovery process with no errors but also tests system functionality after restoring systems. Additionally, confirm that backup processes restored all data to the objective point with appropriate data integrity. Include the time to fix any corrupted data in the time it took to failover. Resolve the underlying issue that caused data corruption to prevent it in the future and improve recovery times.

Who has access to the backups?

Know what actions attackers may take with the credentials they obtain. Consider write-once, read-only backups such as is offered by AWS.[242] Ensure that a single set of administrative credentials cannot change permissions on the backups and delete the data. If they can, store those credentials away and require two parties to access them.

Consider where you store those credentials, so they are available in the event of an emergency. Always use MFA — correctly. Ensure you, rather than the attacker, encrypt backups. In a cloud

---

[242] Create Write-Once-Read-Many Archive Storage with Amazon Glacier https://aws.amazon.com/blogs/aws/glacier-vault-lock/

environment like AWS, you can also apply policies to that encryption key. These and other strategies outlined in this book help ensure your backups are not destroyed or accessed by attackers or malicious insiders.

Also, leverage network defenses to protect backups. Ensure proper controls are in place to prevent backup exposure to the Internet. Use network segregation to ensure that malware cannot infect the backups. Perhaps you have separate people on different networks, maintaining backups and production systems if you have a large organization and highly sensitive data.

Try to catch the problem sooner!

Although this chapter is all about backups, make sure you have the logging and monitoring in place to prevent having to resort to a massive disaster recovery process. Try to catch the problem before it becomes a disaster. Create well-architected systems that self-heal when possible and are resilient to failure. If you want to dive deep into that topic and see some metrics from AWS, check out this blog post by Adrian Cockcroft, former Cloud Architect at Netflix and now Vice President at Amazon Web Services, on "Failure Modes and Continuous Resilience" (Cockcroft, 2019).

16
SECURITY POLICIES THAT REDUCE RISK

Prepare yourself. I'm going to tell you some stories to show that your existing security policies are not working. By the end of this book, I hope to provide strategies that help you fix that problem.

What are your cybersecurity policies?

Most large companies have formal, written cybersecurity policies, standards, and processes. Someone, somewhere, writes down all the things people at the company must do to maintain system security and prevent data breaches. Sometimes these policies are sent to employees to read and sign. In some large organizations, I have had to watch training videos and answer questions. I'm about to tell you why all that is mostly ineffective. I'll also show you how to fix it partially here, but in further detail in chapter 22 which covers security automation.

Typically, an organization has different types of documents, which may include the following as defined by NIST:

Policies:[243] What people should do or not do.

---

[243] Policies https://csrc.nist.gov/glossary/term/information-security-policy

Processes:[244] How people must carry out the policies, step by step, to achieve the objective.

Standards:[245] The specific technology and configurations used to deploy systems, such as the specific configuration of a particular operating system.

Hopefully, your security documents follow security best practices like those defined in the NIST (National Institute for Standards and Technology) Cybersecurity Framework,[246] the Center for Internet Security,[247] or your favored and trusted security organization and references. You could use some of the recommendations in this book to help you formulate a policy. All these recommendations and best practices are great — if you can get people to follow them.

Keeping the policies up to date

After creating policies, standards, and procedures, they need to be updated when industry standards, technologies, and best practices change. I helped with one audit, where I found encryption algorithm standards were out-of-date. The vendors the company was using didn't even offer or support those out-of-date algorithms, but they were still in the policy. I'm sure it was an oversight, as the team was very competent. Make sure that if you have policies and related documents that you provide time to review and update them periodically. If policies are automated, even better as will be explained in a later chapter.

Policy updates include the changes required to operate in cloud environments. One company I worked with enforced specific open-source license policies. Then the company moved into the cloud, and all the developers started using the software tools

---

[244] Process https://csrc.nist.gov/glossary/term/process
[245] Base Standards https://csrc.nist.gov/glossary/term/Base-Standards
[246] NIST Cybersecurity Framework https://www.nist.gov/cyberframework
[247] Center for Internet Security https://www.cisecurity.org/

offered by the cloud provider. When I tried to get one of these tools into our software component repository, it got rejected by the legal team because the license did not meet their policies. I responded that this might be the policy but that thousands of developers throughout the organization were already using the tool and asked what they would like to do about it. As you can imagine, the policy was updated to match reality.

Communicating the policies to those who must comply

Once you have policies and procedures, communicate them to the people who are supposed to abide by them and carry them out. The security team might be passionate about security and sure that their policies are critical because that is the reason their job exists. Now consider the person who works in Human Resources and is trying to get payroll out the door to avoid lawsuits and government fines. How about the developers with a product manager asking, "Is it done yet?" every few hours? These people are focused on other priorities. It's not that they don't care about security. It's just that reading your eloquently crafted security policy document and memorizing every word of it is not high on their agenda.

The other thing is, even if they do read it, is it relevant and meaningful to that person? Do they know why it matters? Can they understand the technical jargon? And will they remember it 24 hours after they signed it? In most cases, probably not.

Examples of security policies that are not effective

Do the employees in your company know what policies and procedures exist? I remember a scenario at one company when my teammate and I had to meet with someone on another team. A meeting appeared on our calendar to meet this person, and we didn't know why. It was some new process, or so we thought.

I had been a development lead at the company for a couple of years. I finagled my way into being able to architect the systems our team developed without involvement by the architecture team for the most part. The architecture team pontificated a lot but didn't build things. I don't think the architects liked this either. However, that was their job — to talk about system designs instead of building systems. I didn't want to be on that team. I wanted to design *and* implement things that solved business problems at that point in my career.

Perhaps they gave me the boring projects initially because I was a woman, and then didn't pay attention to me as a result. I say this because I noticed that the men in the department got what seemed like the company deemed risky projects. Sometimes people acted nervous about giving a project to my team. One of those projects was a major cost-basis tax system upgrade. It went to production resulted in the least complaints during a tax season the company had ever experienced. I must give massive credit for this, in part, to my QA (quality assurance) team at the time who did an excellent job testing every detail and the teams that supported them.

I didn't mind the projects that other people considered boring, and over time our team proved that we could deliver. The projects dealt with massive data sets and interesting nerdy problems from my point of view — taxes for billions of dollars of assets under management and things like that. Eventually, my team went on to implement archiving customer service data into Salesforce, sweep accounts, cost basis, online account transfers, and dividend processing, among other things.

As our team proved to be successful, we got more challenging projects, and it seemed that more and more roadblocks appeared. Finally, I couldn't take it anymore and left, but that is another story and a topic tangentially covered in Chapter 22 when I write about a book by Gene Kim called *The Unicorn Project* (Kim, 2019). His story is my story aligns with my experiences. Too many roadblocks can actually stifle innovation and progress within an organization. However, as policies become less restrictive, it may lead to security problems as will be explained.

Somewhere along the way before that point, one of my team members and I had a meeting appear on our calendars. We went to the meeting. The person who scheduled it seemed very annoyed with us and told us that every project at the company goes through him before any system deployment. OK…the person I went to the meeting with and I didn't even know who he was. It turns out he was a really nice guy. However, no one ever communicated this policy to the people who were supposed to follow it, nor was it enforced. (It was also not the best policy because it created a one-person roadblock).

I later moved to another part of the company and worked on a new, critical initiative. I was concerned about security and asked if I could see the policies that were related to a particular technology implementation. The security professional said that I couldn't see those policies because they were confidential. So, how was I supposed to follow a policy I couldn't read?

In another case, when I asked for the security policies for an issue, the person responsible for that aspect of security sent me a link to a folder. When I looked in the folder, it contained about 50 documents. Yeah. Thanks. I'll get right on reading every last one of those documents.

In other cases, people know that they don't have to follow the rules because no one enforces the policies. I worked with someone who stated in a meeting that it didn't matter if we implemented insecure networking rules because no one was going to check. No one was paying attention. He got promoted that same year.

I witnessed a director state in a training session that security told him not to do something, but that we were going to do it despite these directives — in front of about 100 developers. This blatant disregard for security was running rampant in the organization.

This attitude could be because policies were previously so stringent that the organization had stagnated and couldn't move projects forward. The pendulum swung too far the other direction, and the organization later paid the price for this disregard of fundamental security principles.

I caught a person on the security team bypassing a network compliance tool that would roll back an unauthorized change in three minutes. He figured he could add the unauthorized rule, do what he needed to do, and get out before the rollback. "It's a stupid tool anyway," he said. "Anyone could get around it." I mentioned this to someone else on the security team. Nothing happened.

My feeling on this matter was that it was not necessarily the person's fault. He was assigned work that he was not adequately trained to do. He initially had free reign to build the networking, but he implemented it with Internet access directly to the hardware security modules that stored encryption keys for the company. I already explained in chapter 5 the risk associated with direct Internet access to sensitive data and secrets. He was annoyed when he lost his access to make changes, as people generally are when an organization takes away something they cloud do previously. Had he been properly trained, he would have likely implemented proper networking and maintained his access.

These are all examples that hopefully illustrate the problems with mandated but ineffective security policies. The organization needs to communicate the policies in a way that is relevant to each person's job and point of view. People need to understand why the policies exist to see the value and understand how it prevents a breach. They need to be reasonably easy to follow and not impede people's jobs. As already mentioned, I'll talk more about that in chapter 22 on automation. Finally, people need to know the repercussions of not following the policies — and the organization needs to enforce the policies from the top.

Who writes and enforces these policy documents?

I'm guessing most executives at the highest-level think writing and enforcing security policies is someone else's job; they are doing it, and if something goes wrong, it is that person's fault. Typically, everyone thinks that is the CISO's (Chief Information Security Officer) job if you have one. When the breach occurs, naturally, everyone blames the CISO because he or she is responsible for security. In many of the massive breaches, the CISO loses his or her job or gets demoted.

I mentioned in a blog post while writing this book that you may have noticed CISOs generally only stay in the same role for about two years. A subsequent article came out that backs this observation up with statistics. It states that CISOs remain in a role at the same company an average of just over two years (Cimpanu, Average tenure of a CISO is just 26 months due to high stress and burnout, 2020). Initially, a new CISO can blame anything that goes wrong on the person who formerly held that role. Then, they leave before they get blamed for the next breach. Often, they are in an impossible situation where they are responsible for security with no authority to fix problems. Security staff may want strict security policies, but then business executives force them to loosen them to enable companies to meet business objectives.

In reality, executives at every level who make poor security decisions due to lack of training or other priorities are responsible for breaches. Product managers who forgo security to get a product out the door and project managers who push developers to take security shortcuts to get things done are responsible. Managers who don't send developers to security training are responsible. Top executives who want a "yes" person in the CISO role instead of someone who stands up to them and pushes for secure solutions are responsible. If the CISOs say "yes" when they know they should not, *they* are responsible for the breach. Many CISOs are doing their best to balance cybersecurity with their own job security by not saying "no" too often.

Often, the CISO cannot fix the issue because they lack authority. How can we shift the blame in the next breach to the responsible party? First of all, the company needs a security policy that works and that it can enforce. The CISO needs to get support from the top executives to enforce the policy. The tools need to be in place to gather the appropriate metrics to determine if employees are following the policy or not. When someone does not abide by it, the organization needs to take appropriate actions to make it clear that knowingly and blatantly disregarding the policy has consequences. If you can't do that, forget the policy; it's useless.

Here is an example. A company had a policy to disallow the use of a particular service for corporate data. Let's say it was a cloud document sharing service called BigBin (a made-up company name for this example). The security team had a tool that could tell every time someone went to BigBin on the network. They could technically block access to BigBin using the corporate firewall.

The problem was that the company allowed the use of BigBin for personal use on the corporate network. Some of the top executives in the company used it for personal files and got annoyed when it was blocked. The corporate firewall can't tell whether the files sent to BigBin are business or personal data. Of course, the security team can get into those streams and see what the data is, but that takes a great deal of time. The security team doesn't want to have to access all that sensitive data and look at personal information — especially that of top executives. The intriguing thing was that this company had a network for personal devices. They could have let people use personal laptops, cell phones, or tablets to connect to the personal network and use BigBin. However, no one in the company even knew the personal network existed, and the company wanted to be kind to employees.

This example demonstrates an unenforceable policy. If you have an unenforceable policy, get rid of it. The top executives should sign off on it and accept the risk. If you have a policy but don't enforce it, this could increase the risk for the company. I worked with Mark Baker at SANS Institute while updating the cloud security class labs. He tells a story about how law enforcement showed up at his organization during a security incident. He had to explain to them why the organization wasn't following and enforcing a policy he wrote and was supposed to enforce. He said he learned the importance of policies that day!

When a CISO lacks authority to create effective policy, he or she needs to document recommendations and have the other top executives agree to accept the risk in writing. This approach is a well-known strategy in cybersecurity and something Ira Winkler talked about in the video I referenced in chapter 14 on security testing (Winkler, 2017). When the CEO overrides the recommendation of the CISO, that is acceptance of risk, which then becomes the responsibility of the CEO.

The CEO may think they can always assign blame to the CISO, but as I mentioned in the first chapter, many CEOs end up testifying to congress after a breach. Some of them lose their jobs. How can the CEO avoid this and shift responsibility in the case of a breach? Enforceable policies and metrics can help pinpoint security gaps and policy rule breakers so they can be dealt with appropriately. By showing who is blatantly disregarding the security policy after being provided explicit and easy to follow instructions, executives can not only shift the blame but hopefully improve training and stop the breach from occurring in the first place.

Tracking policy enforcement

Now comes the hard part. The organization needs a means of tracking who is and is not following the policy. I did not learn about risk tracking systems in the cybersecurity master's degree program. The ideas about monitoring and metrics in this book come from my own research and a background in software, financial systems, and security. I think we can reduce breaches by better measuring risk. Part of that has to do with policies.

The steps I propose are simple in concept:

- Understand what is causing data breaches.

- Create policies to minimize those root causes.

- Measure the gaps.

- Continually try to minimize the gaps (i.e., the risk).

The gaps are vulnerabilities that would let someone exploit your systems. The gaps are not missing systems in your system inventory or documents that need to have a classification assigned, such as "Secret," "Top Secret," or "Public." Those things may be helpful. However, when I say gaps, I mean something left exposed that an attacker exploits to get into systems and data, like a CVE, an open network port, or unencrypted data. The policies should focus on eliminating these vulnerabilities. The reports measure how well you have closed the gaps based on what is compliant with the policies or not.

Generate your risk reporting from the systems people already use to do their jobs, not something that creates extra work. Existing systems can generate the data used to produce a holistic report that summarizes overall risk within the company. If they don't, once you ask the questions, you can begin to revise systems accordingly to produce the data you require.

I have never seen a holistic cybersecurity risk reporting system, such as I am proposing, in the companies where I worked or have consulted. I did talk to a CISO of a major telecommunications company at RSA 2017 who had something that was a good starting point. He opened up a mobile app on his phone, showing that all the systems in his company had the latest software patches. He was from another country and could pull up this information wherever he traveled. That was impressive.

One of the reasons comprehensive, automated risk reporting may not exist to the level I am proposing is because no single product (that I know of) exists to do it. Those that exist only help with subsets of the problem or involve a lot of customization and manual effort. The other reason is that this tracking costs time and money to implement and maintain. Security teams don't usually have the resources or authority to track metrics to a meaningful level of detail. Sometimes they don't want to because no one will look at the information, and they feel it won't make a difference.

Although it is not easy, companies can start with basic things like the questions in this book to track the issues most likely to lead to a data breach. Get a macro view of risk at a high level with broad questions that cover the most common causes of security incidents. You can start with a spreadsheet. Over time the organization can build or buy tools that help automate reports.

Credentials exposed via malware, misconfigurations, or phishing are one of your most significant risks, as noted in previous chapters. One of the best ways to protect against these threats is to leverage MFA. Companies also need to know where all the credentials exist to enforce a policy that requires MFA on all accounts. Additionally, tracking all system access allows companies to deactivate all credentials when an employee is terminated or changes roles.

To ensure you know which credentials are active and what they can do, enforce a policy that the company's primary user directory must manage credentials for all systems for the company. Most companies use a product called Active Directory (AD). Single Sign-On (SSO) is the ability for employees to log into any system within the company with a single set of credentials.

One company I know measures how many applications within the organization implement multi-factor authentication (MFA) and SSO (Single Sign-On)[248] as a key performance indicator (KPI)[249]. These KPIs help companies measure how well their business is performing (Marr, 2012). If your policy requires that every application works with MFA and SSO, then track your applications and which ones do or do not implement it. Quantify the risk by calculating the financial loss that would result from a by a breach that leverages the vulnerable credentials. Consider the number of records and the sensitivity data that may be exposed.

It's hard to track all the applications across an organization manually. If possible, implement systems to track risk automatically as people do their jobs and deploy system changes. Track which applications are most risky based on whether or not they comply with security policies. A Cloud Access Security Broker (CASB) can help you find cloud and other applications you don't know are in use within your organization (also known as Shadow IT). Some CASBs associate risk scores with the services they discover but be prepared to hire additional people to configure and manage the system because they produce a lot of data. Implement systems that automate and streamline tracking applications in use and requests to use or deploy new applications. Add monitoring to deployment systems to track new systems coming online.

Distributed responsibility

Some organizations assign the responsibility of tracking whether or not applications meet security policy requirements to a business unit. The responsibility may roll up to a higher-level officer who makes sure each business unit is performing its duties. The individuals responsible for data at the business unit level are sometimes called data stewards. Auditors can validate that

---

[248] Single sign-on https://en.wikipedia.org/wiki/Single_sign-on
[249] Performance indicator https://en.wikipedia.org/wiki/Performance_indicator

security policies follow best practices and each business unit is following them.

When using this distributed approach to track the implementation of security policies, executives need to receive the appropriate security training. Executives may not know what security policies exist or what they mean. Generally, some collaboration must exist between the security or IT department and the business unit to ensure teams implement policies correctly. A business unit may mistakenly believe they have implemented policies correctly when they haven't because they do not fully understand the technical details.

Organizations need to clearly define who is responsible for creating and enforcing policies and accepting configurations that deviate from policies and best practices. Those responsible for enforcing and tracking adherence to policies and making decisions at any level need proper security training, especially if you are distributing this responsibility. Chapter 22 will provide more information about how to create guardrails using technology that tracks compliance with policies, generates data for risk reports, and still allows people to innovate.

17
SECURITY EXCEPTIONS ARE THE NORM

Ideally, a security team writes a perfect policy, and everyone follows it precisely because it is the right thing to do. Anyone working on or with a security team in a large organization knows this does not happen! Exceptions happen.

Rather than defining a policy and expecting everyone to follow it in all circumstances, plan for exceptions in advance. How will people request policy exemptions? Will a system automatically approve and track them? Will exceptions need to go through a formal evaluation and review? Will you have automatic exceptions for specific scenarios? Will exceptions last indefinitely or have a time limit? What if the reasons for which the organization granted the exception change?

Why do we have exceptions?

I would venture a guess based on personal experience, that most exceptions go like this: the security team blocks an initiative. A business executive complains up the chain to top executives about how much business the company will lose if they cannot get an exception. The security team talks about the potential for a security breach, the type of data that will be at risk, and how the attackers can break into the systems if the exception is approved. The executive makes arguments in business terms, while the security team makes arguments in technical terms. The business wins.

Another type of exception I've witnessed involved product managers who did not want to follow best practices they felt would take too long and delay getting a product to market. Although I've heard business executives say they want security and security is a priority, this does not seem to be the case in reality when you dig deeper into business decisions made at all levels throughout the organization. The security speech was just talk, whether the business executive meant it to be or not. The rhetoric coming from leadership was similar at the same time the security policy violations were occurring that I recounted earlier.

Often, at the same time executives are giving the organization speeches about security, teams get conflicting priorities with seemingly equal weight. People have to make choices. Completed features and more money are easy to see and measure. Security is more esoteric and typically not well measured or understood. The debates that lead to exceptions and disputed decisions are often not tracked. When a breach occurs as a result of an exception, it may be hard to determine the decisions that led to the security incident, who made them, and why.

Another type of exception occurs when a parent company forces a change in a business unit that has conflicting security policies. Executives higher up the chain override the business unit's more secure policies. The business unit may have little room to object, and the parent company may not consider it an exception. This scenario occurred at a company where I helped with an audit. An audit gives companies a chance to communicate these issues to higher-level executives.

Yet another common source of exceptions occurs when one

company buys another. Companies may not perform adequate due diligence on the security controls at the company they are purchasing. Sometimes executives accept the risk associated with security problems to get the deal done. In other cases, the acquired company is allowed to operate independently and outside the standard corporate security policies.

Integrating systems and processes upon acquisition of another company is always challenging. Having been through multiple acquisitions, I have witnessed this firsthand. I've seen exceptions to best practices in all these cases to move integration and business deals forward. There may be a good reason for initially accepting the risk, but a plan, with a deadline, should be created to fix it. Whatever the time estimate for that plan is, it likely needs to be doubled or tripled.

Sometimes those who want to make the purchase are overly optimistic when it comes to integration. Later, those same individuals push for cutting corners to meet stated deadlines. Security is usually the first to go, followed by a robust architecture that performs adequately. Integration needs proper testing, including security testing. Neglecting this results in system downtime or security breaches that impact brands and revenue, based on personal experience and publicly available information.

Marriott bought Starwood Hotels after attackers had already infiltrated the company's network. The breach lasted for years (Fruhlinger, Marriott data breach FAQ: How did it happen and what was the impact?, 2018). Possibly, exceptions were made to existing security policies, or perhaps due diligence missed something during the review process. It is sometimes hard to tell what happened based on publicly available information. We do know that the initial breach occurred before the acquisition, and it took years to discover. *The New York Times* writes (Perlroth, Tsang, & Satariano, nytimes.com, 2018):

The assault started as far back as 2014 and was one of the

largest known thefts of personal records, second only to a 2013 breach of Yahoo that affected three billion user accounts and larger than a 2017 episode involving the credit bureau Equifax.

The intrusion went unnoticed for four years by Starwood, which was acquired by Marriott in 2016 for $13.6 billion.

What about tracking exceptions created by vendors accessing company data? Are your vendors following your security policies? Vendors may have a completely different set of security policies and may thereby increase the risk to your business.

Evaluating the risk posed by an exception

Is it wrong to choose business over security when approving an exception? It makes sense that a company would forgo the extra effort to implement security if the security policy creates excessive expenses and delays. If a business doesn't make money, it may not survive much longer.

A problem exists, however, when those who grant the exception do not correctly evaluate the risks and costs associated with the decision to forgo best practices and security team recommendations. In some cases, the better choice for the company is to implement security. However, the calculation of potential loss may not be accurate. The proposed security control may not have been the most cost-effective solution to the problem. A more in-depth analysis may indicate that the overall improvement of security processes and systems would be beneficial when evaluating security holistically throughout the company.

When evaluating a particular exception, were all the potential costs and losses included? Is the cost of implementing proper security more or less than potential losses? Remember to consider the value of stolen intellectual property, infiltrated executive communications, and lost business opportunities while dealing with the breach. Understand that insurance may or may not cover the losses. Consider the much more significant issues in that post related to national security and privacy. If companies do not proactively improve in these areas, governments may step in, and companies are going to face more costs and delays due to increased regulations and fines. Weigh all these potential costs against the cost of implementing proper security instead of allowing an exception.

Cumulative Risk

Those responsible for reviewing exceptions often do so on a case-by-case basis. Organizations need to consider the cumulative risk of many exceptions. Each one increases the chance a company may face an attack or breach, or accidentally expose data. Tracking exceptions throughout an organization helps determine whether the overall risk is going up or down. The increasing risk may indicate a systemic problem.

Tracking security policy compliance should include deviations from those policies in a quantifiable manner. Each of these exceptions should have an associated risk metric. If you have ever read a penetration test report, you may have noticed that the report lists the highest risk items first. Tracking risk associated with exceptions helps you determine where to focus remediation efforts. Quantifying risk is not a perfect science, even with the formulas that help you do so. However, some of the information I have provided throughout this book can help you better understand the threats and associated risks. Using that information, you can perform some simple measurements.

Calculate the potential losses from the risk. No matter how fancy the formula is, it is always subjective and dependent on your organization and the data you store. Hopefully, you have someone who can make an honest attempt to give you an idea of the potential business risk and loss associated with an exception.

I have been in meetings where someone attempted to get a group in agreement by quantifying a decision with numbers. As soon as I entered the room, I knew what was going on. The executive wanted to take a course of action even though I and others had called out security deficiencies with a particular choice. He created categories to evaluate the options, including security and other business factors, and put weights on each. As he took each step to build his metrics, he looked around the room and said, "Right?"

I knew this was an exercise designed to obtain agreement on the desired outcome. By this point in my career, I knew better than to try to sway opinions in such a meeting. The meeting had a specific objective, and dissent would be futile and career-limiting. However, I had probably already limited my career by calling out the security flaws in the desired option in the first place. I nodded with everyone else. "Right." When he got to the end of his analysis, he said, "So we all agree this is the better choice, right?" Everyone in the room nodded. It was obviously the best choice because numbers don't lie. Right?

Alternatively, I could have walked up to the board and slightly altered the weights on a few categories like security issues and flipped the result. I just wanted to get the meeting over with, so I could leave and do something that would be a better use of my time. If people are doing funny math with your risk analysis, it's not useful.

That's why I wrote the questions in this book. They are straightforward ways to quantify cybersecurity and reduce risk at a high level by eliminating some of the most common causes of data breaches. There are nuances and details associated with each question. Still, you can track the questions and eliminate the gaps you find without doing complicated risk metrics and arguing about risk scores, weights, and other subjective matters. I hope the questions are mostly simple enough to track in a way that eliminates obvious security risks such as administrative ports open to the entire Internet.

Tracking exceptions

Here is an example of an exception. Let's say you have a rule that every website in your company must have a web application firewall (WAF)[250] and a Content Security Policy (CSP)[251] with a particular configuration protecting it. You don't need to know what those are to understand this example but know that they help protect websites from vulnerabilities that allow attackers to break in.

Further analysis may prove one system is less risky than others because it is hosting public, static content. It has no forms where an attacker can input malicious characters or content. A static website consists of files that do not have any way for end-users to input data or alter page content. They are read-only files people can download that pose minimal risk because all the content on them is public already. Since the data on the site is publicly accessible, none of the attacks the WAF or CSP protects against are applicable.

For example, an SQL injection attack[252] is used by attackers to steal data from databases. No database exists in this case, so this attack is a non-issue. The site does not have any authentication. It is updated manually. When you scan your site for vulnerabilities using tools like Burp Suite, it warns you if you do not have a CSP, CSRF tokens, HSTS, and XSS headers. These are things you can implement to protect your website from various attacks.

A student in my class scanned the current iteration of my website, and it got an F because I don't have all those headers on my site.

---

[250] Web Application Firewall (WAF)
https://www.owasp.org/index.php/Web_Application_Firewall
[251] Content Security Policy
https://en.wikipedia.org/wiki/Content_Security_Policy
[252] SQL Injection Attack https://www.owasp.org/index.php/SQL_Injection

However, all those attacks they protect against do not apply to the current iteration of my website. This analysis is one of the things a pentester has to know when testing websites — what matters and what doesn't. Some of those things protect against attacks that won't make a difference on my four-page static website. If there's an attack against authentication that leverages cookies for session management and the site uses a different form of authentication, all those cookie attacks don't matter.

Continuing our example scenario, let's say the company wants to avoid the time and cost of implementing the content security policy and WAF. As explained, they do not provide additional benefits in this case. The organization decides to grant an exception for this website, so the developers can save time and get the project out faster.

Track all such decisions for exceptions in your security compliance tracking system, as explained in the last chapter. It could be a homegrown system, an Excel spreadsheet, or an off-the-shelf program. You may also incorporate automated tracking into your deployment systems, a topic to be covered later. Include information like the following, and whatever else you may need to remember later. For example, you might need to recall why the exception is in place, whom to contact about questions, who is responsible for reviewing and updating related information, and when.

- What is the policy related to this exception?
- Why was the exception granted?
- Who requested the exception?
- Who approved the exception?
- Who is responsible for reporting system changes?
- Who is responsible for monitoring the exception?

- What is the associated risk (high, medium, low)?
- What are the potential financial losses?
- When was the exception granted?
- When does it expire?

You may also evaluate other risk frameworks and tools for tracking risk and exceptions. If you want a more formal way to manage risk, consider using the NIST Risk Management Framework,[253] or something similar. Some of these frameworks align with compliance requirements to help you determine if your systems meet compliance standards. However, the focus of this book is on fixing things that commonly cause data breaches, not just achieving compliance. If you use formal methods traditionally tracked with manual documentation, try to find ways to automate the processes and how you gather and report on risk metrics.

If you have defined secure base policies that prevent the top causes of security breaches, the risk associated with compliant systems is hopefully low. Then as you track cumulative exceptions, you can see if your overall risk level is going up or down within the company. You can also monitor the riskiest decision-makers, and which systems, departments, or lines of business pose the most risk to your organization.

Who creates the most exceptions?

When you track exceptions, include who is requesting and who is approving most them. These metrics provide insight to help improve the security and productivity within your organization.

First, in terms of security, you may have a culture or attitude in a

---

[253] Risk Management Framework (RMF) Overview
https://csrc.nist.gov/projects/risk-management/risk-management-framework-%28RMF%29-Overview

particular part of the organization that disregards security. The people making the exception requests or approvals may not understand the risk. Organizations can solve this problem with security training. It can explain why specific actions are risky, show how the vulnerabilities can be attacked, and include case studies, examples, and possibly hands-on labs. I have noticed that real-world stories help best convince people that security risks exist.

A repeat offender may be indicative of another problem: an insider threat or person inside your company whose intent is to steal your data. Foreign governments and criminal organizations offer people money to steal secrets (Kahn, 2017). The person may be using exceptions to create weaknesses and pilfer data from the company for personal use or at the behest of a third party. Alternatively, the person is a risk to your company due to complete disregard of security policies because they think they are unnecessary, or to an inability to follow them.

Exceptions may have other causes that are not the fault of the individual requesting them or generating security violations. A high number of exceptions could be the result of system or network architecture problems that get in the way of people doing their jobs, a misaligned security policy that doesn't work for newer technologies, lack of communication, or a problem with a system or process.

At one company, I got a notice at some point that I had several security violations while using a particular system to make production changes. The root cause was that the company moved me into a role in a hurry to resolve other business issues and provided no training on how to use the system. No one told me that exceeding the time limits set in that system would produce violations. Other people were setting the time limits, and I hadn't even noticed them. Going forward, I was careful to make sure the time limits were appropriate and that I followed the rules.

Everyone had at least *some* dislike for that system, by the way. It was cumbersome to use. No one understood how to get requests into the system without receiving a rejection message, typically devoid of a coherent explanation of why and how to fix it. If you track things like violations of policy and rejected requests, you can find underlying problems that are hurting release cycles and creating angst within your organization. By monitoring exceptions, you can delve into the details to find issues preventing people from working efficiently and look for alternate solutions to improve productivity.

Change management[254] is helpful, and the point when systems change is an excellent time to look for security exceptions. Still, an organization needs to align the process with workflows and technologies so people can follow it with a reasonable amount of effort. Hopefully, your change management system has a decent user interface that is intuitive, and communication on how to use it is clear. Alternatively, you can let people make changes who have the authority to do so, monitor changes, and block unwanted changes automatically.

Expiration

It is a good idea to set a time limit on an exception, especially if it is a risky one. Perhaps an urgent business need exists to migrate or integrate systems due to an acquisition. Set a deadline for resolving the issue that caused the exception.

Periodically review exceptions and perhaps warn people when exceptions are about to expire. Creating a risky exception for something temporary and then never following up to see if it got fixed may lead to an indefinite risk that slipped everyone's mind. Items that organizations set aside to fix later are known as technical debt.[255] Sticking with the analogy, technical debt rarely,

---

[254] Change management https://en.wikipedia.org/wiki/Change_management
[255] Technical Debt https://en.wikipedia.org/wiki/Technical_debt

if ever, gets paid. Put a deadline on it to have a chance that upon revisiting the matter, someone fixes it. When an organization has many exceptions of a single type or category, it may have an opportunity to correct an underlying problem that resolves many exceptions at once.

System changes

Changes to systems and technology are another good reason to set an expiration on an exception. Let's say that the static website I used in the earlier example got moved to a WordPress content management system so the pages could be updated more easily. The pages now contain dynamic content with data stored in a relational database. The developers added a few web forms. WordPress systems have an administration interface for updating content that has been subject to many CVEs over time. When developers implement this system change, the exception is no longer valid. The website implementation should then include a CSP and a WAF.

Who is responsible for revisiting the exception when someone is implementing this change? Will the system developers remember that this site has a security exception? What if a new team is implementing the WordPress site? By having a periodic review of exceptions, hopefully, you can find this issue before an attacker does.

Better yet, use a different architecture to protect the site. That's something I explain in my cloud security class because, at the time of this writing, WordPress and other content management systems are a source of e-skimming breaches. I was recently at a presentation by the U.S. Secret Service and FBI explaining how attackers break into the content management system (CMS)[256] and insert malicious code into the website. The code then steals credit

---

[256] Content Management System
https://en.wikipedia.org/wiki/Content_management_system

card information as people check out on e-commerce web sites. Perhaps you have a policy for securely implementing CMS architectures. A periodic review of exceptions helps you find these types of changes where the risk associated with the exception has increased.

Exception metrics

Organizations may want to track security in a more quantifiable way. The process for doing so is never perfect, and a crafty attacker finds their way around security at some point, no matter what. However, implementing some form of tracking basic security hygiene helps organizations eliminate fundamental security problems and makes it harder for attackers to exploit systems. As organizations improve and mature, attacks require more skill and cost attackers more time and money. At this point, they may even choose to go after easier targets.

My background is not only in security but also software engineering. I've worked in industries and on systems including financial, sales, telecommunications, publishing, healthcare, marketing, retail, oil and gas, manufacturing, security products, venture capital, and many others. I see many ways businesses can leverage automation and deployment systems to improve security and risk reporting. I've helped companies improve marketing metrics, reduce system errors, align technical and business processes for greater efficiency, and improve system performance. I did this using improved communication, training, automation, architectural and user interface changes, and analytics.

All these improvements involve aligning systems and processes and leveraging metrics to measure performance. Organizations can use these same strategies to improve security outcomes. Create security systems and processes that align with business workflows and policies. Track metrics that help pinpoint problems so the organization can fix them and reduce cybersecurity risk.

18
DEPLOYMENT SYSTEMS — DANGER OR DEFENSE

This chapter is related to DevOps and DevSecOps. However, it is not specifically about those particular trends. The things I am going to write about in this chapter apply to systems and processes that existed before those new terms ever existed. Unfortunately, those terms have been misinterpreted, reinterpreted, abused, overused, debated incessantly, misunderstood, despised, and cartoon-ized in less-than-ideal ways [i.e., unicorns excreting rainbows (Cheslock, 2015)]. Instead of using trendy words with varying interpretations, I'm going to write about something tangible. Consider how your software deployment systems will either be a powerful gateway for an attacker or one of your best defenses. For the purposes of this book, I define deployment systems as the applications and processes you use to make changes to software in your organization.

Prior chapters covered security policies, exceptions, and how tracking them helps organizations evaluate risk. Other topics included penetration testing and security assessments. I explained how CVEs could be a source of attacker infiltration, proper use of encryption, and problems with secrets and passwords.

Your deployment system can help you with all those security concerns. It is one of the best tools you have to prevent security misconfigurations and non-compliant software deployments.

Unfortunately, the same tools you use to deploy applications and update software throughout your company may also be leveraged by attackers if they can gain access. Read on to learn how attackers leveraged deployment systems in infamous data breaches and massive ransomware attacks. These systems may have security flaws like anything else. All the security controls I have explained to you need to be applied to them as well. A weak security architecture allows attackers to obtain access via pivoting from other vulnerable systems on the network. Hopefully, your network does not expose your deployment systems to the entire Internet!

The topic of this chapter is related to all the modern development buzzwords in the following list because they involve deploying software. Depending on whom you talk to, you may get a different opinion of what each word means. I've never been a fan of arguing about definitions. I much prefer to fix problems and get things done. I'm not going to try to define all these worlds but mention them here so that people understand that what I am writing about in this chapter is related to them. Modern software and IT operations terminology include:

- DevOps
- DevSecOps
- GitOps
- Rugged DevOps
- All the other -Ops

- Site Reliability Engineering (SRE)
- Continuous Integration (CI)
- Continuous Delivery (CD)
- Infrastructure as Code

If you want to know my impression of DevSecOps, it's in the blog post I mentioned earlier. (Radichel, My History of DevSecOps, 2019). It explains the first time I heard the word DevSecOps at AWS re:Invent and how I got involved in cloud security. I started the Seattle AWS Architects and Engineers meetup which, at the time of this writing, has over 3,000 members. I then helped Capital One move to the cloud. After that, I joined a company as Cloud Architect and later became Director of SaaS Engineering. At this latter company, I was able to architect and direct implementation of a secure DevOps pipeline (deployment system) based on lessons learned at Capital One. I incorporated into it many of the concepts in this chapter. Now I teach people what I learned and continue to research and implement in my cloud security classes.

What does your deployment system have to do with cybersecurity?

Do you remember the movie *Office Space*?[257] If not, I'll tell you the critical part of the plot that relates to what I am about to tell you without giving away the whole story. Two guys come up with a plan to steal money from a company in small increments. They figure that siphoning a small amount of money from the company will go unnoticed (just like the weird guy talking about his stapler that no one realizes still sits in the basement). I'll let you watch the movie for all the rest, but that idea of stealing small bits of money at a time that go unnoticed has a real-word story behind it.

The system they use to try to perform this theft is called the TPS

---

[257] Office Space https://www.imdb.com/title/tt0151804/

system in the movie. Ironically, I worked on a software application named TPS — the transfer processing system — at one company. I often wondered, as I addressed the integrity of the system and fixed numerous reconciliation issues, if the name was indeed a coincidence. If anyone is concerned, those related systems and operations no longer exist. Another company bought those accounts and moved them onto their own platform.

Somewhere along the process of building and deploying financial systems, a developer can leverage rounding or a reconciliation error to move a tiny amount of money to an alternate bank account. The insignificant individual amount goes unnoticed. However, over time, with millions of transactions, the thief makes off with a large sum. *Computer Capers*, by Thomas Whiteside, explains how a programmer at a mail-order company diverted money from rounded-down sales commissions into a phony account for three years before he was caught (Whiteside, 1978).

Whenever I worked on financial systems, which I did for the majority of my career in one way or another, I was always concerned about the deployment systems in large companies. What if someone altered my code and inserted an attack like this, or something else, and made it look like I did it? Then when the crime came to light, I might be blamed! Don't ask me how my mind thinks of these nefarious scenarios. I don't know.

At one company, I watched how changes took place on deployment nights when a bunch of developers, operations, and QA people would have to stay in the office on a Friday night until about 2 a.m. The person who typically ran the deployments was one of the most organized people I know and thoroughly impressed me. She was also exceedingly calm under pressure when something went wrong and knew a lot about the systems so she could fix those problems.

However, I thought about how easy it would be for someone to alter the code during the whole convoluted process, some of which was manual. Updating configurations often resulted in fat-fingering (typing the wrong thing), which, in turn, resulted in failed batch processing jobs the next day. One time a database administrator (DBA) was supposed to make a backup of the database before deploying the new code and backed up the databases in reverse by accident. Other times, operations people copied files to the wrong location. One time, in a pre-deployment meeting, the operations person exposed a production password to everyone in the room. Anyone can make these mistakes. They are all preventable with secure deployment systems, automated deployments, and proper testing in advance of the code release.

Even worse, one time code deployed as part of one of my projects was altered during an evening deployment to remove a database integrity check because something broke. I was the development team lead on that project, but I wasn't present at that particular deployment. Luckily the person in charge of QA contacted me about it the next time we were in the office. He asked if it was OK, and I immediately fixed the integrity check and restored the proper control to make sure invalid data could not enter the system.

Removing this data integrity check would allow the insertion of an invalid beneficiary for an account in the database. The beneficiary is someone who gets money from an account after someone dies. A fake call could be placed to the support team, providing instructions to release funds to the beneficiary on that account, and the wrong person would get the money. I am not saying this was the intent of the change, or that the person was not just trying to fix the problem, but that was a possible outcome.

It always amazed me that in many companies I worked for, though not all, they were generally concerned about the security of the code they were deploying. However, they paid little attention to the security of the processes and systems that deployed changes. So many manual steps occur where someone can insert rogue code or subvert intended controls. Someone who can alter the logs can change them to point the blame to the wrong person. If too many people can modify the code, someone could insert a last-minute unnoticed change. A person could alter previously tested and approved code on its way to the live systems if integrity checking is not in place to ensure that it can't happen.

It could be that changes are so minute that no one ever notices. The person who intentionally did something could claim it was an accident, and they didn't know better, which may or may not be accurate. Of course, someone can make a mistake or be unaware of what they are doing and add your organization to the list of those who have exposed billions of records via misconfigured database security controls. Regardless of the reason for the mistake, try to prevent it. Architect your deployment system in such a way that these types of things cannot happen, as much as possible.

Massive attacks via compromised deployment systems

In addition to all the potential internal security problems related to deployment systems, you also have to worry about external threats. If you have automated your deployments, that automated system is a prime target for attackers. Attackers can use that same automated deployment system that helps you move code into live systems if they can obtain access to deploy malware.

After thinking this was a possibility for years and trying to tell people about it and having them ignore my concerns, I finally got a real-world example. Right about the time I started the SANS master's degree program in 2013, the Target Breach occurred. The attackers stole 40 million credit cards and accessed the personal data of 70 million people (Krebs, The Target Breach, By the Numbers, 2014). The CIO resigned, and the CEO lost his job.

Target did not have a CISO, but some people told me they had many security controls in place. The problem could be that the company purchased security products without enough staff or training to take full advantage of them. Though I don't know what the Target internal network looked like, from my research, it appeared to be lacking network segmentation and well-architected internal security infrastructure. Their staff could have potentially used additional training based on their response to the breach, or at least better coordination with their outsourced security operations center (SOC).

It's easy to criticize after the fact, and from the outside. I'm sure the staff did the best they could in the given scenario. Security is challenging, so I am not going to judge anyone who went through a breach, because I've been there myself. I didn't know anything about security when I faced my first security incident. I never figured everything out because I had no security training, and I knew no security people. I just knew I had eradicated the attackers and prevented them from coming back. I learned how to defend my website, but I wanted to know more about how breaches were happening. That's why I took the master's program. I used this breach as a case study and wrote a white paper about it called "Critical Controls that Could Have Prevented the Target Breach" (Radichel, Case Study: Critical Controls that Could Have Prevented the Target Breach, 2014).

When I started researching for the paper, I didn't know it involved a deployment system, because many news articles had published misinformation and blamed the HVAC system. In reality, it was a sophisticated breach with many factors. However, the point related to this chapter has to do with the fact that the attackers got access to the system that pushed software updates to the point-of-sale (POS) systems. If you've never seen a POS system, it is often a Windows machine with some extra software. It facilitates credit card processing at retail stores and other places that accept credit cards.

Because the attackers got access to the automated deployment system, they could quickly deploy malware all at once to many systems at stores just as the company could do itself. They did so right in the middle of the holiday season rush. This breach led to one of the most infamous cases of stolen credit cards and news organizations widely reported on it. I was not happy about the Target breach. However, I did feel vindicated that my suspicions about the essential nature of deployment system security were accurate.

The Target breach cost close to $300 million according to their financial statements and a report by The SSL Store (Lynch, 2017). Also, the breach occurred in 2013, and that article from May 26, 2017, cites a settlement that same week. That means Target was still spending time and money resolving issues related to that breach four years later.

The NotPetya attack I described previously also involved a deployment system and facilitated ransomware attacks that took down companies around the world. As a reminder, this breach occurred when attackers reportedly associated with the Russian government infiltrated the software update systems of a company called MeDoc in Ukraine. MeDoc produces tax and accounting software used by just about anyone who pays taxes or does business in the country. All those customers of MeDoc need to get software updates. The attackers leveraged the fact that all these systems would allow the MeDoc systems to transfer files to them. The attackers inserted malware into the update process. The malware then automatically tried to pivot on the internal networks of those companies and replicate itself on other systems.

If you think about how malware works, as I wrote about previously, it typically needs to deploy files. A system that is allowed to deploy files to all the other systems in your environment or send updates to many systems from a software vendor is a prime target for attackers. You need to ensure that you have a robust security architecture for your deployment system and proper security controls. That's a complex technical topic that is outside the scope of this book that I cover in my classes.

How your deployment system can improve cybersecurity

Now that you know how important it is to secure your deployment system, I want to explain how it can help you with security. These concepts apply anywhere, not just on platforms like AWS that have built-in automation. The degree to which you can automate deployments depends on 1) the skills of the people deploying the systems, 2) the automation capabilities of the systems you are deploying, and 3) the time and money you can invest.

You may not have much control over the systems that deploy code to your systems from your software vendors. For example, you can't change the way Microsoft and security vendors send software updates. You can implement the controls I've already mentioned for network security to make sure these software updates are coming from a valid source. You can create an architecture which limits how many machines are involved in downloading the updates and then distribute them internally to expose fewer machines to the Internet. Additionally, you can assess your vendor's security practices and their deployment processes.

You have a lot more control over the systems that deploy the custom code your developers write. Your organization can automatically improve compliance with your security policies by automating these deployments, testing them, and building in security checks. At the same time, if you correctly architect and automate your software deployment processes, you can mitigate many of the security issues I have written about in this book. You cannot prevent all architecture and design flaws that lead to security vulnerabilities. However, you can prevent basic misconfigurations and blatantly insecure code from entering your environment.

Think of your deployment system as the luggage scanner at the airport. No one gets into the airport without the security staff at the airport scanning their luggage. It creates a delay, but it is necessary to ensure people do not bring illegal substances onto the plane, or in the worst case, bombs or weapons. People may grumble when there is a long line for the luggage scanning system at the airport. However, they understand the risks associated with letting everyone bypass the scanner, so they put up with it. The scanner is automated, though humans are involved. When people are following the process correctly, things go smoothly, and the scanning doesn't take too long.

What slows down the scanning process? For one thing, the requirement to take off shoes and belts and take laptops out of bags takes time. Some people can bypass this by getting TSA Precheck in the United States.[258] They still must have their bags scanned, but they don't have to take some of the extra steps that those who have not gone through the same background checks and identity verification. You can do the same thing in your deployment system. Figure out which deployments are low-risk, and they can potentially go through faster checks. Higher-risk deployments may need more scrutiny. You can even take the analogy one step further and select random deployments for additional inspection.

The first step in creating a deployment system that can check security is to have a way to deploy software in an automated fashion. It should be easy for people to use and get their jobs done. You should test your deployments the same way you test your system functionality, so they do not fail when they run in a production environment. Production refers to the environment in which your live systems run, not those used by your development and QA teams. The deployment system needs to support building from your development environment to your QA (quality assurance or test) environment without changing the code the developers have written. Then when it goes from QA to production, it should never be altered. If your teams cannot do

---

[258] TSA Precheck https://www.tsa.gov/precheck

that, the system design is incorrect.

Once you have an automated system, you need to ensure that no one can bypass it. If anyone can, all the issues I mentioned above could still happen. When people get frustrated with the automated system, they take shortcuts and bypass it. Then you may end up with security errors, which defeats the whole purpose of the system. Of course, you may need to fix an urgent issue at all costs, and an exception is necessary, but this should require appropriate approvals. Refer to all the information I provided on handling security exceptions.

After you have everyone using the secure, automated system, the security team can inspect the deployments and the logs without interrupting developers to find any security issues. They could do this in the development, QA, and production environments. The security team should be monitoring the deployment system logs along with all the other logs they track. Look for anomalies and suspicious access patterns. Ensure that people are not misusing or bypassing the deployment system. If violations occur, assume good intent. The developer or QA person may have made a simple mistake or didn't understand why what they were doing created a security risk. If you see many violations, there could be a problem with the whole process, as explained in chapter 17 on exceptions. It could be that the development and QA teams need additional security training.

If (when) the security team finds things that are out of compliance, undesirable configurations, architectures, or insecure code, they can work with the team responsible for maintaining the deployment system. They can build in security checks that prevent those issues. Implement security checks carefully, so they do not impact productivity and block everyone who is trying to deploy code. Implement them iteratively. Ensure developers and the security team are working together to create checks that work in a correct, developer-friendly manner. Test with a small group of developers well-versed in security before rolling out blocking security checks to an entire organization.

The security checks in your deployment pipeline can include things like scanning software for security flaws, blocking known CVEs, automated basic penetration testing, and disallowing risky configurations. Adding security checks to deployment pipelines can be very tricky because if implemented poorly or in a draconian manner, this becomes a bottleneck on your productivity. If implemented too loosely and people are free to deploy whatever they want, you have an increased chance for security problems. Someone who can balance these objectives and has proper training should be involved in prioritizing and making security decisions.

Avoid rules that are too strict and end up completely blocking productivity. Blocking work from proceeding often generates animosity in your environment and causes people to try to bypass security controls. You need controls that provide feedback to train people as they make mistakes, prevent egregious errors, and track compliance and risk. At the same time, you need to allow people to make progress and build things. You need to know when and where to block configuration errors throughout the system, and when to create an alert to let someone know that they made a mistake instead of barring them from deploying code. Additionally, security scanning needs to be inserted at the correct point in the process because some of the scanning tools can take a long time to complete. Don't execute them every single time a developer checks in a small piece of code in the development environment.

Communication is another crucial factor. If you apply the rules and don't clearly explain what people need to do to fix the problem, the result may be a great deal of conflict. I used to say to my DevOps team, "If people are complaining, we aren't building it right, or communicating properly." The communication could involve training when people don't understand why the controls exist. Going back to the airport analogy, once you're aware of the importance of scanning your bags, you are more likely to put up with it. I often tell security people, the reason you are having problems with developers is that you're telling them what to do, but you're not explaining why.

Finally, the thing most companies aren't doing is tracking and measuring the risk associated with applications via their deployment and change control systems, if they have one. Your deployment systems produce a great deal of information that can help you monitor and reduce risk in your organization. Many organizations make assumptions about the risk of software deployed within their organizations, rather than measuring it so they can do something about it. Use your deployment system to help track changes that are compliant with security policies and security exceptions.

Change control systems can track changes and corresponding details. You might require people to enter data into a system specifically to track changes. Alternatively, you may allow automatic deployment of changes that are not blocked by security checks. The details about who wrote the code and why they wrote it are in ticketing and source control systems, and the deployments link to those details. Make sure wherever you track this change information, it cannot be altered at any point after deployment by the people making the changes. If exceptions exist, document those. Use all of the data you gather during code deployments to help generate risk reports.

Use your risk reports to determine which high-risk items you must fix right away. Then work to reduce those risks. Chapter 23 provides more information about risk reporting.

Scanning is not perfect!

Be aware that these tactics are not perfect. Someone with purely malicious intentions can obfuscate the code, which is a fancy way of saying they try to make it hard to tell what the code is doing.

For example, you may want to block any JavaScript commands that use the keyword eval:

```
eval(something)
```

You configure your scanner to flag any code that has the word "eval" in it. The attacker can change the code to write out and execute the eval command instead, which has the same result:

```
document.write("e" + "val")
```

This pseudo-code gives you the idea of how code can trick your scanners. If people are doing this intentionally, the policy should enforce the appropriate repercussions.

There are many variations of code that can bypass that same check. Another example would be to turn malicious code into bytecode.[259] If your scanner spots an ampersand (&) in code, and a web browser processes the code, the attacker might use a character code instead. SQL injection or XSS scanners may look for invalid characters. In that case, the person attempting to bypass the scanner "escapes" the character so the scanner can't find it. An escape causes the system to process a special character as a regular character instead of something that is part of the executable code. If the scanner adds a check to see if someone added an escape character, the attacker will simply add another to bypass that check. Whatever type of validation is used to look for bad characters can typically be bypassed by some form of obfuscation. That's why it is better to validate the input conforms to a specific format rather than try to block bad characters.

The other thing you'll need to worry about is malware that your developers don't know the author embedded in the third-party code they downloaded off the Internet. In some cases, fake code libraries with names and links very similar to valid software trick developers into including malicious code in their deployments.

---

[259] Bytecode https://en.wikipedia.org/wiki/Bytecode

Additionally, sometimes they use software because it helps them get things done faster. However, that software embeds things like key-loggers, cryptominers, and credit card stealing malware. Your scanners may or may not catch these issues, depending on how crafty your attacker is.

As you can see, it's going to be challenging to count on scanners when someone is genuinely out to insert something malicious into your code. Defense in depth is important because, at some point, an attacker may bypass one of your defenses. All the controls together in this book will help you thwart their attack.

Another issue with scanners is that some of them produce a lot of false positives. You need someone on staff who understands what is and is not a security problem. Sometimes people brush off issues they don't understand. In other cases, the scanner produces too many false positives, and you spend an inordinate amount of time looking through them. At this point, someone may disregard the scanning and proclaim it is useless. It's not, but it does need tuning to eliminate false reports without eliminating actual problems. I'll be explaining false positives and false negatives in chapter 20 on the efficacy of your security products. In other words, how well they perform their intended function.

Application security resources

There are many great books, resources, and security classes that can help if you want to know more about application security. Here are a few you can use. One of the most well-known is the *Web Application Hacker's Handbook* (Stuttard, September 27, 2011). This book helped me when I was creating my homegrown WAF (Web Application Firewall). The OWASP Top 10 is a great resource, along with many other projects and tools provided by the Open Web Application Security Project. PortSwigger, the company that makes the Burp Suite software, has a Web Security blog that offers many resources for pentesters and developers interested in application security.[260] My friend Tanya Janca, aka

@SheHacksPurple, has a blog series called *Pushing Left Like a Boss*.[261]

Building your deployment pipeline

The information in this chapter is a high-level executive overview of things you need to think about when creating a secure DevOps pipeline. A secure deployment architecture involves multiple types of systems that serve different purposes. One system stores code, another stores application components, and secrets are stored in different vaults for different parts of the software development lifecycle (SDLC).[262] Another system executes deployment jobs. Architects need to think about how to deploy to all environments securely. In my class, we explore misconfigured cloud systems, attacks, and how deployment strategies can prevent security issues.

If you want to know more about deployment systems from a developer perspective, Gene Kim's book, *The Unicorn Project* (Kim, 2019), explains how and why developers and QA teams are bypassing security and IT teams in many cases to get to the cloud. The story demonstrates how a top executive might support an initiative to get things done in ways that thwart old-school security review boards and gatekeepers. Rob Cummings is a former employee of Nordstrom, one of the biggest high-end retailers in the United States. He talked at my Seattle meetup about how he got the company to start using AWS. He convinced some top executives to let him try out the cloud on his corporate credit card. That is how companies are getting to the cloud despite the concerns of security teams and without their input.

I also heard from another person at a large organization when their security team was trying to implement security controls after

---

[260] Port Swigger Web Security Blog https://portswigger.net/blog
[261] Pushing Left Like a Boss https://medium.com/bugbountywriteup/pushing-left-like-a-boss-table-of-contents-42fd063a75bb
[262] Software Development Life Cycle https://en.wikipedia.org/wiki/Systems_development_life_cycle

the fact. This attempt to add security into a cloud environment that did not incorporate it into the initial architecture and deployment led to production incidents. Although he understood that it was necessary, it was also frustrating.

A related issue when companies don't think plan out cloud migrations is that every developer tries to build their own deployment system. The security team has no insight into deployments, and you end up with way too many systems to reasonably manage. The consolidation process then becomes challenging, speaking from experience. Try to get in front of these transformations and get the right people involved in advance.

The software rebellion in Kim's book resonates. It aligns with stories I hear from students in my classes. This exact scenario is happening in many companies today. I highly recommend that security teams read *The Unicorn Project*. If you don't want this to happen in your company in the manner described in the book, get security teams and developers working together to resolve deployment issues. Instead of having a security team that always says "no," try to get them involved with the DevOps team to help design a secure deployment pipeline. Get those developers some security training. If possible, send security teams and developers to security training together. If you train developers about security, they will become some of the best security people in your organization.

19
HOW WELL DO YOU KNOW YOUR VENDORS?

First, a caveat: I wrote this information from the perspective of an organization in the United States. If you live in a different country, the same concepts apply. However, you may have a different viewpoint regarding the location where vendors create and test products and services. Each country has its own political and national security concerns. I reference many news articles because it shows where the data comes from for the points I'm making. However, people in different countries may have different perspectives.

Due diligence on vendor products and services

Your security team hopefully invests a fair amount of time in determining the best policies to keep your organization secure. They take action to ensure that everyone follows the policies, which may include security awareness and training. Then your company hires a vendor or buys an application or security appliance. Maybe a department starts using a cloud service. That vendor gets access to your data. Is that vendor following the same security policies as your company? How do you know?

Do not make assumptions that just because a vendor has a larger organization, more significant customers, or sells security products that they are following best practices. Create a way to evaluate vendors to ensure their security policies align with your own if you are allowing them to have access to your data. If you have critical requirements that mitigate the most significant cybersecurity risks to your organization, make sure your vendors meet those requirements. Ensure your contract with each vendor enforces any agreement to maintain security standards, policies, and best practices.

Vendors and data breaches

Before I explain things to consider when managing risk and vendors, I want to explain why this is an important topic. Let's start by looking at some ways the use of vendor products can and have impacted the security of their customers. When I use the term vendors, I mean anything you buy from a third party, including products, applications, cloud services, or outsourcing IT and security functions. All these vendor interactions can be a point of entry into your organization's network and data.

Attackers sometimes go after vendors that work for or sell products to an organization instead of going after the target company directly. The recent Cloud Hopper campaign, initiated by APT10 in China, is one of the most devastating examples of this type of attack. APT stands for Advanced Persistent Threat.[263] This acronym refers to the kind of organization that may target a victim for years, persistently and in stealthy ways, to obtain information or perform some other type of cybercrime.

APTs are not out for a quick smash and grab to get your data because you exposed it to the Internet. They target victims carefully and go to great lengths to achieve their objectives. Although the term "advanced" exists in the name, they may use

---

[263] APT https://en.wikipedia.org/wiki/APT

very simple attacks on organizations that fail to implement cybersecurity best practices. APTs are often associated with foreign governments or organized crime groups. The topic of APTs and their tactics could fill an entire book. Many stories exist about elite methods to target specific individuals, such as CEOs or government officials. However, in many cases, fundamental cybersecurity practices can limit their ability to achieve objectives.

Some companies outsource IT functions to MSPs (Managed Service Providers) or security to MSSPs (Managed Security Service Providers). Often these companies have remote access and the ability to update the software on client networks. Previous chapters covered risks related to networks, data exposure, and deployment system risk. Also, some vendors store data for their clients.

News agencies, security, and government organizations in the United States and some other countries have accused China of stealing intellectual property for years. A data breach doesn't just cause loss of customer information and fines related to laws like GDPR. The attackers may be stealing your core business value.

The purpose of this chapter is not to prove Chinese espionage exists. You can decide that for yourself. Regardless of who is attacking vendors, a breach may expose your data. Please refer to the following articles about an attack called Cloud Hopper. These articles demonstrate what happens when attackers get access to vendors and, in turn, the data of that vendor's clients.

- "Inside the West's failed fight against China's 'Cloud Hopper' hackers" — *Reuters* (Stubbs, Menn, & Bing, 2019)

- "Uncovering a new sustained global cyber espionage campaign: Operation Cloud Hopper – PWC and BAE Systems" (PWC, 2017)

- "Chinese Cloud Hopper Operation Targets Top Tech Providers in World" — *CPO Magazine* (Lindsey, 2019)

- "Tata Consultancy, NTT Data Among Cloud Hopper Attack Victims: Reports" — *CRN* (Johnson, 2019)

- "UK and US blame China for Cloud Hopper industrial espionage campaign" — *NS Tech* (Williams, 2018)

Other cases exist, not explicitly tied to China, where a compromised vendor allowed an attacker to obtain access to an organization's data. In some cases, the data was stolen; in others, attackers deployed ransomware. New ransomware is not only asking for money to get it back but also threatening to expose data unless the target pays a ransom:

- The breach of a German IT provider affected Airbus, Porsche, Volkswagen, and Toshiba (Winder, Airbus, Porsche, Toshiba And Volkswagen Data Stolen In Massive Breach -- What You Need To Know, 2019)

- "Ransomware at Colorado IT Provider Affects 100+ Dental Offices" (Krebs, Ransomware at Colorado IT Provider Affects 100+ Dental Offices, 2019)

- US-Cert warned of increased attacks on managed service providers and cloud providers in 2019 (US Cert, 2019)

Vendor products — especially network and security

Besides the consultants working for your company or vendors that store your data, be careful with the products you bring into or give access to your environment. Assess any network-connected devices, laptops, and especially network and security appliances. That includes devices that plug into USB ports and network cables. Some types of malware are known as trojan horses[264] because they hide their true intent from people who install the software onto their systems. However, any equipment you install on your network could do the same. Last year at DefCon, a security researcher announced he was manufacturing fake lightening cables designed to compromise systems (Cox, 2019). A lightning cable is used to connect Apple products[265] like iPhones to host computers.

Besides the product itself, you need to understand how and when the vendor will access the equipment and if they are doing so securely. A friend of mine, Bill Knaffl, who helped review this book, told me this story:

> There are *many* cases — some very personal to me — where a vendor was planning to do an upgrade or troubleshooting a huge, expensive piece of equipment. The equipment was on the main program network, and as soon as the vendor plugged in an undeclared laptop to the device, our SOC detected C2 traffic. To avoid that, we ended up creating a policy to disallow this and added it to all support contracts. When vendors arrived, they had to sign off on the policies.

Not only do you have to worry about the equipment itself. You also have to be careful how and when the vendor is accessing that equipment. Do you monitor vendors when they are accessing your network or performing support activities on your products?

Currently, I primarily perform penetration tests on cloud environments and web applications. However, I do have experience and certifications in on-premises and network pentesting. In my advanced pentesting class, I sat next to a woman who tests on-premises primarily in corporate environments. She said she always gets in, usually via the printer. I had a student in a class that formerly worked for a government

---

[264] Trojan horse https://en.wikipedia.org/wiki/Trojan_horse_%28computing%29
[265] Lightning Cable https://en.wikipedia.org/wiki/Lightning_(connector)

agency that made claims about printers. I haven't been able to verify, but let's just say printers may have facilitated some national security initiatives.

Have you inspected your printers lately for vulnerabilities? Do you ask your printer manufacturer how they secure the hardware and software? Do you monitor the network traffic coming out of your printer? I sometimes unplug mine from my network when I'm not using. In a large corporate network, you aren't going to unplug your printer. Hopefully, you are monitoring it and all other devices sufficiently for unexpected network traffic. One article reports that 60% of enterprises suffer data loss due to printer security (CISO MAG, 2019).

Of course, many IoT devices likely exist on your network. Do you ask the vendors who sell you these devices about their security policies and developer training within their organization? Do you request pentest reports? Do you ask them about their supply chain and manufacturing processes? Numerous accounts of compromised IoT devices exist. From cameras to routers, to fish tanks, anything connected to your network can be a source of infiltration, exfiltration, surveillance, denial of service (DoS) attacks, or pivoting. Here are a few examples of cases where IoT devices caused security incidents:

- *The Mirai botnet explained: How IoT devices almost brought down the internet* (Fruhlinger, The Mirai botnet explained: How teen scammers and CCTV cameras almost brought down the internet, 2018)

- *VPNFilter malware infected 500,000 consumer routers all over the world* (Goodin, arstechnica.com, 2018)

- *How a fish tank helped hack a casino* (Schiffer, 2017)

I provided numerous reports about APT 10 attacks and the link to the Chinese government. What about devices manufactured in

China? Could those have embedded malware? Of course. Do they? I don't know. I haven't researched them all personally, but the possibility exists. If you are buying hardware and software manufactured or tested in China, you might choose to perform additional due diligence. If the Chinese government was involved in APT attacks, what stops them from embedding malware in devices manufactured in China? What about patches, updates, and on-going maintenance?

If you are in China, you might be worried about the converse when purchasing equipment from a country that you have proof has stolen proprietary information in the past.

Just because a company has a U.S. office doesn't mean they create hardware and software in the U.S. A recent case against a U.S. company called Adventura Technologies, Inc. claims that the company illegally sold Chinese goods. The company claimed they manufactured the equipment in the U.S. An article states: "Officials say Aventura's actions endangered military personnel on U.S. Navy ships and military bases by selling them Chinese products with known cybersecurity vulnerabilities." (Zialcita, 2019)

Be especially careful when purchasing networking and security products. Do not assume that every developer at a security company has had security training. Also, be aware that some may be very good at security, which could be good or bad depending on their motives. The people who are good at security could insert code that the people who are not so good at security won't catch or understand. Speaking from experience and accounts by other people, every developer in every security company is well-versed in security.

Also, understand that large companies have many different products developed by different teams and lines of business. For example, I know some of the people at Cisco who develop Stealthwatch Cloud and follow people who work on Duo on

Twitter who are very knowledgeable in security. When I worked at a security vendor, teams working on products often operated independently from one another and had different skill sets and approaches to building and deploying systems. For this reason, I wouldn't apply my knowledge of the expertise of the people on a particular team to the entire company. Evaluate different products from the same company independently, as the processes and security knowledge of the development and test teams may vary. Additionally, the location where a company manufactures and tests each product may be different.

Even if an organization develops a product in the U.S., it might test the product in another country. Understand the supply chain for products you buy and the laws in related countries. If an organization tests a security product in China, laws exist that may require a citizen to hand over information to the Chinese government — possibly including security vulnerabilities discovered in the product. It is not that person's fault if that is what they are required to do by law in their country. In fact, foreign nationals working abroad might be required by law to give information to the government of the country where they hold citizenship upon request. Be aware of these issues when you purchase products and how the device might be leveraged to obtain sensitive data.

An interesting debate ensued when Google produced the Titan hardware security key manufactured in China that competes with a YubiKey. The CEO of Yubico, who makes YubiKey, said the device had Bluetooth security deficiencies. (Novet, Google's new hardware security key was made by a Chinese company, 2018). Later, Google did announce a Bluetooth flaw and recalled the devices (Newman, Google Will Replace Titan Security Key Over a Bluetooth Flaw, 2019).

Google has one of the most competent security research teams in the industry — Project Zero.[266] I follow brilliant security researchers at many companies, but I also once worked on a security research team. I cannot tell you how all companies operate. However, just because a company has a brilliant security research team, don't assume everyone at the company has the same level of expertise. The researchers may or may not be involved in product development or influence the day-to-day implementation of products. You should still go through the process to vet the vendor, even if they have a world-renowned research team.

Why network products are so critical

Much debate has ensued over the use of products developed by a company named Huawei to facilitate the implementation of 5G networks. If you think about how network equipment works, all the data on the network flows through it. Some organizations design security products that perform the equivalent of a man-in-the-middle attack so they can inspect traffic and look for security problems.

That means they break the encrypted connection and decrypt the data so they can inspect it for security problems, and then re-encrypt it and forward it along. Even if a networking company is not selling a device for that purpose, the potential exists that they could do the same thing if they can break your encryption. They can also read anything unencrypted and insert attacks into any part of the traffic that is unencrypted.

As mentioned earlier, the Chinese government may force citizens and companies to share data with the Chinese government upon request. The CNBC article below states: "Huawei would have no choice but to hand over network data to the Chinese government if Beijing asked for it, because of espionage and national security laws in the country, experts told CNBC." (Kharpal, 2019) Many countries in Europe are debating the prevention of these products

---

[266] Google Project Zero https://googleprojectzero.blogspot.com/

from infiltrating their networks. Germany is debating whether or not to use devices from Huawei in its networks (Düben & Düben, 2020). Companies in Norway have decided against using Huawei citing security concerns (Nikel, 2019). China is threatening consequences for governments that choose not to use their equipment (Doffman, China Just Crossed A Dangerous New Line For Huawei: 'There Will Be Consequences', 2019).

Some of these are large and complex issues. Substantially vetting every product may be difficult for small organizations. Large companies can do more in-depth security due diligence that helps all the small companies that buy the same product and their customers. They can help find and report vulnerabilities so they can get fixed for everyone.

For example, Starbucks has WiFi hotspots in most of its coffee shops. If they thoroughly scrutinize their network vendors, all Starbucks customers that use Starbucks WiFi benefit. If Starbucks is lax, it potentially hurts customers. If companies that provide Internet connectivity like Comcast Xfinity scrutinize the security of devices that they give their customers, the company and the customers benefit. Citizens in countries making decisions about Huawei benefit from due diligence by experts in cybersecurity — not politicians. In the case of the network backbone in a country, these decisions have a significant impact on national security.

How to evaluate vendors

How exactly can companies evaluate vendors? The following steps help with this process. You may evaluate each vendor more or less extensively. Testing criteria and capabilities may depend on the size of your company, the sensitivity of the data you are storing, and your need to produce business value and complete projects. Taking any or all of these steps can help your overall security and push vendors to improve their security controls.

- Define your criteria

- Research
- Ask questions
- Request documentation
- Validate findings
- Review contracts and insurance
- Monitor

Define your criteria

The first thing you should do is define the criteria by which you evaluate vendors. If you do not specify this in advance, vendor due diligence may be inconsistent. The other advantage of defining criteria upfront is that you can provide a standardized process to members of your organization. Then they understand that the process is not arbitrary but is instead a process required for all vendors. You can also work to streamline that process so you can perform vendor assessments more quickly.

Once again, define and track exceptions. Some vendors may access sensitive data; others will not. You may have different levels of criteria and pre-defined exceptions for certain types of projects. For example, you wouldn't let a one-person company host your sensitive data. However, you might allow a small company with only a few employees or contractors to provide training or specialized consulting that does not involve sensitive data.

If you are not sure where to start when defining a list of questions and criteria for how to select vendors, you can start with the questions in this book. These questions are relatively basic but can get as nuanced as you like based on the supplemental information I provided about each. You can also use other standard assessment frameworks such as the NIST Cybersecurity

Framework, CIS Critical Controls, or the CSA CAIQ (Consensus Initiative Questionnaire)[267] to come up with a standardized checklist for vendor assessments.

Research

The first thing everyone in your organization can do before purchasing a vendor product or service is research. You can find a great deal of information about a company online before you even talk to them. You may determine after initial investigation that they are not a good fit and do not require additional research.

Some things I look at initially before I even consider buying a product include looking at who works at or runs the company and who the investors are. Where do these people work? What is their background? If it is a security or networking product, do they have security expertise? Where did they work previously? How long has the company been in business? Who are their other customers? Do they offer a list of office locations? Does it say where the company develops products and stores your data?

You can also look for statements and reviews from other customers, but be wary of false reviews, or competitor sabotage. As you probably know by now, there is myriad misinformation on the Internet! This information can be helpful but evaluate the source of that information as well and don't use it as your sole judgment on the quality of the company or service.

Look at any available documentation. You can evaluate the product documentation from the company on their website to find out any security information they have publicly available. Also, you can look for any security assessments, audits, or certifications they have, such as SOC2[268] compliance, CSA STAR,[269] ISO.[270] They

---

[267] CSA CAIQ https://cloudsecurityalliance.org/artifacts/consensus-assessments-initiative-questionnaire-v3-0-1/
[268] SOC2 https://www.aicpa.org/interestareas/frc/assuranceadvisoryservices/aicpasoc2rep

may also have other third-party review and validation of their security controls, such as penetration tests.

Read the news. You can easily search for news reports about the company by searching for the company name or product name in Google and then clicking the "News" tab. You can find information about security issues and the company as a whole, but just like the customer reviews, be wary of jumping to a conclusion based on a news article. Some who write about cybersecurity tend to sensationalize issues. Additionally, initial reports may later turn out not to be true.

Investigate the number of vulnerabilities related to the product or service you are using. You can use sources like MITRE's CVE database,[271] a site called CVE Details,[272] and US-Cert Advisories,[273] If a company has repeated, serious vulnerabilities, you may want to ask them about those vulnerabilities, and their internal software development training and practices. Note, also, that companies with no CVEs may merely not be reporting them. They may not have a bug bounty or mechanism for people to report vulnerabilities. At big companies, CVEs may be present in some products more than others. This example demonstrates again why you need to evaluate products independently.

Ask questions

After doing initial research, ask questions. Use the criteria you have defined to ask questions about the vendor's security controls that you could not determine from online resources. Document and track the answers so you can refer to them later. I have helped with audits where the auditors later requested those assessments

---

ort.html
[269] CSA Star https://cloudsecurityalliance.org/star/
[270] ISO https://www.iso.org/home.html
[271] MITRE CVE Database https://cve.mitre.org/
[272] CVE Details https://www.cvedetails.com/
[273] US Cert Advisories https://www.us-cert.gov/ics/advisories

to review them for consistency and accuracy. When asking questions, dive deeper if needed. Instead of asking, "Do you encrypt data?" ask the vendor what encryption algorithms they use, how they protect encryption keys, and who has access to those keys. Sometimes delving into the details reveals vulnerabilities a yes-or-no question would not.

Request documentation

Although your vendor tells you that they have specific security controls, request documentation to back up their claims. Try to get these things in writing if at all possible. Evaluate the documentation for completeness and accuracy. Sometimes documentation is out-of-date or missing the information required to evaluate the product or service thoroughly. Claims that vendors are not willing to put in writing may be suspect.

Validate findings

Validate the findings by testing, when possible. For example, if a vendor gives you a free trial, you may be able to pentest a product and evaluate the security controls in advance of purchase. If you have the expertise, assess the hardware as well as the software. You may be able to perform a security audit or assessment of the vendor environment yourself. Then you can determine first-hand if the claims the vendor is making are valid. You can interview staff and review product and service information at a deeper level. Sometimes when purchasing an expensive piece of hardware or software, vendors will bring in staff to help you get set up and perform your trial and testing. You can also compare new product results to existing products in your environment.

Some vendors may not offer free trials because they don't want competitors to reverse engineer their products. In some cases, the vendor does not allow access to their data centers for security reasons. One great example is AWS data centers. Amazon does not grant access to their data centers because people are only allowed access on a need-to-know basis. Some security professionals complain about this, but my response is if they are letting me into the facility, who else are they granting access? I like that they do not let every random person come in for a tour. How can you deal with situations like this where the vendor does not grant you access to validate security controls yourself?

First of all, if you are big enough, they let you in. The U.S. government did obtain access to assess GovCloud, the environment AWS set up for highly sensitive government data. Whichever company is more prominent and needs the relationship most likely obtains what they request. However, if you cannot gain access, you can request third-party audits, attestations, penetration tests, and certifications. Although you were not able to personally do the evaluation, you can look at the paperwork, who performed the work, and the quality of the results.

Contracts and insurance

With any vendor relationship, the responsibility for security controls may vary. Understand who owns each security control. AWS calls this their shared responsibility model,[274] and the other major cloud providers have adopted something similar. For each vendor, determine what security controls should be in place for the product, service, or work to be performed. Then define who implements and maintains each control. If necessary, go farther and determine how the vendor implements the controls, but be careful with defining specifics that may change over time. For example, instead of defining a specific encryption algorithm, state that encryption algorithms must be industry best practice or acceptable by NIST standards.

Next, make sure your contract addresses these responsibilities. I

---

[274] AWS Shared Responsibility Model
https://aws.amazon.com/compliance/shared-responsibility-model/

told a story about how my contract could have been an important factor when a vendor failed to back up all my data. Just because a vendor tells you they are doing something doesn't mean they are doing it. If they fail to meet those obligations and a data breach ensues, how would a judge decide who is at fault if the case goes to court? In my experience, it comes down to the contract. I have faced issues on both sides of this problem, as a vendor and as a customer. It's an excellent time to have a lawyer tell you which laws apply and how the case may be decided in court if you have questions about enforcement of security policies.

Sometimes companies use insurance to offset the risk associated with vendor data breaches. They may try to get the vendor to cover the deductible that their insurance won't cover and then have insurance cover the rest. Insurance is likely necessary for this day and age of data breaches and cyber threats. However, insurance may not save you in all scenarios. First of all, as noted in previous chapters, the cost of a mega-breach is probably more than most insurance policies cover. Your insurance policy likely covers the average cost of a breach.

Besides the amount of coverage, you need to make sure that you are meeting any of the requirements in your insurance contracts to obtain payment in the case of a data breach. Insurance companies would be wise to request at least basic security controls. Finally, most insurance policies include a clause that excludes "acts of war." What defines an act of war? That gets tricky. Most people say we are already in a cyberwar, as I explained in the [first chapter](#).

Vendor monitoring

Once you have signed a contract with a vendor and start using that vendor, perform on-going monitoring. Many changes can impact your initial risk assessment. Products change over time. Product managers change. Developers change. Executives and company ownership may change. Product services and features change. Certain events may trigger a re-assessment of the vendor relationship. For example, each time you renew a contract, you might want to re-evaluate vendor security. If a company is acquired or executive leadership changes, that may be a good point for another evaluation.

In addition to changes at the vendor, the way your company uses the product or service may change. The original assessment may have approved the product for a particular use case and a specific type of data. Over time, people may start putting more sensitive data into the product, setting up new connections, or using additional features. I talked about monitoring compliance with security policies. This monitoring also applies to the use ofvendor products.

In terms of contractors, monitor both data and network access. Ensure they are using MFA to access your systems. Chapter 21 covers monitoring and incident handling, all of which apply to vendors just as it does to your employees. You also need to monitor your vendor contracts and insurance. As the industry changes, you may need changes to the agreements and level of coverage required to reduce the risk associated with data breaches. Other factors that may impact vendor agreements include new privacy laws like GDPR and the overall political environment if you are dealing with companies in other countries.

Outsourcing and vendor relationships may make sense when the service offered by the vendor is not your organization's core competency. Products and services can help your company create efficiencies, obtain knowledge, improve security, get products to market, and sell them. Make sure that when you purchase products or services from vendors, you perform the appropriate level of due diligence. Allow the business to achieve its objectives while preventing exposure of customer data, business plans, or intellectual property through insecure vendor practices.

20
EFFICACY OF SECURITY PRODUCTS AND SERVICES

Once you have evaluated your security vendors to ensure they are implementing security controls according to your requirements, analyze the effectiveness of the security product itself. When you purchase a security product or service, how do you know if the product is helping?

Just like anything else, you can gather metrics from and about security products. You can do this in advance of purchase and after. The quality of the data depends on the product. The quality of the analysis of the results depends on your security team's knowledge and the amount of time they can spend. If they are always fighting fires related to security incidents, likely they are not spending time analyzing security product effectiveness. If they feel that their analysis of security problems doesn't lead to any improvements, they will probably not want to invest the time.

Researching product effectiveness

Various resources exist to help you determine the effectiveness of the products you want to purchase to protect your organization.

Some companies specialize in rating and evaluating products in different categories. Gartner[275] and Forrester[276] provide research services on products, industries, and companies. Sometimes you can find their reports online for free. These may be helpful but do not go into much detail on exactly how security products work and their effectiveness. IANS also has research reports for customers in their portal, some of which I write.[277] Some of the consultants will also tell you about the products they have used.

Beware that people evaluating products may be influenced by how much the company or product is paying them to perform the evaluation. Some may be hired directly by the vendor. Although I will write or talk about products, I only highlight their features rather than recommend one product over another unless I have invested a significant amount of time into evaluating them. One category of services I research constantly are the major cloud platforms, and I do compare those in my cloud security class.

NSS Labs explicitly tests security products.[278] Before purchase, you may find these reports helpful. A few caveats with these reports, which I learned while working at a company that went through the tests: some have called it a pay-to-play model. Additionally, the companies go through a series of tests, and then they have a chance to fix the problems and rerun the tests. It seemed a bit like a game to me to try to get into the top ranking. NSS Labs tests different categories, such as performance and identification of specific types of malware. Hence, companies end up making products designed to ace those tests. Those tests may or may not be in alignment with your environment and the threats your systems face. However, I still think the work NSS is trying to do is excellent. It's hard for every individual company to run tests like this for all categories of products. I applaud their efforts.

---

[275] Gartner https://www.gartner.com
[276] Forrester https://go.forrester.com/
[277] IANS https://www.iansresearch.com/
[278] NSS Labs https://www.nsslabs.com/

Testing products

A myriad of security products exists for different purposes. It's hard to know in advance if a security product solves your security problems. My biggest recommendation is to try out the product if possible. Otherwise, at a minimum, get a demo of the product in your environment. Every environment is different. Some have more or less data and varying types of network traffic or storage, all of which could affect performance. If you have a large organization, perhaps you can afford to purchase a single piece of hardware or the smallest license options for different products to test them.

You should see if the product finds any existing issues in your environment. It is essential to understand how the product works when formulating your trial or test. Sometimes a product needs to make a baseline of normal traffic and then tell you if there are any anomalies, so you won't see anything immediately. A test like this requires running the product over time.

For example, when we installed Stealthwatch Cloud (formerly Observable Networks) in an AWS account, it didn't find anything initially. Later it alerted us to unwanted traffic going to Brazil. In another test account, someone left a virtual machine running that got compromised at some point after we installed the security product and it alerted us to the problem. These are the types of tests I hope all vendors would let you run with their products to see if they work and find problems.

Be careful when you deploy a security product in your environment. Security products collect and can see a great deal of data. I recommend you do a security evaluation of the vendor first, and that you understand what data is collected, where they store it, and how it is protected. You may want to run the product in a lab environment, where you can evaluate which network ports the product requires you to open and the network traffic produced by the product. If products require too much network access, they may create additional risk at the same time you are trying to increase protection.

Some SaaS (Security as a Service) vendors send all your data to the cloud. Depending on the results of your vendor assessment, you may or may not be OK with this. You should ensure the proper security is in place to make sure other customers and the vendor staff cannot see your data without your permission. If a product stores vulnerability information associated with your environment, that data could be valuable to an attacker. They would know what to attack. If a product stores network traffic logs, those logs may include sensitive data as people send passwords over the network to log into websites or purchase things with credit cards.

Software scanning tools

While completing a research project on code scanning and software vulnerability management, software scanning vendors were, for the most part, unwilling to give out a free trial. It is hard to analyze which one is better for your codebase if a company doesn't offer a free trial. Of course, they don't want you to scan the code and then not purchase the product, but I found that they wouldn't even let me do a free trial on some open-source code or small project. I find this interesting because if you can't test the product and you have to pay thousands of dollars to buy it, you have no way to know in advance if it will work for you.

If I could have tested those products, I would have produced a code base with common sample vulnerabilities. Then I would have scanned that code base with each product to see which ones they found. It would be easy to determine which one was best suited for your environment if you have an accurate and deep enough sample of vulnerabilities.

When choosing software scanners, you'll need to understand what languages they work with and what type of vulnerabilities they find. Some scanners are "linters,"[279] which are focused on evaluating coding best practices for a particular language. They do not usually uncover security flaws. Some scanners only find CVEs in software dependencies. Others try to alert you to vulnerabilities like the OWASP Top 10. Some try to spot malware embedded in your code. Others look for unsafe sources and sinks.[280] The source of a vulnerability is the injection point. The sink refers to data modification to change the behavior of an application. Check to see that the scanner works with the specific programming languages you want to scan.

Networking products

Network security products are interesting because they sit at the edge of your network in some cases. The traffic leaves your network, and then you don't see it after that point. You don't know how that device may have altered the traffic that it processed and sent out. There are a few ways you can test network products. You can set up rules to allow and block traffic and then validate whether those rules worked. Some network products try to identify traffic. You can send various types of traffic through the device to see whether the logs and screen display accurate results. For example, I've witnessed misidentified traffic attributed to the wrong company or cloud service after digging into the details.

When the device is at the edge of your network, you could put another network device in front of the one you are testing to inspect the traffic. You can validate that both logs report the same results. For a cloud network appliance, you can compare the logs of the appliance to the cloud-native network logs. AWS, Azure, and Google Cloud Platform all have the rough equivalent of NetFlow logs (AWS VPC Flow Logs in AWS or similar names in

---

[279] Linters https://github.com/collections/clean-code-linters
[280] OWASP LAPSE Project
https://www.owasp.org/index.php/OWASP_LAPSE_Project

other clouds). Run the device inside a virtual private network in the cloud provider and compare the cloud-native logs to the appliance logs. Set up rules in both and see if any inappropriate traffic slips through the network appliance. You can also do the reverse to test your cloud provider logging services.

Note that just because a vendor sells a product with the same name as the one you get on-premises does not mean they are the same codebase. The vendor often must alter the functionality to get the virtual appliance to work on cloud platforms. Test the on-premises version and the version for each cloud provider independently.

Some network appliances have an intrusion detection or intrusion prevention system function that alerts on or blocks network security problems, respectively. You can create various types of network attacks to see whether the tool catches the issues or not. Some network appliances require a great deal of tuning and configuration to turn on and off all the appropriate features. Running these tests ensures that you have correctly configured the product. Some people buy a network or security appliance and turn it on, leaving all the defaults in place. They may not be getting the full value of the tool they purchased.

I mentioned the tests by NSS Labs. One of the challenges in those tests is the ability to identify all the malware and still achieve the desired performance. As more and more features of a product get turned on, it may limit the amount of data the device can process in a given timeframe. Some products advertise performance results with only a small portion of their complete suite of services enabled. Make sure you test the product with the desired features under the expected load.

Also, consider what type of network protocols you use in your environment. A particular wireless product I evaluated advertised a way to stop malicious behavior in the network. After hearing the details of how it worked, it was clear that all the advertised features would not work on the newer version of the IP protocol (IPV6), found on most networks. The older, much more common version is IPV4. Many organizations don't use, but also don't block, IPV6. That allows attackers to leverage it in attacks, and devices that don't take this protocol into account may have issues.

Products that identify malware

When evaluating products that identify malware, understand what type of malware they catch and how they do it. Some products are signature-based. Some work based on behavioral analysis. Some try to stop a specific type of malware like ransomware or help you reduce phishing in your environment.

Products that perform these functions are in never-ending competition with attackers. The attackers create a new type of attack. The vendors analyze and figure out how to block it. Then the attackers figure out how to bypass the protections. The vendors then develop procedures to prevent the new bypass methods, and so on. I don't know if this is true, but I was watching a presentation by Malwarebytes[281] at an IANS conference. They were talking about the GandCrab ransomware.[282] They said at one point, the attackers put a comment in the code that said, "Hi Malwarebytes." Even if it's not true, I'm sure that's how the vendors and attackers feel about each other at some point.

The effectiveness of your security products depends in part on the strength of the research team. The research team needs to be able to analyze new malware and determine how it works and how to block it. Different types of malware require different kinds of skills to reverse engineer it. Some are simple web code. Some reverse engineering requires a disassembler to view assembly, which is low-level machine code that is not very human-readable.

---

[281] MalwareBytes https://www.malwarebytes.com/
[282] GandCrab https://www.malwarebytes.com/gandcrab/

The team needs to quickly be able to parse what the malware is doing and provide information to the team that updates the products. The process for updating customer systems needs to be efficient so you can get the latest updates to protect your organization as quickly as possible.

Have you ever seen those research reports that express something like a 500-billion percent increase in XYZ malware? Take those with a grain of salt. In light of what I just told you, you can see that the vendors are always playing catchup with the attackers. When you see a significant increase in a particular type of malware, it is likely that the product just started identifying that malware. It probably ramped up at a much slower pace, and it took the vendors a long time to identify it.

True- and false-positives and the need for tuning

Most security products try to identify threats. Often the criteria they have to use has some variance. They produce true-positives, false-positives, true-negatives, and false-negatives as a result of the lack of concrete decision factors.[283]

True-positive: The identified threat or attack was indeed a security problem, and the security appliance or software successfully alerted on or stopped the problem.

False-positive: The security product identified something as a problem, but on further investigation, it turned out to be a non-issue.

True-negative: The potential threat was conclusively determined not to be a problem.

False-negative: This is the worst problem. A security product failed to identify a threat.

---

[283] Sensitivity and specificity
https://en.wikipedia.org/wiki/Sensitivity_and_specificity

As you can imagine, many false positives create a lot of noise and waste time. You can evaluate security products to see how many true- and false-positives they produce. Also, assess how the products can be tuned to reduce false-positives without missing true-positives. It's worse to miss an actual attack than to have many false-positives. At the same time, if you have so many false-positives that people stop responding, then the true-positive is missed anyway. The attackers are always changing their tactics, your environment is ever-changing, and your security vendor adds new alerts from time to time. Make sure you give your security team time to evaluate and tune these products to make sure they provide value.

Determining return on investment

After you have purchased a product or service, decide whether it is helping you. Once you installed the product, how many attacks did it block? These metrics give you some idea of the efficacy of the product and if it was worth the money you paid for it. On the other hand, make sure the things it blocks are things that matter. Your security team can evaluate whether or not the things it blocked would have led to a breach that could have resulted in significant financial loss.

You can also see what things your security product missed. Report those deficiencies back to the vendor so they can improve the product. Some vendors design products to prevent a specific type of malware. Then the malware gets smarter, and the product does not adapt. Evaluating whether or not the security appliances are catching the latest malware helps you determine if you should continue to invest in that product or service.

21
THE ATTACKERS ARE IN YOUR NETWORK — NOW WHAT?

There are two points at which you can respond to a security threat. You can try to prevent it from entering your environment. The other option is to detect it once it has gained entry and then stop it before it can do further damage. I wrote a blog post, called "Defensive cybersecurity strategies: Keep the ball away from the attacker," about how, ideally, I would prefer to stop the threat in the first place if it was possible (Radichel, Cloud Security Defensive Strategies: Keep the ball away from the attacker., 2019). However, trying to prevent every threat is not feasible. If you attempt to stop every one, likely the business will cease to operate effectively and efficiently. As explained throughout this book, attackers go to great lengths to defeat your defenses. At some point, they will get in.

The question becomes what to do once the attackers have breached your security defenses. The first part of this question is, how did you determine they were there in the first place? Someone with proper expertise needs to monitor for cybersecurity threats within your organization. Adequately trained individuals need to respond when tools send alerts. As I explained in the last chapter, this can be an overwhelming task if security products are not sufficiently tuned. In addition to the threats within your network that tools identify, attack vectors may exist that the devices or software scanning products are not finding. How will you find those types of problems?

Many experts have vast amounts of experience dealing with cybersecurity incident response. You might have heard of the company CrowdStrike that responded to the security incident when the U.S. Democratic National Convention's server was breached (Brumfield, 2019). These incident handlers get calls in the middle of the night to respond to a security problem. In some cases, they have bags packed and ready to go to get on planes and fly to different locations within the company or to their customer locations to deal with a security incident.

Incident responders have specific training to handle cybersecurity breaches. They are not software developers or project managers who do this on the side of some other regular job in high-security environments. It is their only job. Incident response requires the ability to correctly assess and deal with an incident, sometimes under a great deal of stress. If you are interested in learning more about the strain on the mental health of cybersecurity incident responders, listen to this podcast with Ann Johnson, Corporate Vice President of Microsoft's Cybersecurity Solutions Group: *Down the Security Rabbit Hole*: "DtSR Episode 312 - Ann Johnson on Mental Health" (Johnson A. , 2018).

Digital Forensics involves capturing cybersecurity evidence to investigate a crime. Incident handlers will typically make a copy of every single bit and byte (the low-level components that comprise the data on a computer hard drive) securely so they can prove no one tampered with the data. I explained in an earlier chapter how to take a hash of a piece of data. People involved in Digital Forensics and Incident Response (commonly referred to as DFIR) will capture the data and then take steps to investigate to determine what happened. That's what CrowdStrike did for the

DNC.

Each chapter in this book could be and has been a book unto itself. I am not going to be able to cover all aspects of DFIR and monitoring in this chapter. The goal is not to make you an expert in these topics in a few pages. I want to provide an executive-level overview so that decision makers understand they need the right resources in place to deal with a security incident. Too many companies don't know when attackers have infiltrated their networks because they fail to ensure they have proper monitoring and staff. Organizations need to have people who can deal with an event effectively on their team— either as full-time employees or via a retainer with a company that provides this service.

Incident handling and monitoring teams

The most critical point for executives to take away from this chapter is to ensure that you have an incident handling team separate from the teams that are building and testing systems, if at all possible. You also need people dedicated to monitoring security incidents and events. At some companies, the group that monitors logs for security events is called a Security Operations Center, or SOC (pronounced "Sock").[284]

Multiple reasons exist for having a separate team or teams for these security functions. Those monitoring logs usually have specialized training in security monitoring and incident handling. This training includes information about how to use security tools like an Intrusion Detection System (IDS) or Intrusion Prevention System (IPS), a SIEM (Security Information and Event Management System), or tools to perform disk and memory capture, memory analysis, and reverse engineer malware. This team should be aware of top threats and how to correctly determine if a suspicious activity in the logs is an event or an

---

[284] Security Operations Center
https://en.wikipedia.org/wiki/Security_operations_center

incident.

Security Event: An event is something that occurs, which may or may not be an actual security problem. An event in the logs may warrant investigation but may not turn out to be a real security problem. For example, several failed logins occur. Upon further investigation, it turns out that one system that integrates with another was misconfigured and repeatedly logging in with the wrong username and password.

Security Incident: A security incident is an event that turns out to be a real security problem. For example, the security team gets an alert because several repeated failed logins have occurred on numerous devices. On further investigation, the organization was experiencing a password spraying attack, and one of the machines on the network was successfully compromised.

Although I highly recommend training developers, QA, IT professionals, and DevOps engineers to learn how to spot security problems in logs, these teams are not focused on this task. They generally focus on building things, and that is a different mindset. Hire people specifically focused on finding security threats and resolving security incidents for the best results.

If you are an executive or business owner, you can probably relate to the fact that context-switching is distracting and can waste time. One minute you are negotiating a contract. Then you are scheduling meetings. Next, you are looking over financials. Then you are preparing a presentation for an upcoming speaking engagement. Someone calls and asks if you can participate in their podcast. You are already overwhelmed. If you also had to watch all your logs for security problems, that would be hard, right? Larger organizations can afford to have people focused on monitoring security logs, and they usually have a separate team for this purpose. Smaller companies can outsource this activity to another company.

The SOC

I don't know what type of security operations center all large companies have, but at one I worked for, it looked like something out of the movies. You walked into a big room with rows of desks pointed towards some large TV screens. The screens were full of news reports, Twitter feeds such as what the hacker group Anonymous was up to, and lots of logs. There was a separate room with no windows or cameras allowed in it. The people that worked in this room performed for need-to-know investigations and employee monitoring.

These teams would try to identify threats in the environment and contact the appropriate group to resolve the problem. For example, if a particular IP address appeared to be infiltrating the network, the people in the SOC would contact the firewall team I worked on to request a rule to block the attack.

Some organizations do not have money for such an extensive facility, so they make do with people at ordinary desks doing what they can to stay on top of the logs and alerts. Others outsource the SOC function to another company. If monitoring security is not the company's expertise, this could be a viable option. Another reason companies may outsource the SOC function would be to establish 24x7 monitoring by hiring a company in a different time zone. Be aware that opening your network and sending logs to third parties brings with it the additional risks I wrote about previously, so make this vendor selection with care.

It is still a good idea to get security training for your internal team. When the outsourced SOC contacts your organization to tell your team about a security event, your team needs to handle it appropriately. Before the Target breach, the company outsourced some of their security monitoring functions to a company in India (Radichel, Case Study: Critical Controls that Could Have Prevented the Target Breach, 2014). The company in India reported suspicious behavior to Target in Minnesota. According to the news media, whoever received that notification did not respond to it in a manner that effectively stopped the breach and limited the number of affected records. Make sure you have enough people trained to handle incidents promptly or a relationship in place with a company that performs incident response on call. It's easy to blame the person that got the call. However, if the company did not provide adequate training or resources to deal with that problem, the responsibility rises to the level of the top executives. That is what ultimately happened.

Logs — all of them

To determine if your organization is under attack or an attacker has breached any systems, the company needs to collect logs — the more, the better. It may not be possible to capture every piece of data from every system event. Still, the company must collect logs from as many of the components within a system as possible to ensure they can adequately determine the cause and impact of a breach. In many cloud environments, I find that companies are not capturing or reviewing all the logs that can indicate that a problem exists in their environment.

In addition to capturing the logs from the correct systems, the company needs to collect the right data. If the logs do not exist or are not capturing the right data, an incident responder doesn't have sufficient evidence to determine what happened. This scenario is problematic for several reasons.

The organization may have been breached but doesn't know it. As I explained, some companies have had attackers inside their network for months or years before discovering their presence. If no logs exist, there is nothing that shows what the attackers are doing. Poorly designed networks can also lead to insufficient information or an overwhelming amount of noise that makes it hard to spot problems in network traffic.

Some breaches incur fines if they expose certain types of sensitive data such as credit card numbers or health data. If no logs exist, the people performing the investigation may not be able to tell how much data the attackers accessed. In that case, the organization must provide the worst-case scenario number of records. That amount may be much higher than the actual number the attackers obtained, and as a result, the company has to pay more than it should have.

If the company wants to take legal action related to a breach, they need proof. The logs provide that proof, showing what activities took place and who did it. If no information about events in the systems exists, there is almost always no way to know what happened.

There are many types of logs. Different logs exist depending on what type of systems you are running and in what environment. All the different infrastructure in an on-premises office, data center, or cloud environment has system logs. Hopefully, every Internet-connected device has traffic, network, or access logs of some kind.

Overview of common types of logs:

Operating system logs: Your laptops, servers, and desktops produce different kinds of logs for different system functionality.

Application logs: Your developers and vendors build logging procedures into their applications. Make sure systems have logging enabled to the appropriate level. Usually, organizations turn off debug logs with detailed error information and possible sensitive data in production.

Server software logs: Turn on logs for web servers, mail servers, DNS servers, NTP servers, and any other type of server software running on your network.

IoT device logs: You may have logs for cameras, printers, automated coffee makers, and even fish tanks. If these devices have access over the network to other systems, make sure the logs are enabled, or at least log network traffic to and from these devices.

Network logs: As data flows through your network and to and from the Internet, it moves between devices that route the packets to the correct destination. These network logs are vital. Even if an attacker gets into an individual device and turns off its logs, the attacker will generally not have access to turn off network logs. I explained previously how network logs helped me identify my first breach, even though I knew little about cybersecurity

Cloud logs: Every cloud service you use should produce logs that tell you who logged in when, what they did, and what data they accessed. Ensuring cloud services can provide the logs you need should be part of your vendor assessment.

All the other logs: Any other device, application, or system connected to your network should have logs, including load balancers, firewalls, security appliances, HVAC systems, voice-enabled devices, alarm systems, mobile devices, and thermostats.

Collecting logs

To get logs from all these devices, you need to make sure the logging functionality is on. The logs need to be secure, so someone cannot change them or delete them. You can replicate live logs to an alternate location. You may want to encrypt them.

Your team needs to understand how the logs work. Is it a daily log file that overwrites itself each day? Is there a file for each day? Does the log file overwrite itself after a certain amount of time? An attacker can generate many events to leverage the way the system works to overwrite the lines that show the actions during the attack if he or she can't overwrite or delete them. Make sure you structure and back up your logs, so this doesn't happen. Also, as explained previously, make sure your backups are sound.

Logs can take up a great deal of space. Organizations need to determine how long they keep log files. Use different types of storage for faster or slower access. That can reduce long term archival costs when logs are required for compliance. Some industries require organizations to maintain logs for a year or longer. Organizations need to make sure they have enough physical hardware to store the files. Alternatively, use a scalable cloud service.

Make sure all the systems have synchronized timestamps. Often, an attacker pivots through an environment, and the people investigating must compare logs from different sources to piece together what happened. If the timestamps are in sync, it is easier to correlate the data in the logs.

Monitoring logs

Now that you have all the logs, someone needs to monitor them. They can also create alerts for suspicious activities and use security tools that help analyze and alert people to suspicious events. I wrote about some of these types of security products in chapter 20.

Another type of security product that companies use to help them monitor logs is called a SIEM (Security Incident and Event Monitor). Companies use this tool to consolidate as many of the logs as possible from different sources. This tool both tracks events and helps security teams find threats and respond to incidents. A SIEM may be used for monitoring by a SOC and help companies with logging requirements for compliance (Pratt, 2017).

Looking for threats in logs is sometimes called "threat hunting."[285]

Ideally, your security products and service find every attack in your environment. However, I already explained why that is not always the case. Training people to look for suspicious activity in your logs helps. You may have a SOC or an incident response team. However, training all your IT and operations team members to be aware of threats helps your organization find a breach faster and shut it down.

Logs can contain any number of suspicious patterns such as numerous failed logins, excessively large data transfers, unexpected long connections. Memory dumps may indicate that malware is attempting to leverage buffer overflows or other types of attacks. Some malware embeds itself deeply into an operating system so that you won't see it in any of the management tools in the operating system itself. However, you can see it on the network as it communicates with other devices if you know what is expected and unexpected, and your logs are clear.

There are so many things in logs that can indicate a problem. Those are just a few to consider. Sometimes, you don't or can't see anything in the logs, but you know something went wrong for some other reason. Perhaps law enforcement came knocking on your door to tell you that someone is selling your data on the Dark Web. That is the place where criminals and people who want to hide transactions do business. Perhaps money is missing from your bank account. Maybe a user is telling you that their machine is "acting funny," or a person thinks someone else is reading their emails based on some external events.

Incident response

Once an organization determines that a security incident has occurred, the process of incident response kicks in. There are different steps in the response process, and you want people who have received proper security training to perform each action

---

[285] Threat hunting https://en.m.wikipedia.org/wiki/Cyber_threat_hunting

correctly. Some people train employees to manage incidents, and others hire companies that specialize in this area of security.

I've already explained why logs are essential in a security incident. Additionally, all logs and data must be accessed, stored, and appropriately transferred, otherwise known as the chain of custody,[286] to be admissible in a court case. If the security incident involves a physical server, an exact copy of the disk is required as well as a hash to prove no one altered it after the point of capture.

Unfortunately, some malware hides traffic within expected traffic or encrypts traffic, in which case an incident handler needs to look at the memory on the system. Some incident responders receive training to capture and analyze system memory to determine if malware exists in the system and what it is doing. The memory is lost as soon as someone shuts down or reboots the system. If the people involved in handling the incident don't know better, they may destroy evidence. They may unplug, reboot, or shut down the hardware or software before the incident responders can capture the evidence and complete their analysis.

Depending on the size and type of security incident, an organization may need to disclose the breach or call in law enforcement. Organizations need to determine how they communicate about the breach and who needs to be involved. One of the reasons for having a separate team handle the incident is in case you have an insider threat. Additionally, external incident handlers might not use the organization's standard means of communication, which helps when attackers have compromised those communication channels.

Preparation

Incident response involves a lot more than what I have covered here. However, as you have probably figured out, you should

---

[286] Chain of custody https://en.m.wikipedia.org/wiki/Chain_of_custody

prepare in advance. Avoid having someone destroy evidence or hinder an investigation by training them upfront.

Ensure that people know what to do and whom to contact when they suspect a security incident. A policy should state the actions people should take if they find or suspect a security problem. Communicate it to the entire organization — and don't expect them to remember it if they watched a video or signed a document. Display the information in places where people will see it. You may have heard the announcement at the airport in the U.S. if you travel, "If you see something, say something."[287] This message is part of a campaign by the Department of Homeland Security. If you remember this phrase, you likely travel a lot as I do (I'm sitting in an airport as I write this), and the announcements reinforce the message over time. Do this with your security policies, and this one.

I worked on a cloud audit at one company where many different departments managed the cloud systems they use. I prepared a list of questions for them regarding their security controls. I also went through the policies the company had created with the help of the auditors. One specified whom to contact in the case of a security incident. When I asked five different teams, none of them gave the correct answer.

Additionally, most of them were not looking at logs, or if they were, they didn't know what to monitor to see if a security problem existed. The security team did not have access to any of the logs. This company could have experienced a breach, and potentially no one would have known. Luckily, they did an audit, and everyone involved wanted to do the right thing. They created a management plan to resolve the issues.

Most security professionals suggest obtaining law enforcement

---

[287] If You See Something, Say Something https://www.dhs.gov/see-something-say-something/about-campaign

connections in advance. Additionally, if you think you may need outside assistance, establish a relationship with that company and have them on call for when an incident occurs.

When a significant incident occurs, the organization may need to disclose information. Someone needs to talk to the press when they call. The organization may need to notify customers through emails, letters, and a statement on the website. Who is responsible for this in your organization, and are they prepared?

You may not want your employees speaking to the press. When I contacted people that I used to work with at Capital One, some of them (not all) said they couldn't speak to me because they were "being monitored." It is probably a good policy to inform people that they should not talk to third parties about an on-going incident or investigation. Others contacted me who'd either already left the company or may not have received those directives. I did not publish everything they told me as I'm not a dirt-digging reporter. Some news outlets may jump to conclusions and write malicious articles that hurt the organization. Communicate to employees what can and cannot be discussed with external sources.

Create a runbook that documents the steps you will take during an incident. It should define who is responsible for which actions and appropriate communication channels. Practice the steps in your runbook in advance. Gather teams to do tabletop exercises. Shelly Giesbrecht, Senior Incident Responder at Cisco, whom I met at BSides Vancouver,[288] wrote a blog post on tabletop exercises (Giesbrecht, 2017) in which she asks:

> You've gone through the work of creating an incident response (IR) plan, created some runbooks to deal with likely, known threats, and you're feeling a lot better about the ability of your organization's ability to detect a cyber incident in your

---

[288] BSides Vancouver https://www.bsidesvancouver.com/

network. But how do you know it works? How can you be sure the teams and individuals named in the plan know their roles and responsibilities, who to report to, or even where the IR documents are stored?

Shelly's questions highlight why it is essential to practice in advance. There are several ways you can practice incident response-related activities. Perform tabletop exercises where you talk through a scenario and your runbook. Hire a red team to infiltrate your network and see how your team responds. Black Hills Infosec produced a card game to practice incident response called "Backdoors & Breaches,"[289] which you can buy on Amazon. Practice capturing evidence such as disk or memory capture. Make sure you have the proper skills and tools to do this effectively without destroying or losing evidence. Executives should participate in incident response preparation and be involved in decisions and communication throughout the process.

---

[289] Backdoors & Breaches
https://www.blackhillsinfosec.com/projects/backdoorsandbreaches/

22
SECURITY AUTOMATION: DO MORE WITH LESS

If you are an executive, you already likely know the power of automation in many other parts of your business. Perhaps you use an automated method to manufacture products. You probably use an accounting program that automatically downloads transactions from your bank, so you don't have to re-enter them. Some companies use robotics to perform certain activities. Some organizations use automation for risky processes, which could cause people to get hurt. If we didn't have calculators, maybe we would all still have an abacus!

Capital One originated from the idea that financial institutions could gain from technological efficiencies. As this article states, "it succeeded in the credit card business due to its use of data collection to target personalized offers directly to consumers." (CFI, 2020) Since then, data science has helped the company evaluate and reduce fraudulent transactions. Online banking might help customers access accounts more easily at any time of day and reduce the need for banking centers and tellers. Using computers to analyze credit card usage over time helps them determine the ideal customer to minimize risk and increase profits.

Cybersecurity efforts can benefit from automation in the same way by leveraging efficiencies obtained through the use of programmatic systems. Automated configurations and deployments can help prevent mistakes. Automated analysis of cybersecurity data helps improve the detection of cybersecurity threats. Programmatic responses help mitigate security incidents faster. Overall, it helps companies do more with fewer resources in this environment where companies complain that there is a shortage of cybersecurity professionals.

The convergence of data, cybersecurity, IT, and software

I remember taking a security class from one of my instructors in my cybersecurity program. I was sitting in the back of the room, very excited to be taking another security class. He asked everyone to introduce everyone and tell each other something about ourselves. I said my name and that I was a software developer leading a team at a major bank. He jokingly said, "What?! Software developers don't come to security classes. What are you doing here?" He was teasing, of course, but his declaration was quite accurate. I met very few software engineers throughout the program. I also got a Master of Software Engineering prior to that, and not once did they mention security. I once heard the CISO of AWS at re:Invent say something to the effect of, "If you find someone who knows both security and software — that's a rare bird."

Later in class, our instructor was showing us how to run many different scripts on a command-line one at a time to execute various functions. I thought that it was incredibly tedious, and my brain immediately went to how I would create a complete script to do all these individual steps for me. When he was walking by at one point, I said, "You don't do all these things manually like this, do you?" He just looked at me. I'm not sure what he thought. I just didn't think people would sit manually running one command at a time the way he was showing us. That would drive me crazy. As fate would have it, this person is now one of the biggest proponents of security automation that I know!

Times have changed in a big way since that moment. I was getting this cybersecurity training to fill in the gaps in my knowledge and put a stamp on my cybersecurity qualifications. People always ask if a degree or certificate is worth it. Sometimes degrees and training cover things you already know or would have known without them, but having that degree helps prove it. It might give you more self-confidence and show people you have put in some time learning things in your field of expertise. I had an interview with someone once, and I didn't make a big deal about my certifications. He said, "Well, do you have any certifications? Because people like to see those letters after your name." I laughed and said, "Yes, I have some letters for you."

At that time, I had eight cybersecurity certifications from SANS, but I am not sure how many of those I will maintain as time goes on. I had never technically had a title that had the word security in it when I started the master's program in information security, even though I had been researching security and attempting to implement secure systems for years. Getting a degree in the topic helped me by providing tangible proof of knowledge and credibility.

I learned a lot in the program from people working across the field of security, which is extremely diverse. No one single person exists who can know everything about cybersecurity. I chose to take classes in a range of topics, including incident handling, network intrusion detection, advanced pentesting, and reverse engineering malware. Since I started, I've had multiple security positions and now run my cybersecurity company teaching security to others and performing penetration tests.

The Master of Information Security Engineering did not mention Security automation in the curriculum in my particular classes, nor was cloud a topic in the books, labs, or tests. I know that changed because later, I taught the SANS Cloud Security Architecture and Operations class, which contained some of my white papers at the time. It *definitely* included security automation!

While I was in the SANS master's program, worlds were colliding and converging in exciting ways. AWS was evolving to the point where it was a viable business option from a security standpoint. About two years prior to this class, when I saw the CIA moving to AWS (Konkel, 2017), I thought to myself, "If the CIA was using AWS, it might be worth another look." This organization certainly requires high security, and they were going to use AWS.

The first time I investigated the cloud, it seemed like a platform full of miscreants attacking my e-commerce sites hosted on other servers. I used to monitor my logs obsessively. As I explained earlier, I had experienced a data breach and was determined not to let it happen again, so I created my Web Application Firewall (WAF). My logs included a way to track every attack and source network, and AWS was often in those logs. At that time, security professionals pointed out that tools did not exist to secure the virtual machines on those cloud hosts properly. I did not want another virtual machine on the same hardware getting into my e-commerce web platform. I had already experienced a breach and did not want another one. Although I helped companies running on these cloud platforms, I did not migrate my systems to them.

After noticing the CIA was using AWS, I went back and read all the AWS whitepapers available at that time (approximately 70).[290] I read fast. Today, there are too many whitepapers for any single normal human to read, most likely. Note that at that time, all the white papers were primarily technical and written by AWS employees. Now some documents are written by vendors selling products or services. After reading the papers, I was convinced

---

[290] AWS Whitepapers https://aws.amazon.com/whitepapers

that the cloud could now provide security benefits that outweigh the risk for a lot of companies. The white paper that influenced me the most was *Amazon Web Services: Overview of Security Processes.*[291] The current version of this paper is from 2017. Since that time, AWS has added new technology that provides increased security benefits.

In 2016, AWS asked me to present a 15-minute lightning talk at AWS re:Invent.[292] That was after I'd written my SANS paper on event-driven security automation in the cloud (Radichel, Balancing Security and Innovation With Event Driven Automation, 2017) and presented it at SANS Networking. I chose the topic *AWS Security Ideas*. I spent 15 seconds on each slide, explaining a security idea that I thought would help people moving to the cloud implement security effectively. This was one of the first presentations where I talked about the convergence of cloud, security, and automation.

This book revolves around the core ideas in these slides, which was not intentional. But it demonstrates that my core ideas around cloud security have remained consistent over time. I would change a few words to more accurately communicate the concept I was attempting to convey, but they still represent the core fundamentals in this book. Each slide presents a topic in this book in a few words. Organizations can leverage these concepts to take advantage of the convergence of automation and security, especially on cloud platforms.

Attackers are using automation — so should you!

Attackers use automation to attack your network and systems. As I explained in other chapters, they are continually scanning the

---

[291] Overview of Security Processes https://d1.awsstatic.com/whitepapers/Security/AWS_Security_Whitepaper.pdf
[292] AWS Security Ideas https://www.slideshare.net/TeriRadichel/aws-security-ideas-reinvent-2016

Internet for flaws in networks and unpatched systems. A lot of exploits arise, not from someone manually running scripts, but because attackers have machines attempting to find these flaws all over the Internet automatically. They may target any address they can or target particular networks.

Criminals design worms to propagate automatically. They attack one system until they successfully exploit and infiltrate a system. Then the malware automatically starts searching for other endpoints to attack. Using these strategies, they can more efficiently take down entire networks, as was the case in the WannaCry and NotPetya attacks. I explained how attackers infiltrated Target and used an automated deployment system to attack all the point-of-sale machines in that 2013 breach simultaneously.

Automation facilitates crafty malware that is hard to detect and can quickly take over a machine. Attackers write code that periodically changes the file name on a system or the layout of the source code, moves a file around, or contacts different domain names in each request using a method called Fast Flux.[293] Ransomware automatically encrypts all the data on a machine. Attackers set up command and control channels that establish connections and automatically report back to the control server.

Attackers use automation to speed up their ability to attack targets. If you cannot respond in kind with a similar level of agility, it could mean that your systems will fall prey to their advances. Ideally, your organization uses automation where you can to prevent the problems that most commonly expose data or allow attackers to breach systems in the first place. However, they will eventually get in. If and when they do, if you are leveraging automation effectively, your organization will be able to spot them faster. Monitoring must be in place to track what the state of the system should be and then report on abnormal variations.

---

[293] Fast Flux https://en.wikipedia.org/wiki/Fast_flux

The benefits of automation

If organizations are using manual methods to try to defend their systems, attackers will win. Automation is faster. If processes are automated and well-tested, you will have fewer mistakes. Automation lets you both innovate faster and lower the risk within your organization at the same time.

Let's do a little exercise using a simple equation to show why and how this is true for basic, repetitive security configurations with repeatable patterns. Think about the systems you use to manage your bank accounts. Imagine somewhere in the system this formula exists:

$$x + y = z$$

People use the system to enter two numbers that affect the balance of your bank account. Let's say the numbers are $x = 2$ and $y = 2$. A properly designed computer processing your data will always produce the correct results under normal conditions. A human could probably do this math pretty quickly and easily as well. Let's say you pass in the numbers $x = 82539822$ and $y = 34589234$. A human will take longer to process the equation than a computer. Humans also might make mistakes if doing math in their heads. This same concept applies to securing configurations and processes. Automation helps prevent mistakes.

The other benefit of this automation is that you could create logs to track every time the numbers x or y changed and who did it. Let's say this calculation is part of the system that tracks the money in your bank account. Suddenly your bank account is short $1,000. Now you can go back and look at the logs to see who changed the numbers that caused the error in the bank account. If you don't have logs — good luck!

In addition to all of the above, companies generally create reconciliation processes for financial systems. These processes add up all the transactions and compare accounts in different ways to ensure that all the entries are accurate at the end of the day. If something is not correct, these reconciliation processes will report problems. Other systems analyze the data for fraudulent transactions and sometimes automatically alert customers when their account may have a problem.

Security is not a one-hundred percent perfect formula. However, a lot of the things that lead to security breaches can be prevented via automated deployments and configuration checks. Organizations can turn repeatable tasks with known good configurations into equations. A human can determine what data to pass in as inputs. The system can produce the results with a well-tested formula. The logs can tell you who did what when, if something goes wrong. We already have some security systems that look for invalid patterns in logs. With a more concrete formula for the inputs and outputs, systems can alert on security configuration problems with much more accuracy.

For example, in my cloud class, I teach people how to create templates to deploy cloud infrastructure, such as S3 buckets. Think of S3 buckets as containers where you can store files in the cloud. You may recall a few security breaches where someone exposed sensitive data in AWS S3 buckets to the Internet. This mistake is entirely preventable if a company has a proper deployment pipeline and security controls! If a company cares about its sensitive data, no valid excuse exists for this type of data breach.

Think about our formula. It has inputs and outputs. A cloud infrastructure template also has inputs and outputs. You can have a team, such as a DevOps team, create a template that deploys an S3 bucket that cannot expose the data to the Internet and prevents unencrypted data from entering the bucket. A security team may define the requirements or even work on the DevOps team to help create these templates. A QA team can test them to ensure no security flaws exist. Next, the developers who are creating S3 buckets to build their applications can use the templates.

The template needs to be as flexible as required without allowing the riskiest mistakes that lead to data breaches. They may allow someone to pass in a valid location for the bucket and the name of the bucket. Then the developers who need to create this S3 bucket use this template to create their buckets for their applications. They are not allowed to change the formula in risky ways, but they are allowed to alter appropriate inputs. They do not have the option to change the bucket to one that is accessible from the Internet.

The developers also do not require a security team to review each change before they can deploy their code if they are using a pre-approved formula. As long as they are using the approved template on the approved deployment system and according to whatever other rules exist, they are free to deploy S3 buckets as needed. This strategy allows developers to innovate and move quickly without exposing sensitive data to the Internet. The security team no longer has to review basic, repeatable patterns that the company allows.

Automation requires investment

The example I provided was an oversimplified example. An organization will not create every single template an organization uses in cloud deployments in advance before developers can deploy infrastructure to the cloud. But this example shows how automation helps you go faster and prevent security problems at the same time. Building automation systems can be tricky because you need to both build in the security, but still allow people to do their jobs. As I mentioned, I told my DevOps team when we built such a deployment system that if people were complaining, we were probably doing something wrong and needed to fix it.

When I joined the Capital One team, a handful of people were building all the cloud templates. As you may recall, there were

11,000 developers at the time. This solution was not scalable. Your automation systems require a proper architecture and forethought to both prevent the security problems while at the same time providing the flexibility needed to get things done. There are different ways to approach this problem, with varying degrees of risk. People making these decisions need to understand the fundamentals in this book to make the right choices when weighing different trade-offs. There is not a one-size-fits-all solution because organizations have data with varying levels of sensitivity, different numbers of employees, and different levels of risk tolerance.

Another common problem exists that leads to problems when trying to implement security automation. The fact that the people who use the system do not understand why the security controls are in place and fight back against them complicates the process. People generally don't like it when you take away their ability to do whatever they want. That's why I recommend security training for all involved. It helps people understand the reasons for the decisions and to be part of them, so they are supportive of this process. Ideally, they help build it, instead of trying to tear things down and thereby create additional risk for your organization.

Security automation is neither a quick fix nor a simple solution. It requires time and money to implement. This investment pays off not only in the prevention of data breaches, but efficiencies that enable the company to be more innovative and get things done faster. The amount of time and money you put in will offset the money you may pay if your company is involved in a data breach. I like to refer to the saying, "Pay now or pay later."

Investment in automation that prevents repeated mistakes will free up time and money for other things. Going back to my financial system analogy, I used to work on back-office systems for a major bank. Often, I had to work with an existing code developed over several years, which had various problems in production. These problems would lead to incidents where someone on the team would have to go in and fix the issue. For example, a file transfer included a number that was too large or had letters instead of numbers. Someone would write a database script to fix the value, and then re-run a job to finish the process. All the while someone was fixing that issue, they could have been working on new features and system improvements. Some of these errors would happen weekly.

Any time our team was assigned to work on a system we had not worked on previously, I would go into the production error log and find all the errors that the system regularly produced. I would account for the time to fix those repetitive errors in our project estimate. As a result, after we added new features to the system, fewer production incidents would occur that would later distract our team, and those supporting production operations. Security automation can do the same for your organization. If repeated events arise, try to find out if there is a way you can leverage automation to reduce the time spent on incidents. That way, your security team can work on something more challenging and productive, like threat hunting and research.

You can also invest in building systems that reduce bottlenecks. When teams complain that security is blocking them, try to find out if there are any parts of reviews or processes that can be further automated. Be careful with this one. Some things are difficult to automate due to all the nuanced explanations I provided to you in this book. Oversimplification of complex security problems can also lead to a breach, but some security approval processes certainly can be, such as the deployment of an S3 bucket template!

Shifting responsibility for a specific part of the process (while also ensuring the person is adequately trained) may help reduce the load on other individuals creating the bottleneck. Creating systems to automate gathering data and validating it in advance of review may simultaneously speed up and prevent errors in review processes. Additionally, systems that track security reviews and decisions can provide metrics that help track risk, as explained in previous chapters.

The people making security architecture decisions also have to understand when automation is overkill, or alternate technology can mitigate security problems, to ensure the level of investment is appropriate. These decisions involve both software architecture and security skills. Both software and security require years of training to obtain expertise in their fields, so you will likely want to engage both your security and software teams. Often each side assumes the other's job is easier than their own or that certain activities are illogical or extraneous. Coming together to solve problems will produce more accurate and effective risk reduction while allowing people to innovate at the same time.

Let me emphasize that automation also needs to be tested. Implementing automation or any haphazardly produced code could lead to devastating results; automation can have harmful as well as beneficial consequences. Failing to take the time to test infrastructure and security automation carefully could lead to new security problems while attempting to prevent old security problems. The level of speed you require will often be proportionate to the risk you incur.

For example, let's say you want to create a script to block malicious traffic automatically. Your team writes the code and puts it into production without first testing to see what traffic it is going to catch in a live production environment. The unintended consequences could include blocking legitimate systems in your network or valid customer traffic. I explained how testing is critical and beneficial in previous chapters, and it is worth repeating here. For automation to be effective, take the time to test it and validate that it works as you expect prior to deploying that automation to production.

Automation does not eliminate the need for people

Automation helps us do things faster, with fewer mistakes. It doesn't mean we don't need people anymore! It means we can do things in such a way that people can focus on more critical problems and innovation while at the same time reducing the risk of mistakes and failure. Automation cannot stop or fix all security issues. Some situations are unique and require someone with the appropriate skill level to analyze variances that do not fit into a strict automation formula. Some problems are simply too complex.

Additionally, once you create your well-intentioned formula for automated approval and system compliance, a scenario will arise that doesn't fit the mold. You will need someone who can decide whether to grant an exception or adjust the system to meet the additional requirements. Anytime you change your automation, your QA team should test it again. Even small changes often have unintended consequences that produce errors. Hopefully, your team has automated testing where possible, so retesting the system will not take too long.

I also mentioned the cat and mouse game that attackers and vendors play when attacking and securing systems. The same may be true of your attempts at automation. Although you try to think of every scenario that can produce a security problem, someone may work around the control either inadvertently or intentionally while trying to get their work done. Attackers may also find a way around your efforts to auto-remediate problems. Someone needs to monitor your automated systems for any issues that arise after deployment.

The most important thing to remember is that the people building the security automation need security training. Many organizations are permitting developers building systems to deploy network changes and create credentials without understanding how their actions could result in a security breach.

Prior to the cloud, when developers built systems on-premises, they were often given a system inside a corporate network where a team well-versed in network and security designed the infrastructure. This shift in responsibilities without corresponding security training may be why so many simple security misconfigurations are causing cloud data breaches. In many on-premises corporate environments, developers are not able to do such things because they don't have access to modify these types of security controls.

When developers deploy applications to the cloud without support from IT and security teams, they probably lack the deep infrastructure and security threat vector training required to understand the implication of risky actions. Although your DevOps team went to some security sessions at a big cloud conference, they may not have the in-depth training that security professionals have after years of researching and dealing with different types of cybercriminals, attacks at different layers in systems and networks, malware, data breaches, and incident response. Anyone creating your security automation can benefit from exposure to these cybersecurity disciplines.

Your security team, on the other hand, can benefit from working with your developers and DevOps team, who are itching to automate all those blockers away! Security teams are often in the habit of saying "no." Developers will ask why and may come up with new and innovative solutions that meet the needs of both sides. Both groups can learn from and help each other.
The executives need to understand both sides at a high level to make appropriate decisions when the teams can't come to an agreement (which will happen, in my experience!) The ability to make the proper decision will keep the business moving forward while keeping risk in check.

23
IS THE LIKELIHOOD OF A DATA BREACH GOING UP OR DOWN?

Often people ask me to answer a question on Twitter that requires an entire chapter from this book to explain. A 280-character Tweet or even multiple Tweets isn't the best place for such answers. Others, especially those who want me to write a blog post or article for them, ask me to provide my "top recommendation" or a "top 10 list." This quandary brings me to one of my favorite quotes, most often attributed to Einstein (Quote Investigator, 2011):

Everything should be as simple as possible, but not simpler.

This book provides a list of 20 questions you can ask your security team. The items on this list are not the only security metrics you use in your organization, nor are they in priority order. An actual security assessment may involve 100 or more questions. The objective of this list is not to fix every security problem. It attempts to provide data to executives on how well the organization is addressing the fundamental security problems that cause the most data breaches at the time of this writing.

I based this list on personal security research following data breaches over time and what causes them. My research includes experience, deep dives into security labyrinths of network traffic and software flaws, and insights from the many sources referenced in this book. I hope you will continue to explore cybersecurity by reading some of the citations and references on which I based this book.

As I have explained, many complexities exist beyond the simple questions. For each one, I presented some high-level information that goes into making decisions about that particular security topic. I don't intend to provide all the answers to cybersecurity problems. As a whole, the book is designed to show executives that security is not a simple problem, and *how to think about security to make better decisions*. It provides some high-level metrics executives can track to determine if cybersecurity gaps exist in their organization. Likely executives will be handing off much of this responsibility to people who will figure out *how* to implement solutions.

Executives can make better decisions with a better understanding of what causes data breaches and metrics on the effectiveness of the organization's steps to prevent and mitigate them. The questions in this book attempt to provide measurements that drive better cybersecurity decisions. Hopefully, they make cybersecurity gaps easier to identify. Often security lists are tactical and tell organizations *what* they should do without explaining *why*. Often, they measure implementation rather than the effectiveness of security controls.

One million events in your security product logs do not demonstrate effectiveness. Sometimes cybersecurity checklists have open-ended questions that are not truly measurable. These lists help get companies thinking about how to improve efforts to secure systems, data, and networks. However, they do not prove security or measure it effectively. Other lists track activities, but not the attack vector that exists. Effective metrics show security gaps that allow attackers to infiltrate systems and may lead to a data breach. Taking actions to reduce the gaps reduces your overall cybersecurity risk and potential losses.

The goal of this book is to help organizations measure cybersecurity risk more effectively and make sure they are validating security. I explained the nuances of testing when I wrote about backups, security testing, and assessing the efficacy of security products. Tests need to measure your top risks accurately. Items need to be appropriately weighted if you choose to assign priorities, or your measurements may be meaningless.

Some cybersecurity decisions will have straightforward answers, but then there are those questions that security people answer with the dreaded, "It depends." I hope this book will help executives understand why security people sometimes give this vague and frustrating answer. It is hard to summarize cybersecurity in a soundbite because so many factors exist. Although the initial questions I presented may seem simple, when you drill down into the details, the considerations can become much more complicated.

Breaking down complexity

In my career, I spent a lot of time dealing with and querying big datasets to find needles in haystacks. One of my strengths appears to be categorizing and pinpointing problems, which helps when trying to analyze network traffic and complex financial data. I remember one time I supported sales and marketing for a medical device manufacturer. An issue existed with integration between two systems, and the marketing people were overwhelmed with all the errors the system was generating. "How will we ever fix all these errors?" they said.

I asked them to give me the list. I took it back to my desk and went through it. By running a simple query, I was able to categorize the items on the report. Three problems caused about

95% of the errors. Once I broke the data down for them this way, it was much less of a daunting task to resolve the system errors. There were about seven problems instead of 3,000, and three of the items would solve most of the issues.

You can do the same thing with your cybersecurity problems. Although there are many nuances and complexities involved in cybersecurity, there are a few top problems that cause a majority of security breaches. By eliminating or at least minimizing these top problems, you can reduce cybersecurity risk. Instead of focusing on every type of attack that could occur at a very detailed level, work on resolving the top issues driving the most risk.

Security people like to say that risk equals likelihood times impact. That means that the more likely something is to happen, the more the risk increases. The resulting damage also increases the risk. I wrote about that in my Target breach paper and am not going to go into too much detail here. You can read my white paper for more on that topic, but I have an alternate point of view you may want to consider. You can spend time arguing about the likelihood and impact of a security incident related to a vulnerability. Another option is to eliminate the question by creating a risk-averse environment where it is easy to get things done. Eliminate complex and subjective decision making and arguments that waste everyone's time.

Here's an example of how you can avoid that scenario. At Capital One, when we moved to the cloud, the CIO said, "Everything will be encrypted." Period. Sometimes encrypting everything comes at an additional cost, affects performance, or adds complexity to an architecture. On the other hand, now there were no questions, discussions, or arguments whether the data went into this category or that category. Does it need to be encrypted or not? Is it sensitive, critical, or public data (or whatever categories you give your data)? People didn't have the chance to make a mistake and miscategorize something that was supposed to be encrypted but wasn't. As I explained, encryption doesn't solve all your problems, but your data is better off with encryption than without it. When it came to auditors and compliance, the answer was simple: Everything is encrypted.

Jeff Bezos made a similar declaration in the early days of developing AWS. He said every point at which two separate systems communicate would be an API (Application Programming Interface) (Mason, 2017). I guarantee you, as a former software engineer, this saved the company hours upon hours arguing over how two systems would integrate.

By having a standard form of communication between systems, it would be easier to monitor traffic between those systems. Programmers can build an API in many different ways, and it is a very flexible form of interaction between two systems. However, it limits interactions to a reasonable standard, which is more manageable. It also enabled systems of any type to communicate with one another because APIs facilitate interoperability. Teams could change the way the systems worked behind the API without affecting systems that use it as long as they don't alter the way the external system calls the API.

If your company can agree on a set of standards, dictated from the top executives, that will set the tone for security in your organization. Clear direction reduces disagreements, conflict, arguments, and politics in decision-making processes. I once read that conflict often ensues when responsibilities are not clearly defined. On the one hand, you need to specify which team is responsible for which activities. On the other hand, overall objectives and responsibilities for security should be clear. The assignment of duties eliminates questions and allows organizations to focus on delivering business objectives.

Once you have defined your standards, the organization should track compliance with those standards. Executives don't need to determine precisely how this gets done. If you explain the data you need to see, then the people in your organization can make that happen. They can tell you why it is hard to do and the challenges they face along the way so you can make appropriate decisions to help them get the data you require.

Many business executives have read the book, *Good to Great*, by Jim Collins (Collins, 2001). I remember that at one point, it explained how a CEO gave all employees insight into the measurements that indicate whether a company is achieving its objectives or not. This insight helps employees understand how their actions fit into the big picture and can provide motivation to help the company meet business targets. Cybersecurity should be one of those targets. Work to create measurable objectives and let employees know if you are hitting those targets or not.

How do you know if employees are doing what they are supposed to do if you don't measure it? Avoid systems that get in people's way and instead extract metrics from the systems that people use to do their jobs and create reports. If the documentation does not give you all the data you need, then fix the systems, not the people. I always remember a quote by Lou Gerstner in the book, *Who Says Elephants Can't Dance?* (Gerstner, 2003). In it, he explained what he did to turn around IBM. At one point, he said, "People do what you inspect, not what you expect." People may not intentionally break the rules. They may not even know the rules exist, as I explained in chapter 16 on policies. However, you won't be aware they are breaking the rules if you don't track policy violations, and you won't be able to address the problem.

By taking this data-driven approach, you will, in turn, drive the development of systems that produce measurable controls. These metrics help you find security deficiencies and vulnerabilities in your environment. As I mentioned in chapter 3 on cybersecurity strategy, by defining the reports in advance of building the system, your data requirements drive the system architecture toward the desired outcome. It explains how the data will be stored and how the systems will function to support the generation of desired reports. You will achieve a better return on security investments if you ensure your security products, processes, and systems deliver data that demonstrate their effectiveness. Improving the efficacy of your security controls will mitigate risk.

Sample reports

The first step in getting the data you need from people in your company is to provide a sample report. Once you have that, you can find out what is and is not possible to collect in your current environment and why. Perhaps the systems are not designed to track security, which is highly likely. Maybe the logs have not all been aggregated into a SIEM or a security data lake, which is a way of consolidating all security-related data in one place (Marty, 2015). Some things may be easier to track than others, so you may want to start with one item at a time.

Let's say you choose to start with MFA because that is a high-risk item for cloud systems. Many cloud providers do not have MFA. Your organization may establish a rule that states going forward any new systems implemented or purchased require MFA capabilities. You may also set a timeline for existing systems to implement MFA. Leverage the strategies from chapter 16 on policies and exceptions to start gathering data. Your initial report can be an Excel spreadsheet, depending on the complexity of your systems and organization.

Department	Systems	% support MFA	% accounts with MFA
Legal	4	75%	50%
IT	23	87%	75%
HR	10	80%	60%
Marketing	16	20%	10%

Create the report format in a way that makes sense and is quick and easy to read on one sheet of paper. That means over time, as your measurements get increasingly complex, you may have a cover sheet of paper with your 20 questions. Supporting documents drill down into the details.

Risk Category	Compliance	Riskiest department
MFA	43%	Marketing
Network Ports	89%	IT
Policy Exceptions	25%	Sales
Automation	50%	Marketing
Security Training	60%	Product Management

That is not a complete list, but it gives you an idea for a possible report format. In this case, an executive could drill down into the details to try to determine what is causing their department to get a low score so they can fix it.

If a breach occurs, it will be apparent where the problem lies. If an executive assigned authority and responsibility to correct a security deficiency to a specific person who did not carry out the assigned task, that person is responsible for the breach, not the executive. If the executive did nothing to monitor and address security weaknesses, he or she might instead be held accountable. The department listed in the report would be the one that owns the system and has the budget and authority to fix the problem. If they do not, the responsibility rises to the level where the power to fix the problem exists.

With these reports, you may want to set target objectives for compliance. Is it 100%? 90%? The data will only help if people see them, and there are repercussions for not meeting the objectives. Organizations can incorporate security targets into bonus structures, just like other types of business targets.

Of course, the company needs to complete projects and make money. However, a data breach could set an organization back millions of dollars, as explained in the first chapter. Also, the loss of business and intellectual property, or the negative impact on the national security caused by a data breach could be even more significant than regulatory fines and legal settlements. The responsible parties need to be aware of these business impacts.

Measuring progress

As you gather reports over time, you will be able to create charts and graphs to indicate whether cybersecurity risk is increasing or decreasing. Hopefully, you will be able to show positive progress. If organizations design systems to report this data automatically, you will quickly spot a negative change. For example, a new system implemented without MFA reduces the total number of MFA-enabled accounts. Design your reports to show when these things occur and document how and why problems exist. Try to fix the issue as quickly as possible and prevent it from happening again.

Even better, systems that track security problems alert people right away when they have taken an action that results in a security violation. This approach helps the person understand that something is wrong immediately so they can fix it. Training people as they are taking action will have an immediate effect versus a video they watch once a year and forget the next day. Most people do not want to be the cause of a data breach or have their names appear on any adverse reports. Likely, they will fix the problem if they know failure to do so has visibility at the highest level and will result in an executive response.

On the other hand, if you produce the reports, but the

organization takes no actions to fix the problems, the information becomes a liability. It proves that problems exist, and the organization was not doing anything about it. Make sure you take action to get the security vulnerabilities fixed. Some companies try to cover up the fact they are not fixing problems by not creating reports that show their systems and networks have security vulnerabilities. In the event of a data breach, not having metrics may be just as damaging as having the data and not doing anything about the problems.

24
CHANGE IS CONSTANT

Then and now — the origins of cybersecurity and malware

Computer mischief started almost as soon as computer networks existed. Stanford and UCLA created the first ARPANET host to host link in 1969, which ultimately led to the Internet as we know it today. The evolution of computer worms and malware started with a program written by Bob Thomas in 1971 called Creeper, which itself was harmless. It would get onto a system, type out the message "I'M THE CREEPER: CATCH ME IF YOU CAN" and then move to another system (Core War, n.d.). Ray Tomlinson (also the inventor of email) changed the program to replicate it from one computer to another rather than move itself. That became the first known computer worm.

The movie *War Games* came out in 1983 (Badham, 1983). A bored student in Seattle uses various techniques to break into systems. First, he figures out where administrators at his school were writing down the password for their computers so he could log in and change his grades. Then he uses a technique called "war dialing"[294] to search for modems he could connect with to get into other systems. By chance, he obtains access to a computer on a military network. He breaks in by guessing the password.

War dialing initially involved modems and rotary phones, the type of phones we used to make calls around the time the first home PCs appeared on the market. I recently realized that some people younger than me don't know how we used to make phone calls. I watched an online video that I found quite humorous, where two 17-year-old boys received a challenge to dial a number on a rotary phone.[295] They didn't know what it was or how to do it. By the end of the video, I was laughing so hard I think tears were coming out of my eyes, as they tried all sorts of unsuccessful methods to dial the number. Although it was funny, it made me feel old at the same time. Oh well.

In the early days of computers, we used dial-up modems to connect computers to remote networks. You can watch the movie to see how they work. We would put our rotary phone receivers into the modem, and the sounds emitted would help one computer connect to another. War dialing is a method of calling many numbers until you find a modem and then attempting to connect to it. In the early days, many modem connections didn't even require a password.

Luckily for me, I did not get into any trouble like the boy in *War Games*. That's because I lived out in the country where long-distance phone calls were expensive, and my dad was the only one who was allowed to use the modem. Instead, I wrote software and stored it on cassette recorders. If you want to see my old computer, the TI/994a, a cassette recorder, and the book that taught me to program, you can find it at the Living Computer Museum.[296] Paul Allen, one of the founders of Microsoft,

---

[294] War Dialing https://en.wikipedia.org/wiki/Wardialing
[295] 17-year-olds dial a rotary phone
https://www.youtube.com/watch?v=1OADXNGnJok
[296] Living Computers museum + lab https://livingcomputers.org/

established it in Seattle in 2012. You'll also find more about *War Games* and other early computer systems there as well.

In *Countdown to Zero Day: Stuxnet and the Launch of the World's First Digital Weapon*, Zetter tells the story of how Ronald Reagan asked his staff after watching *War Games* if such things were possible (Zetter, 2015). This question launched an investigation into proving that it was. I highly recommend reading this book for rest of the story as it is an excellent read. It will help you understand more about cyber threats and why cyberwar is a viable threat. In these early years, very few people knew anything about computers, let alone cyber-attacks.

So, what is still the same after all this time? We still have worms and malware that propagate from one computer to another over networks. We are *still* having problems with passwords! War dialing is the older version of Internet scans looking for open ports that allow attackers to connect to computer systems. Another technique called "wardriving"[297] involves scanning for unprotected WiFi networks. National security still is a concern. Kids are still getting in trouble for computer and security mischief, though in some cases years after the fact. Some of those mischievous kids get arrested, while others become some of the world's most famous researchers — or both.

Security breaches evolve over time

When I started in cybersecurity, I felt like most companies didn't know what was happening on their networks. Many of them were compromised and likely did not know it, as I mentioned. Some still probably are right now. When I talked about cybersecurity to the people I knew, no one cared or understood it. Remember, I didn't know any cybersecurity people. I was figuring things out on my own. For whatever reason, cybersecurity is now more mainstream. More news organizations report on it in, and more

---

[297] War Driving https://en.wikipedia.org/wiki/Wardriving

non-cybersecurity, less technical people are starting to ask questions about how and why this is happening.

I'm not sure exactly why that is, because other massive data breaches occurred in the past. Maybe it has to do with books like those I mentioned earlier from Kim Zetter (Zetter, An Unprecedented Look at Stuxnet, the World's First Digital Weapon, 2014) and Brian Krebs (Krebs, Spam Nation: The Inside Story of Organized Cybercrime-from Global Epidemic to Your Front Door, 2015). The popularity of conferences like DefCon may have some influence. Hackers appear in movies like *The Girl with the Dragon Tattoo*,[298] the James Bond movie *GoldenEye*,[299] and TV shows like *Mr. Robot*. There are many others. People always seem to be intrigued by these characters, and some envision how cool it would be to become hackers themselves.

In reality, as I have explained throughout this book, the job of the defender is infinitely harder. An attacker only has to find *one* hole that lets them in. A defender can't make any mistakes and must plug every hole in a very complicated mesh of interconnected systems and make sure no flaws exist in any software system to prevent an attack. Additionally, many hackers end up in jail because it's difficult to erase all evidence after an attack. The story in Zetter's book is a great example. Eventually, security researchers figured out who did it. The truth is, we need more defenders and people who understand how these attacks infiltrate networks to outnumber the attackers for this reason.

Edward Snowden[300] likely influenced some people as well, whether you agree or disagree with his actions. I asked Jake Williams, another fellow IANS faculty member, about this to get his perspective just as he was about to post a comment on Twitter. As I expected, his response was mixed. Perhaps what the

---

[298] The Girl with the Dragon Tattoo https://www.imdb.com/title/tt1568346/
[299] Golden Eye https://www.imdb.com/title/tt0113189/?ref_=fn_al_tt_1
[300] Edward Snowden https://en.wikipedia.org/wiki/Edward_Snowden

government did was wrong, but Snowden also compromised people's missions and put lives at stake. It's not a simple issue. In any case, it got people's attention. They started to realize that their data was not as private as they assumed. People began to understand how governments spy and surveil.

Additionally, hacktivists like the group Anonymous[301], WikiLeaks[302], and the Shadow Brokers[303] have attracted some people's attention. Anonymous originated in 2003 on 4chan[304], an online forum where people communicate freely about political viewpoints that are far from mainstream and sometimes harmful. 4chan and a related group called 8chan have influenced mass shootings (Palmer, 2019). Anonymous has evolved over the years and has carried out cyberattacks such as DDoS (Distributed Denial of Service) attacks to take down computer systems of organizations in protests with varying political agendas.

Wikileaks tries to expose corruption by posting stolen information online, which may also have harmed U.S. national security (Myre, 2019). WikiLeaks was involved in exposing Hilary Clinton's emails during the 2016 presidential election (Phillip & Wagner, 2016).[305] The Shadow Brokers published stolen exploits used by the NSA (Goodin, NSA-leaking Shadow Brokers just dumped its most damaging release yet, 2017). This led to some of the massive attacks occurring like WannaCry (Newman, The Leaked NSA Spy Tool That Hacked the World, 2018) and NotPetya (Fruhlinger, Petya ransomware and NotPetya malware: What you need to know now, 2017) because the malware in both cases were derivations of the NSA exploits. Other governments and criminal organizations now use these same exploits against victims that have not fully patched systems and locked down networks

---

[301] Anonymous (group) https://en.wikipedia.org/wiki/Anonymous_(group)
[302] WikiLeaks https://en.wikipedia.org/wiki/WikiLeaks
[303] Shadow Brokers https://en.wikipedia.org/wiki/The_Shadow_Brokers
[304] 4Chan https://en.wikipedia.org/wiki/4chan
[305] Hilary Clinton Email Archive https://wikileaks.org/clinton-emails/

(Perlroth & Shane, In Baltimore and Beyond, a Stolen N.S.A. Tool Wreaks Havoc, 2019).

In the past, the government kept things like the fact that China was hacking U.S. companies a secret, and businesses turned a blind eye. As a result, the U.S. government and businesses have lost an untold amount of money in stolen technology, data, and secrets (Sullivan & Shuknect, 2019). I read about things foreign governments were doing on various sources I found on the Internet; cybersecurity specific publications and online forums, not mainstream news channels. I suspected what I was reading was correct based on the traffic in my logs, and the people making the claims seemed credible. I could see traffic and attacks from various networks and countries, and I knew which ones were the worst offenders. If I talked to anyone about it, they typically acted like I was overreacting, including the support people at that large hosting company where I experienced a breach. I couldn't understand why more people didn't realize this was happening and why they weren't doing anything about it. I read about and tried to understand what was going on with the various breaches that occurred.

I remember the "ILOVEYOU" virus, purportedly created by accident, that infected over 10 Million computers in 2000 with a script (Strickland, 2008). I also recall the SQL Slammer virus in 2003 (Vamosi, 2003). Businesses had to care because it was taking down all their SQL server database systems with ports exposed to the Internet. The worm affected over 75,000 machines. Computer systems and networks were grinding to a halt. Of course, I also remember the malware with an embedded Kaspersky virus scanner that spewed out stock spam because it was likely the source of the data breach I experienced.

One particular data breach I recall was the CardSystems data breach in 2005 (Sahadi, 2005) because, to me, it seemed like a big deal that someone stole 40 million credit cards. I happened to be in Australia at the time. When I got back to the United States a couple of months later, no one remembered it. That was the same number of credit cards stolen in the Target breach (Krebs, The Target Breach, By the Numbers, 2014). Perhaps the Target Breach had more impact because it directly affected consumers, whereas most people don't know credit card processing platforms exist, what they do, or how they work. At a Target store, people walk in and physically swipe the card in their hand.

The same may be true in the case of WannaCry. Hospitals had to turn away people who were sick and dying (Brandom, 2017). The impact was visible and directly affected people rather than silently traversing hacked equipment and networks in the background. What executives need to understand is that these silent attacks occurring in their systems may have devastating consequences in the long run if they do not find and stop them.

When I started researching cybersecurity, I found various sites and newsletters that reported breaches, the number of records exposed, and what caused the breach. The Privacy Rights Clearinghouse maintains a list of data breaches dating back to 2005.[306] The most significant data breaches in that list occurred in the last five years. Data breaches and the number of records stolen are definitely on the rise. However, companies are storing more data. The fact that more breaches exist on the list could also be because more companies are reporting them. Regulations exist that require companies to report stolen records and pay related fines. The increase in breaches indicates that we don't understand cybersecurity well enough, and I believe we can do better.

It was in Australia when I first started researching spam and realized that attackers had compromised the systems of many companies. They were sending spam out of their servers, and either didn't know it or didn't care. When I tried to tell them, I got no response in most cases. Only a few times was I able to reach the offending network and get them to stop an onslaught of spam

---

[306] Privacy Rights Data Breach database https://privacyrights.org/data-breaches

emails. If the traffic came from a foreign source, forget it. Any effort to contact those networks was futile, in my experience. Companies need to have avenues for security researchers and customers to report suspicious events — and the staff to react appropriately. In the Capital One breach, their quick response and the speed at which they fixed the vulnerability received praise. Compare this to Equifax, breached months after notification that the vulnerability existed on their network (Otto, 2019).

One thing that has decreased over time is the amount of spam in people's inboxes. Spam filters have gotten much better. Although the number of spam messages appearing in most inboxes is lower than before, the number of phishing attacks has significantly increased. It is one of the primary sources of compromise according to the threat summary on the CIS Benchmarks website.[307]

Sometimes the emails people receive are incredibly targeted and personal attacks, which would be hard to spot. Some attacks may arrive in the form of a calendar invitation (Newman, Tricky Scam Plants Phishing Links in Your Google Calendar, 2019), a claim that the user is in a video (Christensen, 2017), a document, voicemail (Abrams, 2019), or a website. Many companies offer training to help people identify phishing emails. Hence, some people are aware of what phishing is but are often still fooled as the messages are becoming trickier and more targeted.

A defense in depth model is required to protect data. Constant vigilance is necessary to determine what sort of email attacks exist and how they work to thwart this attack vector. Even more importantly, use the MFA strategies in this book to limit the attack if credentials are compromised.

Monitoring changes in the threat landscape

Your organization should be monitoring the on-going

---

[307] Center for Internet Security Cyber Security Threats
https://www.cisecurity.org/cybersecurity-threats/

cybersecurity threats, attackers, data breaches, malware, and other security incidents to understand what types of attacks are affecting organizations most. Threats and attacks are constantly evolving. By understanding how breaches are occurring and how malware is getting into systems, your security team can understand how to stop a new threat. Many organizations already do this, but chances are your security team needs more resources to carry out these activities effectively. It takes a great deal of time, energy, and training to investigate what is going on in your network, if systems are infected, and implement controls that effectively reduce risk.

Besides phishing, the CIS benchmarks threat list at the time of this writing attributes a large percentage of breaches to misconfigurations. IT, network, DevOps, QA, and other technical team members also need training, so they understand if and when they see a security problem that could introduce the latest vulnerability into your production systems. Security teams tell people implementing software and systems to take various actions that help with system security, but they don't know why. As I explained in other chapters, developers often do better with detailed explanations, not just orders.

I just saw a developer ask on Twitter if private networks help security or just make things more complicated. Another person who builds a widely used software framework asked me why I say authentication alone is not good enough to secure systems. I am so happy these people are asking the questions. However, I am afraid they are not always getting the right answers. People building your systems need to be aware of how attacks work and what constitutes suspicious behavior on systems and networks. They need to know what to do if they see something that doesn't look right.

Organizations should monitor legal cases, outcomes, what fines organizations are paying, and how insurance companies are handling the breaches. How much time are companies spending on legal battles? Could this attack impact your company and systems? Do new laws exist that will increase fines? What will companies have to do to comply with these laws? Are attackers targeting your particular industry, and how are they doing it? Are they attacking the type of systems you run? What CVEs are they exploiting? Understanding the cybersecurity threat landscape will help you know what sort of risk your organization faces, perform a more accurate cost-benefit analysis, and make better cybersecurity risk decisions.

Where to monitor for new threats

You can monitor breaches by following people who report on and research security breaches on Twitter. Despite all its idiosyncrasies, Twitter is one of your best real-time threat news feeds. I follow security researchers and news reporters and sometimes provide a brief take on an article or report I have read. I also follow penetration testers to find new attacks that I can use in penetration tests. Many news organizations post cybersecurity-related articles on Twitter. You might want a specific list or a separate account designated explicitly to monitoring security threats. Additionally, I follow news sources all over the world for international events that may be security-related. Leveraging search features in Twitter and Google News can also help you find security threats.

You may also be able to sign up for government- and industry-specific threat reports. For example, US-CERT[308] has a mailing list you can sign up for to find out about new CVE and flaws in security products. Other CERT organizations exist around the world. Many security vendors and other security-related organizations offer newsletters. Government law enforcement agencies sometimes have organizations that companies can join to learn about the latest threats. Infragard is an organization that facilitates information and sharing of information between the

---

[308] US-Cert https://www.us-cert.gov/

government and the private sector.[309] You may be able to get on security mailing lists or Slack channels. Follow security blogs, podcasts, and news organizations that report on the latest security threats.

Numerous cybersecurity conferences exist. One of my favorites is called BSides.[310] These community-led conferences take place in different parts of the world. These conferences cater to security professionals and often have top-notch speakers at a small, low key event. OWASP also offers great events on secure software development.[311] I am a member of the IANS Research[312] faculty and speak at their conferences geared at cybersecurity professionals. ISACA[313] and IIA[314] target auditors. Other events will focus on specific industries, executives, or legal professionals. These events may incorporate a relevant talk about cybersecurity and recent threats.

Vendors often incorporate security into their events. They want to sell you a product, of course, but often offer data about top threats your business may be facing from their perspective. Local business and technical events may exist near you that occur regularly. You can attend or join to help organize events and find speakers. Cybersecurity and technology-focused meetups may have relevant talks on cybersecurity. I often have security topics at the AWS meetup that I run in Seattle,[315] and I attend other security meetups in the area. These are just a few examples. Many more security organizations exist where you can learn more about cybersecurity.

---

[309] Infragard https://www.fbi.gov/about/partnerships/infragard
[310] BSides http://www.securitybsides.com/w/page/12194156/FrontPage
[311] OWASP https://owasp.org/
[312] IANS Research https://www.iansresearch.com/
[313] ISACA https://www.isaca.org/
[314] IIA https://na.theiia.org/Pages/IIAHome.aspx
[315] Seattle AWS Architects & Engineers https://www.meetup.com/Seattle-AWS-Architects-Engineers/

What threats and risks do you need to monitor most?

Although a lot has changed, much remains the same. The attackers are generally still looking for ways to spread from computer to computer. They continue to target software that contains vulnerabilities. War dialing turned into port scanning and wardriving because the technology changed. We no longer use modems to connect to other computer systems. What changes most is the technology and who is managing and making cybersecurity decisions. The other difference is that our systems and networks and connections are becoming more and more complex.

Bruce Schneier, renowned security expert, is often attributed with the following phrase, and you can find it in his blog posts and books (Chan, 2012):

> *Complexity is the enemy of security.*

I explained the exponential nature of complex networks and how each exposure may exponentially increase your cyber risk. The complexity increases the chance that misconfigurations and unpatched security vulnerabilities can expose data. The same concept applies as organizations use more and more technologies and vendors. Each new factor adds to the complexity and management of systems and data.

With each new technology an organization uses, it needs to understand the security best practices and how to configure things properly to prevent a data breach. Assess vendors to make sure they are following best practices. Integrate all systems into the organization's access control and user management systems. IT and security teams should understand what network access is required. Logging and monitoring need to be put in place for that new system to watch for threats and data breaches. The organization should perform threat modeling to understand how the system might be attacked and mitigate those threats. The system, once added, should appear on your risk reports.

The traditional approach of focusing on the most significant risk sounds logical, but simply fixing that risk and leaving many other holes open may add up to a more substantial overall risk. Just as I mentioned with encryption, you can spend a lot of time arguing what should and should not be encrypted. However, if you can afford it and it is feasible, you may save more time and money and simplify management and decision-making if you encrypt everything. When it comes to networking, reduce your attack vector by reducing the number of systems exposed to the Internet, regardless of what they are hosting. As I explained, an attacker can get into one system and then from there access another until they reach your sensitive data. You can construct complex network segregation, but by removing the access points from the Internet, they can't be accessed by external threat actors.

I just read a book called *Atomic Habits* (Clear, 2018) by James Clear. I liked it and already employ many of these strategies. It had some additional insights, research, and helpful reminders to try to combat the things that make us fall back into old habits. In one of the chapters, the author writes about how the British cycling team that went from one of the lowest-ranked teams in cycling to a championship-winning team with team members winning in the Tour de France five years in a row.

They did not do this by making radical changes. They worked on small, cumulative improvements, seeking ways to obtain a 1% improvement in various areas over time. These minor improvements add up. This approach requires attention to detail and continuous monitoring, as I proposed in this book. Rather than focusing on the most significant single risk, focusing on small improvements in all areas may help companies obtain more substantial reductions in cyber risk over time.

How the cloud is affecting cybersecurity

Cloud is one of the areas that exponentially increases the risk for organizations if not carefully managed. Cloud systems open up many new avenues for attacks if not properly understood and assessed before implementation. Before the existence of cloud platforms and services, organizations would deploy systems within networks that at least provided some perimeter protections. Developers could not expose data directly to the Internet if they tried because the corporate network would not allow it.

Now situations exist where one cloud system may, in turn, access another cloud system creating a path for exfiltration. Someone in the organization may grant a vendor access to a cloud application or platform that the organization has not fully integrated with IT and security systems. The access may fall outside the realm which those teams can monitor. Many new threats and network paths may exist as organizations deploy new cloud systems connected to corporate networks. Companies need to watch for this activity and new security threats related to all these connections.

The cloud vendors are creating new services and functionality almost every week that developers may want to use. This technology allows companies to innovate fast. However, as has been shown with some high-profile breaches, failure to perform accurate threat modeling and implement robust security architectures may lead to massive security breaches. When choosing to use new services, the decision-makers need to be able to correctly assess the security of the products, services, and solutions before implementation. Involving security teams will be helpful if security teams and development teams can work together to solve problems, rather than being at odds with one another.

The things you need to secure in the cloud are not much different from anywhere else. You will have network paths between computers and software that attackers may exploit. The people who implement these networks need to be well-versed in network engineering and monitoring. You can still use multifactor authentication to protect credentials and encryption to protect data. You should employ a security team that understands and monitors for threats and attacks. Architectures and processes should include segregation of duties, logging, and monitoring. Your organization requires the ability to perform incident handling and response properly. All the core security principles still apply.

The real difference when it comes to cloud technologies is that many companies are moving so fast. The technology is changing so rapidly that the security teams have not had an opportunity to understand it fully. How can an organization expect a security team to secure something they likely had no say in implementing and have no idea how it works? Sometimes the security team may not even be aware the company is using cloud services. This point is where your system tracking, policies, and risk reporting will be helpful.

The other thing that happens when companies move rapidly is that the people who are implementing core infrastructure lack proper training. Many executives don't understand that cloud systems involve network architectures that used to be designed and deployed by people with years of network engineering and cybersecurity experience. Developers and DevOps teams with far less experience now have this responsibility, and the capability to make a mistake is far easier if not properly managed.

Teams using cloud systems may be exposing data with misconfigurations or creating pivot points between internal and external cloud networks. The cloud vendors may not be following the best practices the security team mandates. The teams implementing cloud systems sometimes don't even understand when they have deployed something that has exposed the company to increased risk. The appropriate people do not have access to or understand all the cloud logging systems, and in some cases, no one is monitoring for data breaches.

As explained, the cloud can also help cybersecurity by leveraging the tools available from the cloud providers and the benefits offered by some platforms. Implement strong cybersecurity policies and automation to create guardrails to prevent mistakes. Leverage the event-driven nature of the cloud to respond to cyber threats automatically. Focus on a secure deployment system that blocks non-compliant implementations as much as is reasonable. Add monitoring and alerts before and after deployments so your security team can investigate suspicious behaviors.

By leveraging automation and the built-in cybersecurity and monitoring of cloud platforms, companies may be able to do more with less. Stephen Schmidt, CISO of AWS, claimed, in an interview on the importance of security automation, that they have no SOC and one person monitors all their operations (Swinhoe, 2018):

> We don't have a SOC. We don't have a room that has, you know, the big TV monitors in it and people watching them and that sort of thing," Schmidt says. "I have a single on-call security engineer who is responsible for watching the automation and making sure it's functional. That rotates every six hours around the world to make sure we've got coverage in people's day times.

Automating security has created even more buzzwords, like SOAR (Security Orchestration, Automation, and Response).[316] I didn't dive into this too much in the earlier chapters because I think it's another case of creation of buzzwords to sell something that already has a name: security automation. However, maybe it will catch on. I've already seen it in a few articles.

---

[316] SOAR https://resources.infosecinstitute.com/security-orchestration-automation-and-response-soar/

Cloud platforms can apply artificial intelligence and machine learning technologies to massive amounts of logs and data to try to uncover security threats experienced across their entire customer base. They turn around and incorporate alerts and security features into the platform to help their customers stay more secure.

Cloud networking has driven changes to on-premises networks that are now becoming more agile and able to create more finely-grained networking rules. Software-defined networking allows organizations to deploy virtual networking, automate, and make changes more quickly.[317] Networks are more scalable and enable zero-trust models that weren't feasible before.

Technically, if you could manage to host all your systems in a physical data center properly with all the best security practices, your organization would have more control over security and less chance of a data breach. If you could have private lines between every organization and location you do business with, you could be more reassured rogue actors were not getting into your communications.

Unfortunately, the ability to do so *correctly* with *no implementation flaws* and all the required staff and technology to move quickly is cost-prohibitive for most organizations. They do not have enough resources or expertise in many cases, and managing cybersecurity and technology is not the core business of many organizations. In this case, it may make sense to outsource some of these functions.

As the book explains, however, choose vendors, products, and services with care. You still need to manage what you deploy on these systems. You still need to understand where your data is and who can access it. You need to take steps to implement cybersecurity fundamentals for the parts of the implementation

---

[317] Software-defined networking https://en.wikipedia.org/wiki/Software-defined_networking

that fall within your area of responsibility. Ensure contracts are clear on these points and what will happen in the event of a data breach.

In summary

The underlying conceptional mechanisms for attacks don't change over time, but the specific tactics do. Even if you are not the hands-on-keyboard person implementing cybersecurity controls, you can understand how attacks work at a high level and monitor broad statistics to help lower your cyber risk. Then, train your team to implement the details correctly. You've learned about the basics of cybersecurity throughout this book. Whether you are implementing systems in the cloud, your office, or a data center, these cybersecurity principles still apply.

Use the questions in this book, along with input from your security team if you have one, to create metrics and monitor whether cybersecurity risk is increasing or decreasing. Ensure you measure *gaps that can lead to a security incident*, rather than cybersecurity activities. The point of the questions in this book is to *reduce the vulnerabilities that make data breaches possible*. This approach differs from lists that measure whether you are taking actions that are important for cybersecurity implementation and monitoring but do not measure things that are the root cause of data breaches. The more avenues attackers have to get into your systems, the higher the chance they will.

Create policies and procedures aligned with the risk metrics you capture. Automate enforcement and tracking as much as possible. Monitor deployments to detect attacks and prevent security mistakes. Leverage these strategies to minimize risk while still allowing people to innovate and grow the business. Use data from deployment, change management, and ticketing systems to feed into your cybersecurity risk reporting. New risks may surface when organizations implement new technology. Fixing one problem may introduce another. Conversely, the point of change may fix security issues and reduce cybersecurity risk.

As explained, one of the ways to help reduce risk is by ensuring as many people as possible have security training. Raise awareness of security threats in your organization by sending people to classes or have your security team do internal training. Each line of business or department should be responsible for making sure their decisions align with security best practices as defined by the organization to maintain an acceptable level of risk. The security team can't do it alone and trying to solve these problems completely using technical solutions will create bottlenecks and roadblocks.

Create a security culture within the organization by defining rules and policies, but also by teaching people how to make better choices. Create tracking mechanisms that transparently show who is making cybersecurity decisions that increase risk within your organization. Hold those people accountable, rather than having this accountability rise to the top executive level because no one was informed, and no repercussions exist for failing to follow policies.

When you don't have the appropriate people on staff, call in external companies who have that expertise if needed. Ensure your organization does proper due diligence on these companies, products, and services. Whether it is a contractor, penetration tester, security researcher, vendor, or product, verify that you are working with someone who has the qualifications and security practices you require. If possible, do tests on products but otherwise read reviews and investigate reports that show whether products and services are trustworthy. Be aware of the global political environment and understand where security vendors are manufacturing and testing security products if this concerns you.

Monitor cybersecurity news and reports for new threats and attack vectors that may affect your organization. Perhaps you don't have time to do this yourself; then delegate this function to someone who regularly reports this information to you and anyone else making cybersecurity decisions within your company. Track the systems in your organization, changes, and new threats introduced by those changes. By keeping your decisions-makers informed of the latest cyber threats, they can choose implementation options that avoid additional risk and perhaps even improve the security of your systems and networks.

Thank you for taking the time to read this book. I sincerely hope you found it beneficial and that it helps reduce risk and limit the attack vectors that lead to data breaches within your organization. You can follow me on Twitter for cybersecurity updates and additional resources

ABOUT THE AUTHOR

Teri Radichel is the CEO of 2nd Sight Lab, a cloud and cybersecurity training and consulting company. She has a Master of Software Engineering, a Master of Information Security Engineering, and over 25 years of technology, security, and business experience. Her security certifications include GSE, GXPN, GCIH, GPEN, GCIA, GCPM, GCCC, and GREM. SANS Institute gave her the 2017 Difference Makers Award for innovation in cybersecurity. She is a member of the IANS (Institute for Applied Network Security) faculty and previously taught and helped with curriculum for cloud security classes at SANS Institute.

Teri started the Seattle AWS Architects and Engineering meetup in 2012 and was later designated an AWS Hero by Amazon. Capital One asked her to be on the original cloud team, where she helped with security and networking. Since then, she has helped many other companies with practical cloud security consulting and training. Teri is a sought-after public speaker on the topics of cloud and cybersecurity. She has presented at conferences such as RSA, AWS re:Invent and re:Inforce, Microsoft Build, ISACA Congress, IANS, OWASP AppSec Day, ServerlessDays London, and BSides conferences.

You can follow her on Twitter @teriradichel

Bibliography

Abrams, L. (2019, October 31). *New Office 365 Phishing Scams Using Audio Voicemail Recordings*. Retrieved from bleepingcomputer.com: https://www.bleepingcomputer.com/news/security/new-office-365-phishing-scams-using-audio-voicemail-recordings/

Allen, K., & Radichel, T. (2018, February). *Red Team vs. Blue Team on AWS*. Retrieved from RSA: https://www.rsaconference.com/industry-topics/presentation/red-team-vs-blue-team-on-aws

Armansu, L. (2018, July 19). *News Backdoors Keep Appearing In Cisco's Routers*. Retrieved from Tom's Hardware: https://www.tomshardware.com/news/cisco-backdoor-hardcoded-accounts-software,37480.html

Arnold, C. (2017, September 26). *Equifax CEO Richard Smith Resigns After Backlash Over Massive Data Breach*. Retrieved from NPR: https://www.npr.org/2017/09/26/553799200/equifax-ceo-richard-smith-resigns-after-backlash-over-massive-data-breach

AWS. (2020). *KSP and CNG Providers for Windows*. Retrieved from docs.aws.amazon.com: https://docs.aws.amazon.com/cloudhsm/latest/userguide/ksp-library.html

Badham, J. (Director). (1983). *War Games* [Motion Picture].

Barth, B. (2019, August 8). *Selling zero-days to governments takes some business savvy, says former bug broker*. Retrieved from SC Magazine: https://www.scmagazine.com/home/security-news/vulnerabilities/selling-zero-days-to-governments-takes-some-business-savvy-says-former-bug-broker/

Bartlett, G., & Inamdar, A. (2016). *IKEv2 IPsec Virtual Private Networks: Understanding and Deploying IKEv2, IPsec VPNs, and FlexVPN in Cisco IOS (Networking Technology: Security)*. New York: Cisco Press.

BBC. (2019, April 30). *Vodafone denies Huawei Italy security risk*. Retrieved from BBC: https://www.bbc.com/news/business-48103430

BBC News. (2014, May 5). *Target's chief executive resigns*. Retrieved from BBC News: https://www.bbc.com/news/business-27283872

Benner, K. (2020, February 10). *U.S. Charges Chinese Military Officers in 2017 Equifax Hacking*. Retrieved from nytimes.com: https://www.nytimes.com/2020/02/10/us/politics/equifax-hack-china.html

Brandom, R. (2017, May 12). *UK hospitals hit with massive ransomware attack*. Retrieved from The Verge: https://www.theverge.com/2017/5/12/15630354/nhs-hospitals-ransomware-hack-wannacry-bitcoin

Brewster, T. (2018, December 12). *We Broke Into A Bunch Of Android Phones With A 3D-Printed Head*. Retrieved from Forbes: https://www.forbes.com/sites/thomasbrewster/2018/12/13/we-broke-into-a-bunch-of-android-phones-with-a-3d-printed-head/#3c5955113307

Brown, D. J. (2014). *The Boys in the Boat*. New York: Penguin Books.

Brown, J. (2019, Aprial). *New Australian Law Threatens Prison for Tech Execs Who Allow Violent Content on Their Platforms*. Retrieved from Gizmodo: https://gizmodo.com/new-australian-law-threatens-prison-for-tech-execs-who-1833806676

Brumfield, C. (2019, December 3). *CrowdStrike, Ukraine, and the DNC server: Timeline and facts*. Retrieved from csoonline.com: https://www.csoonline.com/article/3482006/crowdstrike-ukraine-and-the-dnc-server-timeline-and-facts.html

Burgess, C. (2017, December 11). *Espionage: Germany unmasks fake Chinese LinkedIn profiles*. Retrieved from csoonline.com: https://www.csoonline.com/article/3241239/espionage-germany-unmasks-fake-chinese-linkedin-profiles.html

Burgess, C. (2018, March 21). *Former employee visits cloud and steals company data.* Retrieved from CSO: https://www.csoonline.com/article/3265109/former-employee-visits-cloud-and-steals-company-data.html

C, V. (2019, April 27). *How I hacked 50+ Companies in 6 hrs.* Retrieved from medium.com/@cvignesh28: https://medium.com/@cvignesh28/how-i-hacked-50-companies-in-6-hrs-3866b61cfdcc

California State Legislature. (2018, 06 29). *Assembly Bill No. 375.* Retrieved from leginfo.legislature.ca.gov: https://leginfo.legislature.ca.gov/faces/billTextClient.xhtml?bill_id=201720180AB375

Campbell, M. (2020, January 7). *Burner phones are an eavesdropping risk for international travelers.* Retrieved from Help Net Security: https://www.helpnetsecurity.com/2020/01/07/burner-phones-eavesdropping-risk/

Captain, S. (2020, January 2). *What California's new privacy law really means for you.* Retrieved from Fast Company: https://www.fastcompany.com/90445374/what-californias-new-privacy-law-really-means-for-you

Carr, N., Goody, K., Miller, S., & Vengerik, B. (2018, August 01). *FireEye.* Retrieved from On the Hunt for FIN7: Pursuing an Enigmatic and Evasive Global Criminal Operation: https://www.fireeye.com/blog/threat-research/2018/08/fin7-pursuing-an-enigmatic-and-evasive-global-criminal-operation.html

CFI. (2020). *Capital One Financial Corp.* Retrieved from corporatefinanceinstitute.com: https://corporatefinanceinstitute.com/resources/careers/companies/capital-one-financial-corp/

Chan, C.-S. (2012, December 17). *Complexity the Worst Enemy of Security.* Retrieved from schneier.com: https://www.schneier.com/news/archives/2012/12/complexity_the_worst.html

Cheslock, P. (2015, May 4-5). *Why We Can't Have Nice Things, A Tale of Woe and Hope For the Future.* Retrieved from Vimeo: DevOps Days: https://vimeo.com/129822165

Christensen, B. M. (2017, January 14). *Beware of Scam "YouTube Video" Facebook Messages*. Retrieved from hoax-slayer.net: https://www.hoax-slayer.net/beware-of-scam-youtube-video-facebook-messages/

Cimpanu, C. (2019, November 17). *Chrome, Edge, Safari hacked at elite Chinese hacking contest*. Retrieved from zdnet.com: https://www.zdnet.com/article/chrome-edge-safari-hacked-at-elite-chinese-hacking-contest/

Cimpanu, C. (2019, November 19). *Major ASP.NET hosting provider infected by ransomware*. Retrieved from zdnet.com: https://www.zdnet.com/article/major-asp-net-hosting-provider-infected-by-ransomware/

Cimpanu, C. (2019, January 9). *New tool automates phishing attacks that bypass 2FA*. Retrieved from zdnet.com: https://www.zdnet.com/article/new-tool-automates-phishing-attacks-that-bypass-2fa/

Cimpanu, C. (2019, September 12). *Simjacker attack exploited in the wild to track users for at least two years*. Retrieved from zdnet.com: https://www.zdnet.com/article/new-simjacker-attack-exploited-in-the-wild-to-track-users-for-at-least-two-years/

Cimpanu, C. (2019, June 3). *Wave of SIM swapping attacks hit US cryptocurrency users*. Retrieved from zdnet.com: https://www.zdnet.com/article/wave-of-sim-swapping-attacks-hit-us-cryptocurrency-users/

Cimpanu, C. (2020, February 12). *Average tenure of a CISO is just 26 months due to high stress and burnout*. Retrieved from zdnet.com: https://www.zdnet.com/article/average-tenure-of-a-ciso-is-just-26-months-due-to-high-stress-and-burnout/

CISA. (2019, June 22). *CISA Statement on Iranian Cybersecurity Threats*. Retrieved from dhs.gov: https://www.dhs.gov/news/2019/06/22/cisa-statement-iranian-cybersecurity-threats

CISO MAG. (2019, February 26). *60% of enterprises suffer data loss due to printer security breaches*. Retrieved from cisomag.com: https://www.cisomag.com/60-of-enterprises-suffer-data-loss-due-to-printer-security-breaches/

Clear, J. (2018). *Atomic Habits: An Easy & Proven Way to Build Good Habits & Break Bad Ones.* New York: Avery; 1st edition.

Clover, J. (2017, July 6). *Security Researchers Don't Think Apple Pays Enough for Bug Bounties.* Retrieved from macrumors.com: https://www.macrumors.com/2017/07/06/apple-bug-bounties-dont-pay-enough/

Cockcroft, A. (2019, November 11). *Failure Modes and Continuous Resilience.* Retrieved from medium.com/@adrianco: https://medium.com/@adrianco/failure-modes-and-continuous-resilience-6553078caad5

Collins, J. (2001). *Good to Great: Why Some Companies Make the Leap and Others Don't.* New York: Harper Business.

Conrad, E., Misenar, S., & Feldman, J. (2015). *CISSP Study Guide (Third Edition).* New York: Syngress.

Core War. (n.d.). *Core War: Creeper & Reaper.* Retrieved from corewar.co.uk: https://corewar.co.uk/creeper.htm

Corfield, G. (2019, May 20). *Vengeful sacked IT bod destroyed ex-employer's AWS cloud accounts. Now he'll spent rest of 2019 in the clink.* Retrieved from The Registere: https://www.theregister.co.uk/2019/03/20/steffan_needham_aws_rampage_prison_sentence_voova/

Cox, J. (2019, Septebmer 30). *Legit-Looking iPhone Lightning Cables That Hack You Will Be Mass Produced and Sold.* Retrieved from vice.com: https://www.vice.com/en_us/article/3kx5nk/fake-apple-lightning-cable-hacks-your-computer-omg-cable-mass-produced-sold

Crenshaw, A. (2014, December 29). *Dropping Docs on Darknets: How People Got Caught.* Retrieved from YouTube: https://www.youtube.com/watch?v=eQ2OZKitRwc

Düben, B. A., & Düben, B. A. (2020, January 9). *thediplomat.com.* Retrieved from Try as It Might, Germany Isn't Warming to Huawei: https://thediplomat.com/2020/01/try-as-it-might-germany-isnt-warming-to-huawei/

Doffman, Z. (2019, December 16). *China Just Crossed A Dangerous New Line For Huawei: 'There Will Be*

Consequences'. Retrieved from forbes.com: https://www.forbes.com/sites/zakdoffman/2019/12/16/china-just-crossed-a-dangerous-new-line-for-huawei-there-will-be-consequences/#19362c2175a3

Doffman, Z. (2019, August 4). *New Data Breach Has Exposed Millions Of Fingerprint And Facial Recognition Records: Repor*. Retrieved from Forbes.com: https://www.forbes.com/sites/zakdoffman/2019/08/14/new-data-breach-has-exposed-millions-of-fingerprint-and-facial-recognition-records-report/#ab2b28c46c60

Doffman, Z. (2019, November 14). *Secret Iranian Network Behind 'Aggressive' U.S. Cyberattacks Exposed In New Report*. Retrieved from Forbes: https://www.forbes.com/sites/zakdoffman/2019/11/14/secret-iranian-network-behind-aggressive-us-cyberattacks-exposed-in-new-report/#1e4f4f43579c

Dunham, K. (2008). *Mobile Malware Attacks and Defense*. New York: Syngress.

Dunn, J. E. (2018, May 16). *Serious XSS vulnerability discovered in Signal*. Retrieved from nakedsecurity.sophos.com: https://nakedsecurity.sophos.com/2018/05/16/serious-xss-vulnerability-discovered-in-signal/

European Union. (2016, April 27). *REGULATION (EU) 2016/679 OF THE EUROPEAN PARLIAMENT AND OF THE COUNCIL*. Retrieved from eur-lex.europa.eu: https://eur-lex.europa.eu/legal-content/EN/TXT/PDF/?uri=CELEX:32016R0679&from=EN

Fazzini, K. (2019, June 17). *Email sextortion scams are on the rise and they're scary — here's what to do if you get one*. Retrieved from CNBC: https://www.cnbc.com/2019/06/17/email-sextortion-scams-on-the-rise-says-fbi.html

Fazzini, K. (2019, March 7). *Equifax CEO testifies company took security seriously before its massive breach in response to scathing Senate report*. Retrieved from CNBC: https://www.cnbc.com/2019/03/07/equifax-marriott-ceos-testify-in-senate-over-data-breaches.html

Fazzini, K. (2019, November 12). *Iowa paid a security firm to break into a courthouse, then arrested employees when they succeeded.* Retrieved from https://www.cnbc.com: https://www.cnbc.com/2019/11/12/iowa-paid-coalfire-to-pen-test-courthouse-then-arrested-employees.html

FBI. (2018, December 28). *Chinese Hackers Indicted: Members of APT 10 Group Targeted Intellectual Property and Confidential Business Information.* Retrieved from fbi.gov: https://www.fbi.gov/news/stories/chinese-hackers-indicted-122018

Feiner, L. (2019, October 30). *Twitter bans political ads after Facebook refused to do so.* Retrieved from CNBC: https://www.cnbc.com/2019/10/30/twitter-bans-political-ads-after-facebook-refused-to-do-so.html

Fontana, J. (2015, February 23). *LinkedIn will pay $1.25 million to settle suit over password breach.* Retrieved from zdnet.com: https://www.zdnet.com/article/linkedin-will-pay-1-25-million-to-settle-suit-over-password-breach/

Foote, A. (2018, June 14). *Encrypted Messaging Isn't Magic.* Retrieved from Wired: https://www.wired.com/story/encrypted-messaging-isnt-magic/

Fruhlinger, J. (2017, October 17). *Petya ransomware and NotPetya malware: What you need to know now.* Retrieved from csoonline.com: https://www.csoonline.com/article/3233210/petya-ransomware-and-notpetya-malware-what-you-need-to-know-now.html

Fruhlinger, J. (2018, September 8). *Marriott data breach FAQ: How did it happen and what was the impact?* Retrieved from CSO: https://www.csoonline.com/article/3441220/marriott-data-breach-faq-how-did-it-happen-and-what-was-the-impact.html

Fruhlinger, J. (2018, March 9). *The Mirai botnet explained: How teen scammers and CCTV cameras almost brought down the internet.* Retrieved from CSO: The Mirai botnet explained: How teen scammers and CCTV cameras almost brought down the internet

Galeotti, M. (2017, June 12). *The Kremlin's Newest Hybrid Warfare Asset: Gangsters*. Retrieved from Foreign Policy: https://foreignpolicy.com/2017/06/12/how-the-world-of-spies-became-a-gangsters-paradise-russia-cyberattack-hack/

Gallagher, S. (2013, November 6). *Googlers say "F*** you" to NSA, company encrypts internal network*. Retrieved from arstechnica.com: https://arstechnica.com/information-technology/2013/11/googlers-say-f-you-to-nsa-company-encrypts-internal-network/

Gallagher, S. (2013, 10 31). *How the NSA's MUSCULAR tapped Google's and Yahoo's private networks*. Retrieved from arstechnica.com: https://arstechnica.com/information-technology/2013/10/how-the-nsas-muscular-tapped-googles-and-yahoos-private-networks/

Gallagher, S. (2019, September 13). *Check the scope: Pen-testers nabbed, jailed in Iowa courthouse break-in attempt*. Retrieved from arstechnica.com: https://arstechnica.com/information-technology/2019/09/check-the-scope-pen-testers-nabbed-jailed-in-iowa-courthouse-break-in-attempt/

Garrett, G. M. (2017, December 13). *How a Dorm Room Minecraft Scam Brought Down the Internet*. Retrieved from Wired: https://www.wired.com/story/mirai-botnet-minecraft-scam-brought-down-the-internet/

Gatlan, S. (2019, July 5). *Automated Magecart Campaign Hits Over 960 Breached Stores*. Retrieved from Bleeping Computer: https://www.bleepingcomputer.com/news/security/automated-magecart-campaign-hits-over-960-breached-stores/

Gatlan, S. (2019, February 22). *Tax Returns Exposed in TurboTax Credential Stuffing Attacks*. Retrieved from bleepigncomputer.com: https://www.bleepingcomputer.com/news/security/tax-returns-exposed-in-turbotax-credential-stuffing-attacks/

Gaus, A. (2020, February 15). *Cloud Battle Between Microsoft and Amazon Enters New Phase After Judge Orders Suspension of JEDI Contract*. Retrieved from TheStreet:

https://www.thestreet.com/investing/judge-halts-microsoft-pentagon-worth-signaling-tough-battle-ahead-with-amazon

Gerchow, George, Radichel, T., & Hansen, J. (2019, 06 10). *Masters of Data Podcast*. Retrieved from Security Experts Panel - Second Edition: https://www.podbean.com/media/share/pb-zrcjt-b3b7ab

Gerstner, L. V. (2003). *Who Says Elephants Can't Dance?* New York: Harper Business.

Giesbrecht, S. (2017, March 27). *Tabletops Aren't Just For Eating Dinner On.* Retrieved from Cisco Blogs: https://blogs.cisco.com/security/tabletops-arent-just-for-eating-dinner-on

Goodin, D. (2017, October 16). *Millions of high-security crypto keys crippled by newly discovered flaw.* Retrieved from arstechnica.com: https://arstechnica.com/information-technology/2017/10/crypto-failure-cripples-millions-of-high-security-keys-750k-estonian-ids/

Goodin, D. (2017, April 14). *NSA-leaking Shadow Brokers just dumped its most damaging release yet.* Retrieved from arstechnica.com: https://arstechnica.com/information-technology/2017/04/nsa-leaking-shadow-brokers-just-dumped-its-most-damaging-release-yet/

Goodin, D. (2018, May 23). *arstechnica.com.* Retrieved from Hackers infect 500,000 consumer routers all over the world with malwar: https://arstechnica.com/information-technology/2018/05/hackers-infect-500000-consumer-routers-all-over-the-world-with-malware/

Goodin, D. (2018, May 3). *Facebook security analyst is fired for using private data to stalk women.* Retrieved from Ars Technica: https://arstechnica.com/information-technology/2018/05/facebook-fires-security-analyst-accused-of-using-access-to-stalk-women/

Goodin, D. (2019, May 23). *Why a Windows flaw patched nine days ago is still spooking the Internet.* Retrieved from Ars Technica: https://arstechnica.com/information-technology/2019/05/why-a-windows-flaw-patched-nine-days-ago-is-still-spooking-the-internet/

Greenberg, A. (2020, January 12). *Iranian hackers have been "password spraying" the US grid.* Retrieved from Ars

Technica: https://arstechnica.com/information-technology/2020/01/iranian-hackers-have-been-password-spraying-the-us-grid/?comments=1

Greenburg, A. (2018, August 22). *The Untold Story of NotPetya, the Most Devastating Cyberattack in History.* Retrieved from Wired: https://www.wired.com/story/notpetya-cyberattack-ukraine-russia-code-crashed-the-world/

Grimes, R. A. (2015, December 15). *Why identity is the new security.* Retrieved from CSO: https://www.csoonline.com/article/3014725/why-identity-is-the-new-security.html

Heller, M. (2019, June 28). *Another Amazon S3 leak exposes Attunity data, credentials.* Retrieved from Tech Target: https://searchcloudsecurity.techtarget.com/news/252465992/Another-Amazon-S3-leak-exposes-Attunity-data-credentials

Henmi, A., Lucas, M., Singh, A., & Cantrell, C. (2006). *Firewall Policies and VPN Configurations.* Rockland: Syngress.

Higgens, K. J. (2006, September 28). *HD Moore Unplugged.* Retrieved from Dark Reading: https://www.darkreading.com/risk/hd-moore-unplugged/d/d-id/1128332

Holmes, A. (2019, October 17). *Business Insider.* Retrieved from Tech execs who lie about privacy violations could face 20 years behind bars under a newly proposed Senate bill: Tech execs who lie about privacy violations could face 20 years behind bars under a newly proposed Senate bill

Honig, A., & Sikorski, M. (2012). *Practical Malware Analysis.* Sebastopol: O'Reilly.

Hulquist, J. (2020, January 5). *'All the information is gone': U.S. cybersecurity expert on Iran's cyberwar capabilities.* Retrieved from MSNBC: https://www.msnbc.com/msnbc/watch/-all-the-information-is-gone-u-s-cybersecurity-expert-on-iran-s-cyberwar-capabilities-76087365872

Hunt, T. (2019, January 17). *The 773 Million Record "Collection #1" Data Breach.* Retrieved from troyhunt.com: https://www.troyhunt.com/the-773-million-record-collection-1-data-reach/

Hutchins, E. M., Cloppert, M. J., & Amin, R. M. (2010). *Intelligence-Driven Computer Network Defense Informed by Analysis of Adversary Campaigns and Intrusion Kill Chains*. Retrieved from lockheedmartin.com: https://www.lockheedmartin.com/content/dam/lockheed-martin/rms/documents/cyber/LM-White-Paper-Intel-Driven-Defense.pdf

Identity Theft Resource Center. (2016). *Identity Theft: The Aftermath 2016™*. Retrieved from idtheftcenter.org: https://www.idtheftcenter.org/images/page-docs/AftermathFinal_2016.pdf

Ikeda, S. (2019). *2019 Sans Institute Cloud Security Survey Reveals Top Threats, Which Surprisingly Are Not DDoS Attacks*. Retrieved from CPO Magazine: https://www.cpomagazine.com/cyber-security/2019-sans-institute-cloud-security-survey-reveals-top-threats-which-surprisingly-are-not-ddos-attacks/

Ikeda, S. (2020, February 11). *Ransomware Attacks Are Causing Cyber Insurance Rates to Go Through the Roof; Premiums up as Much as 25 Percent*. Retrieved from Databreaches.net: https://www.databreaches.net/ransomware-attacks-are-causing-cyber-insurance-rates-to-go-through-the-roof-premiums-up-as-much-as-25-percent/

Ilascu, I. (2019, November 28). *Dutch Govt Warns of 3 Ransomware Infecting 1,800 Businesses*. Retrieved from bleepingcomputer.com: https://www.bleepingcomputer.com/news/security/dutch-govt-warns-of-3-ransomware-infecting-1-800-businesses/

Ilascu, I. (2019, April 30). *Emotet Trojan Is the Most Prevalent Threat in Healthcare Systems*. Retrieved from bleepingcomputer.com: https://www.bleepingcomputer.com/news/security/emotet-trojan-is-the-most-prevalent-threat-in-healthcare-systems/

Irish Central Staff. (2019, April 5). *Facebook founder Mark Zuckerberg visits Ireland to talk regulation*. Retrieved from technology.inquirer.net: https://technology.inquirer.net/84930/mark-zuckerberg-visits-ireland-to-discuss-facebook-reform-pledge

ISACA. (2019). *Cyber Security Audit.* Retrieved from isaca.org: https://isaca.org/About-ISACA/advocacy/Documents/CyberSecurityAudit_mis_Eng_1017.pdf

Islam, A., Oppenheim, N., & Thomas, W. (2017, May 26). *SMB Exploited: WannaCry Use of "EternalBlue".* Retrieved from Fireeye: https://www.fireeye.com/blog/threat-research/2017/05/smb-exploited-wannacry-use-of-eternalblue.html

Iyengar, E. J., & Thomson, M. E. (2020, January 8). *QUIC: A UDP-Based Multiplexed and Secure Transport.* Retrieved from quicwg.org: https://quicwg.org/base-drafts/draft-ietf-quic-transport.html

Johnson, A. (2018, September 5). *DtSR Episode 312 - Ann Johnson on Mental Health.* Retrieved from https://podtail.com/podcast/down-the-security-rabbithole/: https://podtail.com/podcast/down-the-security-rabbithole/dtsr-episode-312-ann-johnson-on-mental-health/

Johnson, O. (2019, June 26). *Tata Consultancy, NTT Data Among Cloud Hopper Attack Victims: Reports.* Retrieved from crn.com: https://www.crn.com/news/channel-programs/tata-consultancy-ntt-data-among-cloud-hopper-attack-victims-reports

Kahn, R. A. (2017, May 18). *Economic Espionage in 2017 and Beyond: 10 Shocking Ways They Are Stealing Your Intellectual Property and Corporate Mojo.* Retrieved from americanbar.com: https://www.americanbar.org/groups/business_law/publications/blt/2017/05/05_kahn/

Kanno-Youngs, Z., & Perlroth, N. (2020, January 8). *The New York Times.* Retrieved from Iran's Military Response May Be 'Concluded,' but Cyberwarfare Threat Grows: https://www.nytimes.com/2020/01/08/us/politics/iran-attack-cyber.html

Kennedy, D. (2020, January 6). *Iran's key cybersecurity threat is ransomware: Former NSA hacker.* Retrieved from cnbc.com: https://www.cnbc.com/video/2020/01/06/irans-key-cybersecurity-threat-is-ransomware-former-nsa-hacker.html

Kerner, S. M. (2019, April 15). *Microsoft's Cloud Email Breach Is a Cause for Concern.* Retrieved from eweek.com: https://www.eweek.com/security/microsoft-s-cloud-email-breach-is-a-cause-for-concern

Kharpal, A. (2019, March 5). *Huawei says it would never hand data to China's government. Experts say it wouldn't have a choice.* Retrieved from cnbc.com: https://www.cnbc.com/2019/03/05/huawei-would-have-to-give-data-to-china-government-if-asked-experts.html

Kim, G. (2019). *The Unicorn Project.* Oregon: IT Revolution Press.

Kindervag, J. (2010, November 5). *Build Security Into Your Network's DNA: The Zero Trust Network Architecture.* Retrieved from virtualstarmedial.com: http://www.virtualstarmedia.com/downloads/Forrester_zero_trust_DNA.pdf

Kirk, J. (2018, May 24). *FBI Seizes Domain Controlling 500,000 Compromised Routers.* Retrieved from Bank Info Security: https://www.bankinfosecurity.com/experts-brace-for-new-round-router-cyberattacks-a-11030

Kirtley, J. E. (2019, December 6). *Getting to the Truth: Fake News, Libel Laws, and "Enemies of the American People".* Retrieved from ABA: https://www.americanbar.org/groups/crsj/publications/human_rights_magazine_home/the-ongoing-challenge-to-define-free-speech/getting-to-the-truth/

Konkel, F. R. (2017, November 20). *Amazon Web Services Announces Secret Cloud Region For CIA.* Retrieved from nextgov.com: https://www.nextgov.com/it-modernization/2017/11/amazon-web-services-announces-secret-cloud-region-cia/142662/

Kosewski, L., Ramanujam, A., Behnam, N., Blohowiak, A., & Probst, K. (2018, March 12). *Project Nimble: Region Evacuation Reimagined.* Retrieved from The Netflix Tech Blog: https://medium.com/netflix-techblog/project-nimble-region-evacuation-reimagined-d0d0568254d4

Kravets, D. (2008, July 15). *San Francisco Admin Charged With Hijacking City's Network.* Retrieved from WIRED: https://www.wired.com/2008/07/sf-city-charged/

Krebs, B. (2014, May 14). *The Target Breach, By the Numbers*. Retrieved from krebsonsecurity.com: https://krebsonsecurity.com/2014/05/the-target-breach-by-the-numbers/

Krebs, B. (2015). *Spam Nation: The Inside Story of Organized Cybercrime-from Global Epidemic to Your Front Door*. Chicago: Sourcebooks.

Krebs, B. (2019, November 19). *110 Nursing Homes Cut Off from Health Records in Ransomware Attack*. Retrieved from krebsonsecurity.com: https://krebsonsecurity.com/2019/11/110-nursing-homes-cut-off-from-health-records-in-ransomware-attack/

Krebs, B. (2019, April 15). *Experts: Breach at IT Outsourcing Giant Wipro*. Retrieved from Krebs on Security: https://krebsonsecurity.com/2019/04/experts-breach-at-it-outsourcing-giant-wipro/

Krebs, B. (2019, December 07). *Ransomware at Colorado IT Provider Affects 100+ Dental Offices*. Retrieved from krebsonsecurity.com: https://krebsonsecurity.com/2019/12/ransomware-at-colorado-it-provider-affects-100-dental-offices/

Krebs, B. (2020, January 20). *Iowa Prosecutors Drop Charges Against Men Hired to Test Their Security*. Retrieved from krebsonsecurity.com: https://krebsonsecurity.com/2020/01/iowa-prosecutors-drop-charges-against-men-hired-to-test-their-security/

Kumar, M. (2019, August 07). *TSMC Chip Maker Blames WannaCry Malware for Production Halt*. Retrieved from The Hacker News: https://thehackernews.com/2018/08/tsmc-wannacry-ransomware-attack.html

Lawrence, J. (2018, November 2). *How the US lost the propaganda war in Afghanistan*. Retrieved from stripes.com: https://www.stripes.com/lifestyle/how-the-us-lost-the-propaganda-war-in-afghanistan-1.554778

Lepido, D. (2019, April 29). *Vodafone Found Hidden Backdoors in Huawei Equipment*. Retrieved from Bloomberg: https://www.bloomberg.com/news/articles/2019-04-

30/vodafone-found-hidden-backdoors-in-huawei-equipment

Lewis, D. (2014, September 2). *iCloud Data Breach: Hacking And Celebrity Photos.* Retrieved from forbes.com: https://www.forbes.com/sites/davelewis/2014/09/02/icloud-data-breach-hacking-and-nude-celebrity-photos/#1968069a2de7

Liebetrau, E. (2018, June 22). *How Google's QUIC Protocol Impacts Network Security and Reporting.* Retrieved from fastvue.co: https://www.fastvue.co/fastvue/blog/googles-quic-protocols-security-and-reporting-implications/

Lindsey, N. (2019, July 11). *Chinese Cloud Hopper Operation Targets Top Tech Providers in World.* Retrieved from cpomagazine.com: https://www.cpomagazine.com/cyber-security/chinese-cloud-hopper-operation-targets-top-tech-providers-in-world/

Lopez, N. (2020, January 21). *Report: Apple drops plan to encrypt iCloud backups after FBI protests.* Retrieved from thenextweb.com: https://thenextweb.com/insider/2020/01/21/report-apple-drops-plan-to-encrypt-icloud-backups-after-fbi-protests/

Lubold, G. (2018, December 14). *Chinese Hackers Breach U.S. Navy Contractors.* Retrieved from WSJ: https://www.wsj.com/articles/u-s-navy-is-struggling-to-fend-off-chinese-hackers-officials-say-11544783401

Lynch, V. (2017, May 26). *Cost of 2013 Target Data Breach Nears $300 Million Read more at: https://www.thesslstore.com/blog/2013-target-data-breach-settled/.* Retrieved from thesslstore.com: https://www.thesslstore.com/blog/2013-target-data-breach-settled/

Mackenzie, J. (2017, September 5). *U.S. forces apologize for 'highly offensive' Afghan propaganda leaflet.* Retrieved from reuters.com: https://www.reuters.com/article/us-afghanistan-coalition-leaflet/u-s-forces-apologize-for-highly-offensive-afghan-propaganda-leaflet-idUSKCN1BH0M5

Marczak, B., & Scott-Railton, J. (2016, August 24). *The Million Dollar Dissident: NSO Group's iPhone Zero-Days used against a UAE Human Rights Defender*. Retrieved from citizenlab.ca: https://citizenlab.ca/2016/08/million-dollar-dissident-iphone-zero-day-nso-group-uae/

Marty, R. (2015). *Security Data Lake*. Sebastopol: O'Reilly.

Mason, R. (2017, August 25). *Have you had your Bezos moment? What you can learn from Amazon*. Retrieved from cio.com: https://www.cio.com/article/3218667/have-you-had-your-bezos-moment-what-you-can-learn-from-amazon.html

McNeil, A. (2017, May 19). *How did the WannaCry ransomworm spread?* Retrieved from MalwareBytes: https://blog.malwarebytes.com/cybercrime/2017/05/how-did-wannacry-ransomworm-spread/

Merriam-webster. (2020). *hacker*. Retrieved from merriam-webster.com/dictionary: https://www.merriam-webster.com/dictionary/hacker

Metcalf, S. (2018, August 4-9). Retrieved from From Workstation to Domain Admin: Why Secure Administration Isn't Secure and How to Fix It: https://i.blackhat.com/us-18/Wed-August-8/us-18-Metcalf-From-Workstation-To-Domain-Admin-Why-Secure-Administration-Isnt-Secure.pdf

Microsoft. (2019, July 8). *A world without passwords with Azure Active Directory*. Retrieved from docs.microsoft.com: https://docs.microsoft.com/en-us/azure/security/fundamentals/ad-passwordless

Microsoft. (2019, August 21). *Backup and recover account credentials using the Microsoft Authenticator app*. Retrieved from docs.microsoft.com: https://docs.microsoft.com/en-us/azure/active-directory/user-help/user-help-auth-app-backup-recovery

Microsoft. (2019, October 6). *docs.microsoft.com*. Retrieved from Configurable token lifetimes in Azure Active Directory (Preview): https://docs.microsoft.com/en-us/azure/active-directory/develop/active-directory-configurable-token-lifetimes

Microsoft. (2019, August 09). *Remote Desktop*. Retrieved from docs.microsoft.com: https://docs.microsoft.com/en-us/windows/security/identity-protection/hello-for-business/hello-feature-remote-desktop

Mihalcik, C. (2019, July 27). *Trump says Apple won't get tariff relief for Mac Pro parts made in China*. Retrieved from cnet.com: https://www.cnet.com/news/trump-says-apple-mac-pro-wont-be-excluded-from-china-tariffs/

Miller, G. (2020, February 11). *For decades, the CIA read the encrypted communications of allies and adversaries*. Retrieved from washigntonpost.com: https://www.washingtonpost.com/graphics/2020/world/national-security/cia-crypto-encryption-machines-espionage/

Morris, A. (2020, January 4). *@Andrew__Morris*. Retrieved from Twitter: https://twitter.com/Andrew___Morris/status/1213501291122565123?s=20

Mozur, P. (2020, February 13). *With Harsh Words, China's Military Denies It Hacked Equifax*. Retrieved from nytimes.com: https://www.nytimes.com/2020/02/13/business/china-equifax-deny.html

Mozure, P. (2019, April 14). *One Month, 500,000 Face Scans: How China Is Using A.I. to Profile a Minority*. Retrieved from nytimes.com: https://www.nytimes.com/2019/04/14/technology/china-surveillance-artificial-intelligence-racial-profiling.html

MS-ISAC. (2019, 01). *MS-ISAC Multi-State Inforamtion Sharing & Analysis Center*. Retrieved from cissecurity.org: https://www.cisecurity.org/wp-content/uploads/2019/01/Security-Primer-EternalBlue.pdf

Myre, G. (2019, April 12). *How Much Did WikiLeaks Damage U.S. National Security?* Retrieved from npr.org: https://www.npr.org/2019/04/12/712659290/how-much-did-wikileaks-damage-u-s-national-security

Newman, L. H. (2016, August 19). *Hackers Trick Facial-Recognition Logins With Photos From Facebook (What Else?)*. Retrieved from wired.com: https://www.wired.com/2016/08/hackers-trick-facial-recognition-logins-photos-facebook-thanks-zuck/

Newman, L. H. (2017, May 9). *Fixing the Cell Network Flaw That Lets Hackers Drain Bank Accounts*. Retrieved from

Wired.com: https://www.wired.com/2017/05/fix-ss7-two-factor-authentication-bank-accounts/

Newman, L. H. (2018, March 7). *The Leaked NSA Spy Tool That Hacked the World*. Retrieved from wired.com: https://www.wired.com/story/eternalblue-leaked-nsa-spy-tool-hacked-world/

Newman, L. H. (2019, May 22). *Facial Recognition Has Already Reached Its Breaking Point*. Retrieved from WIRED: https://www.wired.com/story/facial-recognition-regulation/

Newman, L. H. (2019, May 15). *Google Will Replace Titan Security Key Over a Bluetooth Flaw*. Retrieved from wired.com: https://www.wired.com/story/google-titan-security-key-recall-ble/

Newman, L. H. (2019, June 17). *Tricky Scam Plants Phishing Links in Your Google Calendar*. Retrieved from wired.com: https://www.wired.com/story/phishing-links-google-calendar-invites/

Newman, L. H. (2019, May 6). *What Israel's Strike on Hamas Hackers Means For Cyberwar*. Retrieved from Wired: https://www.wired.com/story/israel-hamas-cyberattack-air-strike-cyberwar/

Newman, L. H. (2020, February 8). *How to Get Your Yahoo Breach Settlement Money*. Retrieved from Wired: https://www.wired.com/story/how-to-get-yahoo-breach-settlement-money/

Nikel, D. (2019, December 16). *Huawei Loses Out to Ericsson for Telenor 5G Network*. Retrieved from www.lifeinnorway.net: https://www.lifeinnorway.net/huawei-loses-out-to-ericsson-for-telenor-5g-network/

NIST. (2012, September). *Guide for Conducting Risk Assessments*. Retrieved from nvlpubs.nist.gov: https://nvlpubs.nist.gov/nistpubs/Legacy/SP/nistspecialpublication800-30r1.pdf

NIST. (2015, August 5). *NIST Policy on Hash Functions*. Retrieved from csrc.nist.gov: https://csrc.nist.gov/Projects/Hash-Functions/NIST-Policy-on-Hash-Functions

NIST. (2017, June 22). *Digital Identity Guidelines*. Retrieved from pages.nist.gov: https://pages.nist.gov/800-63-3/

NIST. (2019, July). *Guideline for Using Cryptographic Standards in the Federal Government: Cryptographic Mechanisms*. Retrieved from nvlpubs.nist.gov: https://nvlpubs.nist.gov/nistpubs/SpecialPublications/NIST.SP.800-175Br1-draft.pdf

Novet, J. (2018, August 30). *Google's new hardware security key was made by a Chinese company*. Retrieved from cnbc.com: https://www.cnbc.com/2018/08/30/google-titan-made-by-chinese-company-feitian.html

O'Donnell, L. (2019, May 22). *Google Stored G Suite Passwords in Plaintext Since 2005*. Retrieved from threat post: https://threatpost.com/google-stored-passwords-in-plaintext/144967/

O'Flaherty, K. (2019, March 10). *Why The Citrix Breach Matters -- And What To Do Next*. Retrieved from Forbes.com: https://www.forbes.com/sites/kateoflahertyuk/2019/03/10/citrix-data-breach-heres-what-to-do-next/#11d124691476

Ollam, D. (2017, December 11). *Wild West Hackin' Fest*. Retrieved from I'll Let Myself In: Tactics of Physical Pen Testers: https://www.youtube.com/watch?v=rnmcRTnTNC8

Osborne, C. (2019, July 24). *AT&T fails to have $24 million SIM-swap attack lawsuit dismissed*. Retrieved from zdnet.com: https://www.zdnet.com/article/at-t-fails-to-have-24-million-sim-swap-attack-lawsuit-dismissed/

O'Sullivan, D. (2020, January 2). *A fake Twitter account stirred tensions between Jews and African Americans. Trolls celebrated*. Retrieved from cnn.com: https://www.cnn.com/2020/01/02/tech/twitter-fake-account-anti-semitic-new-york-attacks/index.html

Otto, G. (2019, August 2). *What Capital One's cybersecurity team did (and did not) get right*. Retrieved from cyberscoop.com: https://www.cyberscoop.com/capital-one-cybersecurity-data-breach-what-went-wrong/

PCI Security Standards Council. (2018, July). *PCI DSS Quick Reference Guide*. Retrieved from pcisecuritystandardscouncil.org:

https://www.pcisecuritystandards.org/documents/PCI_DSS-QRG-v3_2_1.pdf

Perlroth, N. (2012, October 23). *In Cyberattack on Saudi Firm, U.S. Sees Iran Firing Back*. Retrieved from nytimes.com: https://www.nytimes.com/2012/10/24/business/global/cyberattack-on-saudi-oil-firm-disquiets-us.html?mtrref=undefined&assetType=REGIWALL

Perlroth, N., & Shane, S. (2019, May 25). *In Baltimore and Beyond, a Stolen N.S.A. Tool Wreaks Havoc*. Retrieved from nytimes.com: https://www.nytimes.com/2019/05/25/us/nsa-hacking-tool-baltimore.html

Perlroth, N., Tsang, A., & Satariano, A. (2018, November 30). *nytimes.com*. Retrieved from Marriott Hacking Exposes Data of Up to 500 Million Guests: https://www.nytimes.com/2018/11/30/business/marriott-data-breach.html

Perrin, C. (2008, January 22). *How to spoof a MAC address*. Retrieved from techrepublic.com: https://www.techrepublic.com/blog/it-security/how-to-spoof-a-mac-address/

Pham, T. T. (2015, January 12). *Stolen Passwords Allowed Hackers to Steal Over One Billion Rubles*. Retrieved from duo.com: https://duo.com/blog/stolen-passwords-allowed-hackers-to-steal-over-one-billion-rubles

Phillip, A., & Wagner, J. (2016, October 12). *Sections Democracy Dies in Darkness Politics Hacked WikiLeaks emails show concerns about Clinton candidacy, email server*. Retrieved from washingtonpost.com: https://www.washingtonpost.com/politics/hacked-wikileaks-emails-show-concerns-about-clinton-candidacy-email-server/2016/10/12/cdacbbd0-908f-11e6-a6a3-d50061aa9fae_story.html

Ponemon Institute, IBM. (2018, July 11). *IBM Study: Hidden Costs of Data Breaches Increase Expenses for Businesses*. Retrieved from prnewswire.com: https://www.prnewswire.com/news-releases/ibm-study-hidden-costs-of-data-breaches-increase-expenses-for-businesses-300679124.html

Poremba, S. (2018, August 10). *Identity Is the New Perimeter — But Where's Its Firewall?* Retrieved from SecurityIntelligence: https://securityintelligence.com/identity-is-the-new-perimeter-but-wheres-its-firewall/

Positive Technology. (2016). *PRIMARY SECURITY THREATS FOR SS7 CELLULAR NETWORKS.* Retrieved from ptsecurity.com: https://www.ptsecurity.com/upload/ptcom/SS7-VULNERABILITY-2016-eng.pdf

Pratt, M. K. (2017, November 28). *csoonline.com.* Retrieved from What is SIEM software? How it works and how to choose the right tool: https://www.csoonline.com/article/2124604/what-is-siem-software-how-it-works-and-how-to-choose-the-right-tool.html

Puig, A. (2019, July 22). *Federal Trade Commission Consumer Information.* Retrieved from Equifax Data Breach Settlement: What You Should Know: https://www.consumer.ftc.gov/blog/2019/07/equifax-data-breach-settlement-what-you-should-know

PWC. (2017, April). *Operation Cloud Hopper.* Retrieved from pwc.co.uk: https://www.pwc.co.uk/issues/cyber-security-data-privacy/insights/operation-cloud-hopper.html

Quote Investigator. (2011, May 13). *quoteinvestigator.com.* Retrieved from Everything Should Be Made as Simple as Possible, But Not Simpler: https://quoteinvestigator.com/2011/05/13/einstein-simple/

Radichel, T. (2014, August 5). *Case Study: Critical Controls that Could Have Prevented the Target Breach.* Retrieved from sans.org: https://www.sans.org/reading-room/whitepapers/casestudies/case-study-critical-controls-prevented-target-breach-35412

Radichel, T. (2017, September 7). *Are Social Media Bots Influencing You?* Retrieved from Secplicity: https://www.secplicity.org/2017/09/07/social-media-bots-influencing/

Radichel, T. (2017, March 12). *Balancing Security and Innovation With Event Driven Automation.* Retrieved from sans.org:

https://www.sans.org/reading-room/whitepapers/incident/balancing-security-innovation-event-driven-automation-36837

Radichel, T. (2017, August 10). *Packet Capture on AWS.* Retrieved from sans.org: https://www.sans.org/reading-room/whitepapers/detection/packet-capture-aws-37905

Radichel, T. (2017, December 22). *People Do What You Inspect, Not What You Expect.* Retrieved from Infosecurity: https://www.infosecurity-magazine.com/opinions/people-do-what-you-inspect-not/

Radichel, T. (2017, October 17). *The Problem with Hacking Back: It Might Be Your Network.* Retrieved from Secplicity: https://www.secplicity.org/2017/10/17/problem-hacking-back-might-network/

Radichel, T. (2017, October 3). *Where in The World is That Network Traffic Coming From?* Retrieved from Secplicity: https://www.secplicity.org/2017/10/03/world-network-traffic/

Radichel, T. (2018, December 21). *Just-in-time VPN access with an AWS IoT button.* Retrieved from AWS News Blog: https://aws.amazon.com/blogs/aws/just-in-time-vpn-access-with-an-aws-iot-button/

Radichel, T. (2018, December 17). *Why use a VPN for remote access in the cloud?* Retrieved from medium.com/cloud-security: https://medium.com/cloud-security/cloud-security-why-use-a-vpn-e0c9a059e6f8

Radichel, T. (2019, September 1). *Amazon DocumentDB Network Access—Why the VPC?* Retrieved from medium.com/cloud-security: https://medium.com/cloud-security/amazon-documentdb-network-access-why-the-vpc-1090a4b978e9

Radichel, T. (2019, February 6). *Cloud Security Defensive Strategies: Keep the ball away from the attacker.* Retrieved from medium.com/cloud-security: https://medium.com/cloud-security/cloud-security-defensive-strategies-58d7079535d9

Radichel, T. (2019, November 25). *Effective Security Testing.* Retrieved from medium.com/cloud-security:

https://medium.com/cloud-security/effective-security-testing-93aff57b2858

Radichel, T. (2019, December 18). *My History of DevSecOps.* Retrieved from medium.com/cloud-security: https://medium.com/cloud-security/my-history-of-devsecops-58defb149804

Radichel, T. (2019, August 23). *Pentesting CORS: Give me all your cookies! OK.* Retrieved from medium.com/cloud-security: https://medium.com/cloud-security/pentesting-cors-890010f8ef77

Radichel, T. (2019, August 1). *What's in your cloud?* Retrieved from medium.com/cloud-security: https://medium.com/cloud-security/whats-in-your-cloud-673c3b4497fd

Radichel, T., & Janca, T. (2019, May 6). *Do it Yourself Security Assessment.* Retrieved from medius.studios.ms: https://medius.studios.ms/Embed/video/B19-CFS2013?l=22.733844444444443

Raymond, E. S. (2001). *How To Become A Hacker.* Retrieved from http://catb.org/~esr/faqs/hacker-howto.html#what_is: http://catb.org/~esr/faqs/hacker-howto.html#what_is

Riley, D. (2017, November 21). *Uber fires security chief over cover-up of hack involving 57M customer records.* Retrieved from Silicon Angle: https://siliconangle.com/2017/11/21/uber-fires-chief-security-officer-cover-hack-involving-56m-customer-records/

Risk Based Security. (2019, November). *Data Breach QuickView Report 2019 Q3 trends.* Retrieved from https://pages.riskbasedsecurity.com/data-breach-quickview-report-2019-q3-trends

Roccia, T. (2017, May 16). *Malware Packers Use Tricks to Avoid Analysis, Detection.* Retrieved from McCafee: https://www.mcafee.com/blogs/enterprise/malware-packers-use-tricks-avoid-analysis-detection/

Rudis, B. (2019, July 30). *BlueKeep Exploits May Be Coming: Our Observations and Recommendations.* Retrieved from RAPID7 Blog:

https://blog.rapid7.com/2019/07/31/bluekeep-cve-2019-0708-for-windows-rdp-what-you-need-to-know/

Russo, K. L. (2017, January 11). *Obfuscation and Polymorphism in Interpreted Code.* Retrieved from sans.org: https://www.sans.org/reading-room/whitepapers/ActiveDefense/obfuscation-polymorphism-interpreted-code-37602

Sahadi, J. (2005, July 27). *40M credit cards hacked: Breach at third party payment processor affects 22 million Visa cards and 14 million MasterCards.* Retrieved from money.cnn.com: https://money.cnn.com/2005/06/17/news/master_card/

Samuel, H. (2018, October 23). *Chinese spies fooled 'hundreds' of civil servants and executives, France reveals.* Retrieved from telegraph.co.uk: https://www.telegraph.co.uk/news/2018/10/23/chinese-online-spies-fool-hundreds-totally-unprepared-top-french/

Sanger, D. E. (2012, June 1). *Obama Order Sped Up Wave of Cyberattacks Against Iran.* Retrieved from The New York Times: https://www.nytimes.com/2012/06/01/world/middleeast/obama-ordered-wave-of-cyberattacks-against-iran.html

Schiffer, A. (2017, July 21). *How a fish tank helped hack a casino.* Retrieved from washingtonpost.com: https://www.washingtonpost.com/news/innovations/wp/2017/07/21/how-a-fish-tank-helped-hack-a-casino/

Schneier, B. (1996). *Applied Cryptography.* Hoboken: John Wiley & Sons.

Schneier, B. (2018, December 24). *MD5 and SHA-1 Still Used in 2018.* Retrieved from Schneier on Secruity: https://www.schneier.com/blog/archives/2018/12/md5_and_sha-1_s.html

Seals, T. (2019, February 12). *Double-Stuffed: Dunkin' Hit by Another Credential-Stuffing Attack.* Retrieved from Threat Post: https://threatpost.com/dunkin-credential-stuffing/141754/

Secureworks Counter Threat Unit Research Team. (2015, May 28). *Living Off the Land.* Retrieved from Secureworks: https://www.secureworks.com/blog/living-off-the-land

Sharton, B. R., & Stegmaier, G. M. (2018, August 21). *Breaches in the boardroom: What directors and officers can do to reduce the risk of personal liability for data security breaches.* Retrieved from Thomson Reuters: https://legal.thomsonreuters.com/en/insights/articles/board-liability-reduce-risk-for-data-security-breaches

Shaw, K. (2018, October 22). *The OSI model explained: How to understand (and remember) the 7 layer network model.* Retrieved from Network World: https://www.networkworld.com/article/3239677/the-osi-model-explained-how-to-understand-and-remember-the-7-layer-network-model.html

Sheridan, K. (2019, May 16). *Google to Replace Titan Security Keys Affected by Bluetooth Bug.* Retrieved from darkreading.com: https://www.darkreading.com/endpoint/google-to-replace-titan-security-keys-affected-by-bluetooth-bug/d/d-id/1334742

Spadafora, A. (2020, January 01). *WannaCry was the most common crypto ransomware attack last year.* Retrieved from techradar pro: https://www.techradar.com/news/wannacry-was-the-most-common-crypto-ransomware-attack-last-year

Spitzner, L. (2019, June 27). *Sans.org.* Retrieved from Time for Password Expiration to Die: https://www.sans.org/security-awareness-training/blog/time-password-expiration-die

Stødle, D. (2005, May 26). *Ping Tunnel.* Retrieved from mit.edu: https://www.mit.edu/afs.new/sipb/user/golem/tmp/ptunnel-0.61.orig/web/

Stahie, S. (2019, December 9). *Windows Hello for Business Affected by Serious Vulnerability; Microsoft Issues Advisory.* Retrieved from securityboulevard.com: https://securityboulevard.com/2019/12/windows-hello-for-business-affected-by-serious-vulnerability-microsoft-issues-advisory/

Stewart, J. (2006, November 13). *SpamThru Statistics.* Retrieved from Secureworks: https://www.secureworks.com/research/spamthru-stats

Stockler, A. (2019, 12 3). *MIT DEEPFAKE VIDEO 'NIXON ANNOUNCING APOLLO 11 DISASTER' SHOWS THE POWER OF DISINFORMATION*. Retrieved from Newsweek: https://www.newsweek.com/richard-nixon-deepfake-apollo-disinformation-mit-1475340

Stockley, M. (2016, December 15). *Yahoo breach: I've closed my account because it used MD5 to hash my password.* Retrieved from nakedsecurity.sophos.com: https://nakedsecurity.sophos.com/2016/12/15/yahoo-breach-ive-closed-my-account-because-it-uses-md5-to-hash-my-password/

Strickland, J. (2008, August 29). *10 Worst Computer Viruses of All Time*. Retrieved from computer.howstuffworks.com: https://computer.howstuffworks.com/worst-computer-viruses2.htm

Stubbs, J., Menn, J., & Bing, C. (2019, June 26). *Inside the West's failed fight against China's 'Cloud Hopper' hackers.* Retrieved from reuters.com: https://www.reuters.com/investigates/special-report/china-cyber-cloudhopper/

Stuttard, D. (September 27, 2011). *Web Application Hacker's Handbook, 2nd Edition*. Hoboken: Wiley; .

Sullivan, L., & Shuknect, C. (2019, April 12). *As China Hacked, U.S. Businesses Turned A Blind Eye*. Retrieved from npr.org: https://www.npr.org/2019/04/12/711779130/as-china-hacked-u-s-businesses-turned-a-blind-eye

Swinhoe, D. (2018, November 1). *Automating security at AWS: How Amazon Web Services operates with no SOC.* Retrieved from csoonline.com: https://www.csoonline.com/article/3317702/automating-security-at-aws-how-amazon-web-services-operates-with-no-soc.html?upd=1581846501248

Talbot, S. (2004, August 1). *Reagan and Gorbachev: Shutting the Cold War Down*. Retrieved from Brookings.edu: https://www.brookings.edu/articles/reagan-and-gorbachev-shutting-the-cold-war-down/

Taleb, N. N. (2005). *Fooled by Randomness: The Hidden Role of Chance in Life and in the Markets (Incerto)*. New York: Random House Trade Paperbacks.

Targett, E. (2020, January 8). *Las Vegas Hacked: Quick Reactions Save Sin City from Outages.* Retrieved from CBR: https://www.cbronline.com/cybersecurity/breaches/las-vegas-hacked/

Thompson, N. (2018, December 17). *How Russian Trolls Used Meme Warfare to Divide America.* Retrieved from wired.com: https://www.wired.com/story/russia-ira-propaganda-senate-report/

Tolkien, J. R. (1900). *The Hobbit; or, There and Back Again.* Boston: Houghton Mifflin Harcourt.

Troy, M. (2018, March 29). *Google login #phishing sites hosted on @digitalocean gapps[.]site gmail-accounts-m[.]com goooigle[.]com safepassword[.]ru.* Retrieved from Twitter: https://twitter.com/bad_packets/status/979555331113013251

Tyldum, M. (Director). (2014). *The Imigation Game* [Motion Picture].

U.S. Army. (2005, July 13). *Army approves plan to create school for Red Teaming.* Retrieved from web.archive.org: https://web.archive.org/web/20110617105841/http://www.tradoc.army.mil/pao/tnsarchives/July05/070205.htm

US Cert. (2019). *APTs Targeting IT Service Provider Customers.* Retrieved from us-cert.gov: https://www.us-cert.gov/APTs-Targeting-IT-Service-Provider-Customers

Vamosi, R. (2003, January 27). *SQL Slammer: How it works--prevent it.* Retrieved from zdnet.com: https://www.zdnet.com/article/sql-slammer-how-it-works-prevent-it/

Venezia, P. (2014, June 23). *Murder in the Amazon cloud.* Retrieved from InfoWorld: https://www.infoworld.com/article/2608076/murder-in-the-amazon-cloud.html

Verizon. (2013). *2013 Data Breach Investigations Report.* Retrieved from eventtracker: http://www.eventtracker.com/eventtracker/media/eventtracker/files/collateral/verizon-data-breach-2013.pdf

Verizon. (2019). *2019 Data Breach Investigations Report.* Retrieved from Verizon:

https://enterprise.verizon.com/resources/reports/2019-data-breach-investigations-report.pdf

Whiteside, T. (1978). *Computer Capers: Tales of Electronic Thievery, Embezzlement, and Fraud.* New York: Ty Crowell Co. Retrieved from Computer Capers: Tales of Electronic Thievery, Embezzlement, and Fraud.

Williams, O. (2018, December 21). *China's Cloud Hopper campaign branded "one of the worst cyber intrusions to date".* Retrieved from tech.newstatesman.com: https://tech.newstatesman.com/security/china-cloud-hopper-campaign

Winder, D. (2019, May 4). *Airbus, Porsche, Toshiba And Volkswagen Data Stolen In Massive Breach -- What You Need To Know.* Retrieved from Forbes: https://www.forbes.com/sites/daveywinder/2019/05/04/airbus-porsche-toshiba-and-volkswagen-data-stolen-in-massive-breach-what-you-need-to-know/#29b60201701c

Winder, D. (2019, August 20). *Data Breaches Expose 4.1 Billion Records In First Six Months Of 2019.* Retrieved from Forbes: https://www.forbes.com/sites/daveywinder/2019/08/20/data-breaches-expose-41-billion-records-in-first-six-months-of-2019/#c280973bd549

Winkler, I. (2017, October 31). *Ira Winkler, Spies Among Us ~ Cyber Threat Summit 2017.* Retrieved from ICTTF You Tube: https://www.youtube.com/watch?v=yHowdR7h_bs

Wong, E. (2019, August 27). *How China Uses LinkedIn to Recruit Spies Abroad.* Retrieved from nytimes.com: https://www.nytimes.com/2019/08/27/world/asia/china-linkedin-spies.html

Wong, J. C. (2019, May 14). *WhatsApp urges users to update app after discovering spyware vulnerability.* Retrieved from theguardian.com: https://www.theguardian.com/technology/2019/may/13/whatsapp-urges-users-to-upgrade-after-discovering-spyware-vulnerability

Yamanouchi, K. (2019, September 18). *As Delta Air Lines Expands Face Recognition, Criticism Grows.* Retrieved from govtech.com: https://www.govtech.com/products/As-

Delta-Air-Lines-Expands-Face-Recognition-Criticism-Grows.html

Zetter, K. (2014, November 3). *An Unprecedented Look at Stuxnet, the World's First Digital Weapon.* Retrieved from Wired: https://www.wired.com/2014/11/countdown-to-zero-day-stuxnet/

Zetter, K. (2015). *Countdown to Zero Day: Stuxnet and the Launch of the World's First Digital Weapon.* Portland: Broadway Books. Retrieved from https://www.amazon.com/Countdown-Zero-Day-Stuxnet-Digital/dp/0770436196

Zialcita, P. (2019, November 7). *U.S. Company Accused Of Illegally Selling Chinese-Made Security Products To Military.* Retrieved from npr.org: https://www.npr.org/2019/11/07/777374783/u-s-company-accused-of-illegally-selling-chinese-made-security-products-to-milit

Made in the USA
Monee, IL
21 January 2021